ALMOST HOME

Almost Home

||||||||||||||||||||||||||||||||||||||||||||||||||||

*America's Love-Hate Relationship
with Community*

DAVID L. KIRP

Princeton University Press, Princeton, New Jersey

Library of Congress Cataloging-in-Publication Data
Kirp, David L.
Almost home : America's love-hate relationship with community /
David L. Kirp   p. cm.
Includes index.
ISBN 0-691-04973-4 (cl. : alk. paper)
1. Community life—United States.   2. United States—Social
conditions—1980–   I. Title.
HN90.C6 K57 2000
307'.0973—dc21   99-046064

This book has been composed in Palatino

www.pup.princeton.edu

Printed in the United States of America

1   3   5   7   9   10   8   6   4   2

To my godparents Jakie and Frank
and to my godson Aaron

CONTENTS

CONTENTS

ALMOST HOME

Community Theater

In democratic countries, knowledge of how to
combine is the mother of all other forms of
knowledge; on its progress depends that of all
the others.

Alexis de Tocqueville, *Democracy in America*

1

On a warm September afternoon a few weeks into the
fall 1999 term, Berkeley's Sproul Plaza teems with life.
Students scurry between classes or head toward Tele-
graph Avenue. The quintessentially Berkeley characters are on the scene—the preacher cajoling, the man
with the fake microphone crooning off-key, and the
drummer pounding away.

In this scruffy square, the cultural revolution had its
tumultuous start with the Free Speech Movement. But
now that seems like ancient history. Mario Savio, the
personification of the Movement, has been transformed into an icon, his death mourned by a chancel-
lor whose predecessor sicced the police on him. When
compared with the 1960s, the occasional protests over
the demise of affirmative action or the university's unwillingness to let its teaching assistants unionize are

timid affairs. A small circle embedded in the Plaza is inscribed with the words "This Space Is the Territory of No Nation," but to the oblivious passersby, that circle—with the utopian fantasy that it represents—is just part of the pavement.

On this Indian summer day, student organizations are recruiting new members. Tables have been set up along the edge of Sproul Plaza—an astonishing one hundred seventy-six tables—manned by students who together represent a benign Babel. Campus Greens are here as well as Campus Republicans. So are the Undergraduate Minority Business Association and the Pre-Med Honor Society; the New Life Christian Club, the Asian Baptists, and the Bahai Club; the Taiwanese Student Association and La Familia; Cal Dykes and Chi Phi; the Golden Bear Victory Fellowship and Food Not Bombs; Swingin' Out and Take Back the Night. The hockey team hopes to convert roller-bladers into goalies; the debating society hopes to lure silver-tongued orators.

Students wander slowly past these tables, as if window-shopping for an identity, deciding how to choose among their multiple selves. One of them might be black and Latino, a practicing Catholic, a Go player and a soccer nut. Another could be a lesbian whose politics are libertarian and whose passion is square dancing.

Literally thousands of personal decisions about which groups to join, or whether to join at all, will be made this afternoon and in the coming days. Out of this crucible of choice will emerge small communities rooted in common interests—a network of associations that closely resembles the vision of democracy made small that Alexis de Tocqueville found so distinctive and so praiseworthy.

Directly underneath Sproul Plaza, a very different scene is being played out. In a darkened room as claustrophobic as a prison cell and as hushed as a cloister, students sit hunched over the latest generation of electronic games, Tomb Raider or Quake or Warcraft. They are intent on the task at hand, deadly earnest as they commit virtual mayhem on the bad guys and the evil empires. No one is talking—indeed, there is no sound at all except the electronically created voice of the machines. The civil society that is in the process of being formed on the Plaza is just a few feet away, but the psychological distance can be reckoned in light years.

These are two distinct worlds, two very different conceptions of the individual: the citizen of the commonweal and the solitary self. But when students emerge from the electronic cave, blinking in the dazzling sunshine, some of them will join the crowds checking out the myriad campus organizations. And some of those who are staffing the tables on the Plaza will find their way downstairs. They find pleasure both in solitary pursuits and in sociability—and in having the chance to choose between those pleasures, to construct the shape of their lives.

2

The pull and tug of isolation and communion, freedom and commitment, contained in this vignette tells a tale of America in miniature.

There is a ton of prose on the idea of community, and mostly it is passionately opinionated. Community is praised and damned—a haven in a heartless world or a prison of conformity; a place where habits of the heart are nurtured or a seedbed of intolerance; a place to which you can't return or else a place from which you'd gladly flee. The word *community* itself is a Rorschach blot upon which myriad hopes and fears are projected. Communitarians versus libertarians, the advocates of identity politics versus those who embrace the idea of a common vision—the antagonisms are deep, the arguments as fierce as wildfire.

These thirteen tales scrutinize the minute particulars of time and place, telling stories about how people live together. The settings range from Los Angeles to East Harlem, from the Berkeley hills, lovely and decimated, to a Miami far from the palm-shaded beaches; from a New Jersey suburb with pretensions to exclusivity to a hardscrabble southern town. The communities include long-settled neighborhoods and experimental schools, Fortune 500 corporations and fledgling social movements. Sometimes the focus is on a response to crisis, at other times on the pull and tug of everyday life.

There are heroes in the narratives—among them one of America's most remarkable education reformers and a woman who deserves to be spoken of in the same breath as Rosa Parks—as well as a handful of villains. Mostly, though, the inhabitants of these communities are ordinary people, neither more nor less virtuous than the rest of us, who happen to get caught up in extraordinary events. Their voices contribute to the making of decisions in the practice of community—and those decisions in turn reshape the participants.

Taken together, these stories offer a snapshot of a diverse array of contemporary American communities. Because the histories are imbedded in an ongoing intellectual conversation about the meanings of community in America, it makes sense to begin by situating them, briefly and with some unavoidable oversimplification, in the slipstream of that conversation.*

3

Ever since the colonists won their independence more than two centuries ago, individual rights have been the touchstone of the American creed. Personal liberty, the opportunity freely to pursue one's own life course, has been thought to be the surest path to a better society. The dangers of tyranny were intimately understood, the blessings of freedom regarded as important enough to merit putting one's life and one's "sacred honor" at risk. The bravura Declaration that announced the new nation embraces the Enlightenment's hostility toward tradition and its commitment to emancipation through acts of self-discovery. It speaks of liberty and the pursuit of happiness, not duty or obligation. The Constitution, with a Bill of Rights to protect the citizenry from an overreaching national government, reflects those beliefs, and they were suffused through the land. Where else but in

---

*Caveat reader: If you have no patience with abstract argument, you should skip to page 18.

America would a state adopt as its motto "Don't Tread on Me"?

In this rights-based world, the job of government is not to foster virtue but to act as a neutral, a referee. "Since people disagree about the best way to live," Michael Sandel writes in *Democracy's Discontent*, describing this set of beliefs, "it should not affirm any particular vision of the good life. Instead it should provide a framework of rights that respects persons as free and independent selves, capable of choosing their own values and ends." In the marketplace, laissez faire operates as the economic counterpart of political liberty. Through the working of Adam Smith's invisible hand, unfettered pursuit of personal gain is supposed to translate automatically into greater wealth and happiness for the greatest number. In the market as in politics, there is no conception of a public interest distinct from the sum of individual interests.

Over the course of our history, these ideas have captured the American imagination. If you ask middle-class Americans what they regard as the defining characteristics of the nation, as Alan Wolfe does in *One Nation, After All*, most of them cite economic individualism and political democracy. A commitment to liberty in the political and economic spheres has also become America's preeminent export, as more and more nations, disillusioned with the systems under which they have lived, have taken the procedural republic as their model.

But freedom in action, even though deeply loved by Americans, can also be troubling. The people with whom Alan Wolfe talked, while committed to liberty, were also abidingly aware that, as one of them put it, "the same things that can make America a better place can also make it a worse place." Unchecked, economic freedom degenerates into "the worship of shallow material things over deeper spiritual values." Political freedom, out of control, produces a Hobbesian war of all against all. Unfettered moral freedom means "only think[ing] in terms of 'I.'"

IN WANTING the best of both worlds—liberty without license, virtue without imposition—these citizens echo a tension that has been evident since the first days of the Republic. The commitment to individual rights, though pivotal, represents only one strand of the American creed. The founding generation also believed that the political community should nurture civic virtue—that, as Michael Sandel puts it, "liberty depends on sharing in self-government."

How this should be accomplished was less clear. One school of thought favored a schoolmaster state that would "convert men into republican machines." Voluntary associations of the like-minded potentially represented a far less coercive training ground in civic virtue, but they too were controversial. George Washington worried about the baleful effects of "self-created societies" with political purposes; James Madison sought to curb the power of "factions" to influence government.

By the time Alexis de Tocqueville, America's most prescient observer, arrived half a century later, events had overtaken, and allayed, these concerns. Americans form associations at "all ages, all stations in life, and

9

all types of disposition," Tocqueville marveled in *Democracy in America*. "Moral, serious, futile, very general, and very limited, immensely large and very minute [associations] . . . Americans combine to give fetes, found seminaries, distribute books . . . hospitals, prisons, and schools take shape that way."

If this variety of associations was impressive, its implications for the practice of citizenship and for the health of the nation were profound. "The art of association becomes the mother of action, studied and applied by all." In this respect, as with the commitment to the primacy of individual rights, the American experience was special. There were few "partial publics" in other countries, Tocqueville pointed out, few institutions (aside from the hierarchical Church) that occupied the terrain between the individual and the state. Political parties, associations in the sphere of government, could take on this responsibility as the "great free schools to which all citizens come to be taught the general theory of association."

Move the calendar up a century and a half, and Tocqueville's testimonial to voluntarism looks hopelessly dated. "While the voluntary association would continue to flourish," Michael Schudson notes in *The Good Citizen*, "it would also come up against social problems to which its participatory form was not a very effective solution. As the locus of authoritative decision-making moved increasingly to Washington . . . the petition gave way to the lobby." The only checks on centralized power were individual rights decreed by an activist judiciary. Although these new rights formally enfranchised groups that had effectively been excluded from political life—blacks, women, and the disabled—in practice they sometimes proved chimerical.

The public embrace of community turned into a rhetorical trope—a nostalgic fantasy and a political weapon. Ronald Reagan's 1980 platform stoutly pledged to "reemphasize those vital communities like the family, the neighborhood, and the workplace" that lie "between government and the individual," and to promote the "rebirth of citizen activity in neighborhoods and citizens across the land." But as Christopher Lasch acidly observes in *The True and Only Heaven*, "Reagan's rhetorical defense of 'family and neighborhood' could not be reconciled with his championship of unregulated business enterprise, which has replaced neighborhoods with shopping malls and super-highways."

4

The only thing we really know about the future is that it will look different from the present. Even as would-be Tocquevilles were decrying the death of community a generation ago, the idea was making its reappearance on the public stage. Old arguments were trotted out and new ones fashioned to commend the virtues of association and the capacity of associations to promote public virtue.

Voices on both ends of the political spectrum joined the chorus, although for diametrically opposed and equally implausible reasons. The Left was anxious to maintain political and moral laissez faire despite the sometimes-destructive identity politics that it generated, but the Left rightly feared the power of an unchecked market to overwhelm everything else. The Right envisioned an unregulated market somehow coexisting with a renewed commitment to civic virtue, forgetting that entrepreneurs had no use for sentimental attachments that came without a price tag.

The Puritans' aspiration to build a new city upon a hill, though long overshadowed by the exercise of do-your-own-thing, don't-tread-on-me freedom, never disappeared. What caused its resurfacing was the growing recognition of how problematic a society dedicated to individualism can be. In *Habits of the Heart* (a phrase from *Democracy in America*), published in the mid-1980s, Robert Bellah and his colleagues discovered a gnawing dissatisfaction with rootless individualism, an inchoate longing for a public life, among the people they interviewed. Remarkably, this book, published by a university press with a modest first printing, became a best-seller and spawned groups of devotees across the country.

In the years since then, the centrality of community has been the driving force for a host of new schools of thought and new political movements. Although the labels are different and the affinities usually go unacknowledged, this is the narcissism of small differences or else the lamentable consequence of overspecialization.

Republican theory, a term out of favor since the founding of the nation, has been rediscovered by scholars across an array of disciplines. "Central to republican theory," writes Michael Sandel in *Democracy's Discontent*, "is the idea that liberty depends on sharing in self-government . . . deliberating with fellow citizens about the common good and helping to shape the destiny of the political community. . . . It requires a sense of belonging, a concern for the whole, a moral bond with the community whose fate is at stake." Similarly, "deliberative democracy"—an "exciting development in political theory," James Bohman and William Rehg observe in the eponymous volume—contends that "legitimate lawmaking issues from the public deliberation of citizens. . . . It presents an ideal of political autonomy based on the practical reasoning of citizens."

All this comes straight from the groves of academe. But those who think about, and sometimes involve themselves in, public policy want to bridge the gap between thought and action. They too are promoting the idea of deliberation. In *The New Politics of Public Policy*, Martin Shapiro points out that "for a great many years, students of politics and policy neglected moral philosophy as both a way of evaluating policy and a motivating force in politics." No longer. "A [new] methodological faith is proclaimed. If persons of good faith engage in a mutual exchange of tentative claims about the good . . . they will arrive at statements of the good (or public policies) that are different from and more agreed to be true than the initial claims made. These statements or policies will contain an element of moral truth above and beyond the mere summation of the pleasure-pain preferences of those making the initial claims."

13

"It is something of an unfair parody of the new fascination with deliberation," Shapiro adds, "to say that it seeks to turn the legislative chamber and the administrative agency into philosophy department seminar rooms." Though the case studies in the volume mostly ignore "high-stakes interests" prone to faith in "the democratic wish," they do focus on the messy practical business of rethinking environmental policy and reforming the tax code.

The New Politics of Public Policy is aimed at politicians and policy wonks inside the Beltway. By contrast, the intellectual activists who line up behind the banner of the civil society, as well as those who refer to themselves as communitarians, focus on more local associations. They also have a much wider audience in mind. Their shared ambition is to use their texts as tools in an organizing campaign—an attempt to launch nothing less than a movement that is centered on commitment to community.

In *America's Promise*, a civil society manifesto, Don Eberle describes the fledgling movement as "reflecting a search for a new citizenship that is less self-centered, more civil, and civically engaged. It is an attempt to draw Americans together again . . . to transcend political differences in order to become neighbors again." Borrowing a line from Tocqueville, Eberle speaks to those who would come together "in civil association with his fellows." Amatai Etzioni, in *The Spirit of Community*, emphasizes different aspects of what is essentially the same idea. At the core of the communitarian movement, he writes, is the need to correct "the current imbalance between rights and responsibilities."

Etzioni's book is nothing less than a call to arms. "We can act without fear that attempts to shore up our values, responsibilities, institutions, and communities will cause us to charge into the dark tunnel of moralism and authoritarianism that leads to a church-dominated state or a right-wing world."

5

Why all this intellectual ferment and these efforts to mobilize the citizenry—and why now?

In many and varied corners of the republic, from seminar rooms to the living rooms visited by Robert Bellah and, latterly, Alan Wolfe, unhappiness with corrupted individualism is widely heard. Even as social scientists argue with one another over whether Americans are really less trusting of one another, less association-minded, the belief that more and more we are "bowling alone," and that we are worse off because of it, has captured the popular imagination. Individualism has acquired a harsh edge as people grow overly self-centered, uncivil, and civilly disengaged.

The unhappy consequences of the regime of hyperrights are entirely familiar because we are living with them. Money talks in an ever-louder voice. Businessmen spend tens of millions trying to buy their way into governors' mansions or seats in Congress. Political action committees, originally intended to democratize politics, have had the perverse effect of concentrating power. The corporate gigantism brought about by the recent wave of mergers is creating powerful new players on the Washington scene. It is no surprise that three-quarters of the American population believes that public officials are not interested in ordinary people—up from 58.9 percent in 1973, when Watergate and Vietnam sorely tested Americans' faith in their leaders.

In the borderland between public and private life, the entrepreneur has elbowed the citizen aside. With the triumph of exit over the exercise of voice, let alone loyalty, the public square is stripped clean as if by vultures. Parents demand vouchers or charter schools, not public schools, for their children and so public education suffers from malign neglect. Barnes & Noble and www.bn.com replace the public library and the local bookstore. Wal-Mart undermines Main Street. Private security guards outnumber public police officers. An estimated three million American households live in gated communities—twenty thousand of them—protected by the apparatuses of surveillance from the outside world. Even towns planned according to the citizenship-minded tenets of the New Urbanism are mainly run by rules—no laundry hanging in the backyard—and not by those who live in them.

More and more we join health clubs, nodding hello to the person on the next Stair-Master, and mail checks to organizations like the Sierra Club. Is that what civic life has been reduced to?

THE litany of woes attributed to hyper-individualism is seemingly endless. Out of frustration the idea of community, with its promise of a better society, has reemerged. But "community" turns out to be a protean term, susceptible to myriad readings, and it is hardly devoid of problems.

The reinvention of association, its boosters variously claim, will boost trust among the citizenry and so promote nation-building. . . . It will allow discussion among equals. . . . It will serve as boot camp for citizenship, converting rent-seeking individuals into civic republicans. . . . It will produce better policy outcomes. . . . It will clarify differences. . . . It will promote consensus as reasoning together leads people to change their minds. . . . It will improve civility by making appeals to selfishness or bigotry literally unspeakable. . . . It will direct conflict into peaceable channels. . . . and so forth and so on.

So the theory goes. If wishes were horses—but of course they are not. This wish list overpromises and so invites disillusionment. Some of the promises are improbable or at least very hard to demonstrate. How would we prove that a particular policy was better than another? How might equality of status be assured? Other promises are incompatible. Deliberation cannot both yield consensus and specify differences. How are the trade-offs to be made? How, even in an ideal world, does one value the relative importance of good discussion and good outcomes?

Life in tight-knit associations can be a miserable experience—which, after all, is why liberty has meant so much to Americans. Since Cotton Mather's time, intentional communities have not looked kindly on dissenters. Congregations of the like-minded are susceptible to acting coercively. For all the nostalgic allure of the Amish, imagine what it would be like to grow up as an independent spirit in that environment. For all the social solidarity of ultra-Orthodox Jews, imagine being a woman who desperately wants a divorce, which she will get only if her husband deigns to consent. Even the tens of millions of Americans who belong to homeowners associations know the sting of ostracism when they defy the majority on a matter as trivial as picking paint colors for their houses.

One of the tasks of community is setting boundaries. Members of tight enclaves are often inclined to exclusivity, building walls that separate the members from everyone else. The walls may be literal, as in gated communities, or else figurative but no less formidable, as in chilly suburbs that use zoning laws to repel outsiders or private schools that make it plain that only the right kind of children will be welcome.

However strong the ties of community may be, however well intentioned the members, the amount that any small-scale association can accomplish is necessarily limited by the unchecked and uncheckable growth of a national, and increasingly international, political economy. Associations can reshape the lives of their members. But it is merest nostalgia to believe that the deep structural problems of the society—the growing inequality of wealth and power—can be settled locally.

6

These crosscutting ideas come up again and again in the specific depictions, as the theater of community is performed on its many stages.

Some of these stories reveal the darker side of neighborliness. In the New Jersey suburb of Mount Laurel, wealth is equated with membership, with no room for loyalty. Announcing the town's rejection of affordable housing, the mayor tells a congregation of black and mostly poor families who trace their ancestry in the township to the seventeenth century, "If you folks can't afford to live here, you'll just have to leave our town." *Our* town, not yours. Residents of the Berkeley hills vow, after a fire destroys their neighborhood, to build a new utopia. But once the insurance checks start arriving, many of them succumb to unneighborly selfishness. A middle-class San Francisco neighborhood regards itself as a gorgeous mosaic, but when a black adolescent murders his gay white next-door neighbor, it learns that no cement keeps that mosaic together. And a teenager with AIDS is run out of a fearful Southern town.

Yet this same teenager finds a home in another town a hundred miles away. There, a stranger takes it upon herself to become his surrogate mother and the school administration decides to offer him sanctuary. At their best, communities—neighborhoods, schools and community colleges, workplaces, and social movements—bring out what's finest in us. In a down-at-the-heels corner of San Francisco, two families come together to talk out disagreements that threaten to escalate into violence. Similar scenes are repeated thousands of times every year under the auspices of an organization called Community Boards, as volunteer mediators from a neighborhood coax the warring tribes into listening to one another.

The drawing of boundaries can invite people into the fold. Although Pacific Bell does not have a reputation for corporate progressivism—in the past it has been the target of protests by minority groups alleging bias—in responding to the AIDS epidemic the company listened to insiders who advocated company-sponsored education and inclusion. In East Harlem as well as Los Angeles, small public schools have transformed themselves into nurturing communities where intimacy of scale is linked with excellence in instruction. The community college in Miami, the nation's largest, delivers the kind of instruction needed by new immigrants who barely speak English as well as by students who need second and third chances to succeed. What explains the path that these different communities take? A look at how places across the country have responded to the controversial policy of needle exchange offers an answer whose implications extend beyond the specific circumstances.

Associations are formed as previously isolated individuals join forces. People with hemophilia, who for years were entirely dependent on their doctors, came to realize that the doctors hadn't warned them of the deadly danger of blood-clotting products contaminated with HIV. Like gay men earlier in the epidemic, they transformed themselves into a social movement. Their lives changed dramatically—and so did blood policy, not only in the United States but also in dozens of other countries.

The complexities of community are not just artifacts of the external world. As the tale of the two Sproul Plazas suggests, each of us is an amalgam of internalized communities, a complexity of identities. Richard Rodriguez—a writer and TV essayist who is Latino, devoutly Catholic, and gay—and Shelby Steele, a child of a racially mixed marriage who refuses to see things in black and white: both individuals embody the varieties of personal history and the difficulties of crossing one's own psychological boundaries.

THE stories that follow play off one another, moving between the personal and the political, in the process showing the pulls and tugs of civitas and citizenship.* They highlight pivotal moments when borders are blurred or solidified, parochialisms tested, and identities confirmed or remade.

These telling moments in the annals of our contemporary public preoccupations have meanings beyond their particulars. They afford us a glimpse of who we really are.

---

*These pieces were written over the span of a decade. In some instances, factual material has been updated, but the core meanings of these stories remain unchanged.

Our Towns

||||||||||||||||||||||||||||||

Ironies in the Fire:
After the Berkeley-Oakland
Conflagration,
a Man-made Nightmare

STANDING in the fourth-story tower of his startling new home, his untamed beard flying off in every direction, psychotherapist Michael Lesser resembles an Old Testament prophet looking out over the Promised Land. His house is one of nearly three thousand newly built in the hills of Berkeley and Oakland, California, not as part of a planned development but rather one by one, on three square miles reduced to ashes in October 1991 by one of the most destructive wildfires in the nation's history.

The fire raged for three days. Before it leveled the pine and eucalyptus trees, thick foliage blocked all but the minutest of views from what was then the Lessers' home. Now the vista is almost unimpeded, and Michael Lesser finds himself pleased by the distant and ennobling sight of San Francisco Bay. "It was God," he said during one of my many visits to these charred hills, "who gave us a magnificent 360-degree view."

The new houses vary from near-duplicates of those destroyed in the fire to insistently postmodern residences intended for glossy display in the architecture magazines. The Lessers' house was designed by noted Bay Area architect Stanley Saitowitz. Like all of Saitowitz's buildings, it is meant to make a statement, and in this, at least, it succeeds. Most of the Lessers' neighbors liken the massive gunship-gray building to a motel. The more whimsically minded see a submarine encased in stucco, run aground on a sloping suburban lot.

All the windows in the Lessers' house are positioned to prevent the eye from gazing downward at the tangle of weeds and debris that chokes the rest of their property. The view instead is entirely upward, east toward a treeless landscape of cracked foundations, tall grasses, and fire-twisted ruins. The middle distance is filled with architectural contraptions risen crazily from the ashes, their variegated roofs (flat and mansard, bowed and peaked) overshadowed, a bit farther up the hillside, by the immense backsides of the boxy new constructions commonly called "monster houses."

The sight startles everyone who encounters it for the first time. It's as if, after the eruption of Vesuvius, Pompeii had reinvented itself as Las Vegas. I came to these ominous hills in hopes of understanding how this happened—how so many seemingly well-intentioned people, most of them possessed of large sums of insurance money and the aspiration to do well for themselves by doing good, could make such a shambles of what was once a lovely hillside.

THE inferno of 1991 is the most literal, but not the only, trial by fire through which Berkeley has passed. Berkeley is among the best-known cities of a hundred thousand souls anywhere on the planet, and certainly the most willfully controversial. Its university is world-class; its cultural offerings rival those of cities fifty times its size; its street-theater politics, although muted in recent years, play two standard deviations to the left of Democratic Party orthodoxy; and its capacity to embrace the artistic avant-garde is legendary. The city trades on this reputation, writing and rewriting advertisements for itself as "the conscience of the white Western world" and "the intellectual epicenter of the United States."

Berkeley's professed radicalism makes it a refuge for the mad and the visionary alike, for Nobel Prize laureates and lawyers who have seen the transcendent light. Despite this, it remains a socially divided community where geography recapitulates demography. The flatlands that fan out from the university campus west to San Francisco Bay suffer the deprivations that beset every American city. Crowded with modest workingman's bungalows built half a century ago, the flats are social light-years removed from the serene hills on the city's southeastern corner, where the average house sells for half a million dollars and the views reach as far as the Golden Gate Bridge.

The October 1991 fire did not scorch the flats. It was the hills, covered with 1,800 acres of brush and scrub, parched by six years of drought, that burned. Winds blew at thirty-five miles an hour; tree branches shot

27

flames like spears across two major freeways and a reservoir. During the three days that the fire raged out of control, 3,354 single-family homes and 456 apartments situated along the hilly ridge of Berkeley and Oakland were destroyed. One hundred and fifty people were seriously injured. Twenty-five were killed. So complete was the devastation that observers invoked the image of bomb-blasted, smoldering Dresden.

For a few short months after the fire, the residents of the Berkeley hills behaved in an exemplary manner. Those who had lost their houses insisted on being called survivors, not victims, and the distinction wasn't merely semantic. They would return, they said, hardy pioneers determined to make this charred desert bloom again. The Berkeley fire survivors saw themselves in noble contrast to more materialistic California disaster victims. After a 1993 inferno in Malibu, a local paper carried a story about two intrepid matrons who piled their jewels and dogs into kayaks and set out to sea, where they were rescued by bronzed and heroic lifeguards. Lost in the celebratory telling was the news that the women had abandoned their Hispanic maids.

An impromptu meeting at nearby Montclair Presbyterian Church, held just two days after homeowners were allowed back into the burn zone, attracted a crowd of nearly two hundred, anxious for news of their neighbors. At the next meeting, a week later, six hundred people turned up, accompanied by a bevy of TV news trucks. A newly invented newspaper, the *Phoenix Journal*, supplied badly needed information as well as tales of heroism, a platform from which to promote the survivors' cause, and a billboard for merchants eager to tempt these affluent homeless with everything from stress-relieving chiropractic to Turkish kilims.

People who had been burned out of their homes painted ceramic tiles to memorialize what they had lost: Grandma's fine china and the grand piano that went up in flames, the tabby cat that had gone missing, "the squirrels who used our telephone lines as a highway." A ten-year-old's tile contained just a single word: "Why?" The tiles, two thousand in all, were joined together in a mosaic 9 feet high and 104 feet long, a memorial, displayed at the BART station on College Avenue, whose message carries an emotional punch akin to the AIDS quilt.

Many of these new refugees saw their loss in almost mystical terms. Barely three weeks after the fire, Deirdre English, a onetime editor of *Mother Jones*, published an essay in a local weekly, the *East Bay Express*, describing how she had "floated above the smoldering ruins in a state of effortless Zen detachment." The firestorm had swooped down upon her house, obliging her to flee for her life, abandoning every material possession as well as the manuscript of a book in progress.

At first, she recalled, those material losses felt liberating, part of a new awareness that "attachment to things is a futile denial of death." But Zen masters live hardscrabble lives, and the East Bay hills weren't filled with the sound of one hand clapping. Very quickly, Deirdre English sensed in herself the temptation to "start denying death all over again from the starting line: by madly consuming." In this she was not alone.

29

1

A sexual division of labor asserted itself among the refugees. While the women mostly concentrated on keeping their families intact amid all the uncertainties—finding places to live and clothing to wear, swapping sorrows in emotional support groups—the men set out to engineer a new public order. They organized self-help groups, about fifty in all, known as Phoenix neighborhood associations. These newly minted activists weren't interested in reviving the barn-raising tradition of an earlier West, summoning the unscathed to pitch in and rebuild what their neighbors had lost. Instead, they conceived their mission as one of persuading state and federal politicians to amend the tax codes and so rescue the former residents from the calamity of having to pay hundreds of millions of dollars in capital-gains taxes.

When the refugees turned to local public agencies for emergency relief, they offered their suffering as proof of their worth and courage. They said, in effect, "We've been through hell. Now we deserve all the help you can give us." But because California cities are routinely bankrupt, some of the demands could be accommodated only by subtracting services from the residents of the flatlands.

In a city as racially segregated as Oakland, where the fire did its worst work, the fire survivors' plaint reawakened long-abiding hostilities between the less-affluent majority who lived in the flats and those who lived in the hills. In a letter to the *Oakland Tribune*, flat-lander Joyce Owens-Smith insisted that she wouldn't pay "for people in the hills to have a clean, safe environment while I and the other poor, minority people live in squalor, abandoned by the same government and corporate entities making this audacious request."

Such thinking wasn't well received at the higher elevations. "We've paid for *their* police protection and fire protection long enough," the prevailing argument went. "Now it's *our* turn." A group of hillside residents proposed seceding from Oakland and founding a new city named Tuscany. Oakland, it was said, was famous only for "baseball scores and murder counts."

Flatlands residents recalled the scant attention paid by government officials to the people made homeless by the 1989 Loma Prieta earthquake, and they remembered bitterly that in 1978 the precincts in Oakland that voted for Proposition 13, the initiative forcing California's cities to cut property taxes, were situated in the hills. Now these same landowners were appealing to the municipality they'd helped to bankrupt, asking and receiving help from a city with a reputation for shabby public services. The bitterness of the flatlanders was ignored. Retired Admiral Robert Toney, president of the Oakland Chamber of Commerce, told the *Montclarion*, a local paper, that the refugees were "a very desirable part of the population," leaving the flatlanders wondering just how the admiral regarded *their* presence.

To THE insurance companies the homeowners presented a united front, banding together, in groups with acronyms like FIRE and MIFFED, to negotiate bigger settlements. Insurance claims ran to $1.6 billion, nearly half a million dollars for each household. Property owners complained that claims adjusters were low-balling them, discounting their damage estimates. The insurance companies responded by pointing to a handful of rapacious residents who claimed they'd lost possessions, even entire floors of houses, that in fact had never existed.

Many homeowners discovered after the fire that they carried woefully inadequate coverage—one policyholders' group named itself the Unexpectedly Underinsured Allstate Policyholders—but by drawing on the force of their unified, well-connected voice, as well as on the support of the state's populist insurance commissioner, they wrung an astonishing concession from their insurers. Policies were upgraded retroactively, boosting the amount a homeowner could recover by an average of $200,000.

As Deirdre English learned, the lessons of the disembodied spirit taught by the old Japanese Zen masters translated with remarkable ease into the Zen of insurance settlements. "Just when the fire experience is encouraging you to detach from worldly possessions, purify your intentions, and all that," she wrote, "the realpolitik of your insurance policy rises up to inflame pride, greed, guilt, and every other unenlightened emotion you can think of.

"Experience the guilt," she counseled her fellow refugees—but still "fight for your price."

Once in receipt of their insurance settlements, most residents stopped participating in the Phoenix neighborhood associations. Some householders who had been leaders in their insurance groups cut their own backroom deals, agreeing not to reveal the terms of their settlement to anyone else in their own group. As the checks began to roll in, the neighborhood associations collapsed, and the residents turned their attention toward rebuilding what they had lost.

2

On the slopes untouched by the fire, the Berkeley and Oakland hills look the way they did generations ago: pleasant homes, many in the Arts and Crafts style that defined progressive architecture in the early years of the century, situated amid informal gardens, framed by sycamores and eucalyptuses grown grand with age, on winding streets that encourage the sense of neighborliness.

That landscape didn't come about by lucky accident. It was the realization of a philosophy about how houses, and entire neighborhoods, should be designed—a philosophy clearly set forth in a slim volume, published in 1904 and titled *The Simple Home,* by a young Berkeley poet named Charles Keeler, who propounded what was for the time and place a radically different vision of home, a "simpler, a truer, a more vital art expression." During the early decades of the century, this craftsman's ethos emerged in the designs of a new generation of Berkeley architects, among them Bernard Maybeck and Julia Morgan.

Eight weeks after the fire of 1991, the residents of the hills, with the assistance of local architects, published their own book, *Community Voices,* that laid out their "sense of the larger landscape." By and large the

new plans matched Keeler's old metaphysical blueprint. Although the citizens suggested modest improvements—sidewalks in some neighborhoods, more
attractive street lighting in others—they placed their
emphasis on restoring, in spirit if not in specifics, what
had been consumed in the fire.

What *wasn't* wanted had a specific name: Blackhawk. In that gated community twenty miles to the
east, beyond the hills, homes, which cost an average of
$600,000, run upwards of four thousand square feet.
Their architecture tends toward the ersatz, and they
are arranged with an eye to golf-course proximity
rather than the natural patterns of the landscape. Blackhawk looks like all the Brobdingnags rising across
America, where new houses keep getting bigger and
contemporary means kitsch.

In keeping with their reputation as exemplars of the
nation's better self, the Berkeley refugees meant to
prove themselves more visionary than the philistines
of Blackhawk. Local architects hoped aloud that the
onetime homeowners would do for a new generation
as Maybeck and Morgan had done in the aftermath of
a 1923 inferno, making a poetic correlation in time and
space. Their circumstances provided them with a
chance seldom available in a country where individually designed homes have become a rarity for middle-
class families. Even for the well-to-do, building a new
house usually comes down to a matter of choosing one
of three or four standardized models in a real estate
developer's catalogue. But the princely sums of insurance money that were paid out placed good architecture within reach of people who weren't Fortune

500 CEOs. "Here was an educated crowd," Berkeley architect Thaddeus Kusmierski told me as we walked through the generously proportioned rooms of his new home, adapted from the plans of his Maybeck-designed house that had been incinerated. "Here were people with taste as well as money."

Shortly after the fire, Christopher Alexander, a Berkeley architect and planner whose influential book *A Pattern Language* offers prescriptions for timeless houses and entire cities alike, took up Charles Keeler's turn-of-the-century campaign for simple homes in soul-nurturing neighborhoods. The Berkeley hills had been "an organic and precious thing," Alexander pointed out in a lengthy radio interview on KPFA-FM in Berkeley. While those "lovely and informal places" had been leveled, the streets themselves, the stairway paths that climbed the hills, the foundations of houses—the vital patterns—all remained intact.

"The idea at every point," Alexander said, "is to make a thing that has life by adding to and elaborating on its structure." The right course of action was to design new homes to fit the footprints of the old.

YET even as Alexander offered his counsel, homeowners were straying off the path of spiritual enlightenment. After the fire, four residents in ten decided not to return, and many who came back did so because they believed that they had to rebuild in order to get the biggest possible insurance settlement. They weren't the kind of clients that architects refer to as "new home people," the ones who keep notebooks filled with sketches of their fantasy houses and file folders stuffed with articles from *Metropolitan Home*. They were "old home people," who knew little about architecture and were in no mood to learn. Even though they were nostalgic about the houses they'd lost, the very fact of suffering and loss led them to want—to believe that they were entitled to—more than they'd had. Their specifications, often based on casual conversations with friends or quick perusals of architectural magazines, tended to reflect the thoughtless hodge-podge that goes by the label "contemporary": Gropius married to Colonial, Palladian windows affixed to medieval turrets.

Hundreds of architects and as many contractors have labored to remake the hillsides since the conflagration, and the result is a muddle. Lacking the kind of shared aesthetic derived from a common culture, unaware of what had gone into the design of the built landscape of the hillsides, many residents equated "better" with bigger and fancier, and their new homes feature four and five bathrooms, three- and four-car garages, double front doors that belong in an expense-account restaurant. The people who built smaller houses, respectful of the historic scale of the neighborhood, found themselves with what appear to be the cabanas of the monster houses that literally overshadow them.

Some architects treated the damaged landscape as a blank page on which to doodle eccentric fantasies. None went about this task more exuberantly than Ace Architects, a local firm that for one fire-zone client radically reconceived a Bernard Maybeck chapel, supplying the original design with acid-washed copper fish

scales on its sides and a balcony modeled after a basketball hoop. For another client, a jazz musician, the
firm provided a residence painted in Day-Glo colors,
with a megachimney that mimics the curved bell of a
mammoth saxophone and twin star towers shaped
like trumpets tooting at the sky.

Ace Architects reserved the most daring of its plans—
"a house that was really *about* the fire!"—for David
Roth, a young attorney with a professed fondness for
new ideas and a handsome insurance settlement, part
of which had gone to purchasing a level lot with a fine
view. Ace partner David Weingarten recognized him
as the perfect client for his own incendiary vision.

And what a vision! The shell of a concrete barbecue
would remain, "like Grecian ruins," Weingarten told
me when I visited his bizarre office building, dubbed
the Leviathan, near the Oakland waterfront. The house
itself would be made up of three separate buildings,
each embodying a different moment in post-fire history: a tower made of copper, which would eventually
blacken to take on a charred appearance and thus recall the period immediately after the inferno, when
chimneys stood out from the landscape; a rectangle
clad in plywood left deliberately rough to symbolize
the process of rebuilding; and a stuccoed structure facing the street, looking more or less like a traditional
home, though with Pegasus-like wings. Surely such a
residence was destined for the pages of *Architectural
Design*.

The work of construction, however, forced artistic
compromise. The old barbecue, Weingarten's "Grecian
ruins," had to be removed when a neighbor's contrac-

tor backed into it with a tractor. The three parts of the house were physically joined, collapsing the conceptual stages of post-fire history. The plywood box looks less like an unfinished construction than an ordinary wooden rectangle. While the copper tower remains, it's by no means unique: towers are everywhere in the burn zone, the new design cliché. As seen from the street, the most distinctive feature of David Roth's residence are those wings. It's no longer a house with a story line but one that looks ready to fly away.

Just a few lots down the street from Roth's house in Oakland, Stanley Saitowitz, the architect responsible for Michael Lesser's submarine-run-aground, produced a long narrow building and dressed it in aluminum squares of silver and gray. Some neighbors call it the Air Stream, and it does resemble those vintage 1950s trailers. To others it's a sardine tin whose lid, a roof that swoops skyward, has come partway off. Around the corner sits a massive steel structure that looks like a Silicon Valley semiconductor plant.

Such buildings would stick out almost anywhere. They're especially noticeable in a neighborhood where most of the residents, older people who have lived there for years, opted to build versions, albeit somewhat bigger, of the pleasant homes they'd occupied before the fire. When an Air Stream house and a winged tower–house suddenly appear, it's as if strangers had crashed their garden party and upset all the furniture.

David Roth wanted his new neighbors to like his house. He showed them the model, hoping they'd be reassured, but its strange shapes only made them angrier. The old residents wanted things to be as they had been, with a Swiss-style chalet, circa 1910, reconstructed on the site, not a pyrotechnical folly.

"Never has anyone been quite so rude to me in all my life," said Roth, shaking his head at the memory as we walked through his still-unfinished house. Considering that he makes his living as a lawyer, that's saying a great deal.

3

"Boxes," "monster houses," "motels," "houses on steroids," "mushrooms springing up in charcoal," "factories," "trailers," "visual indigestion," "icons of kitschitecture"—there's no end to the catalogue of insults, printable and otherwise, appended to these new constructions. An inviting hillside of winding roads, thick foliage, and informal houses has been transformed, at a cost of more than a billion dollars, into the kind of place that nobody supposedly wanted—a variation on the grandiose theme of Blackhawk, the impact of excess only magnified by the denuded landscape.

If any corner of the burn zone should by rights have escaped so dismal a fate, it's the Berkeley neighborhood where Michael Lesser lives with his fire-made 360-degree view. Elsewhere in the hills people reported meeting their neighbors for the first time as they picked through the wreckage, but the families who lived near the intersection of Alvarado and Vicente roads were hardly strangers. They had keys to one another's houses; they gossiped about, and would say they looked out for, one another. Over the years, some of them had become intimate friends. They were drawn together as well by the recognition that they lived in an ecologically fragile place that obliged them to act together as a neighborhood. In 1978 several of these families joined in the purchase of three acres of land in the middle of the neighborhood, preserving a swath of open space as a "sacred place."

The rules for designing new homes established by the Berkeley planning commission after the 1991 fire seemed tailor-made for this little group of neighbors. Berkeley normally requires a public hearing before issuing a building permit, even if no one objects to the plan (a facet of Berkeley-style socialism, life in a world of endless meetings), but in a rush of sympathy for the refugees, this requirement was waived. Residents were made sovereign, given the authority to pass judgment on their neighbors' designs.

The lower stretches of Alvarado Road were untouched by the fire, but as the road makes a wide curve half a mile or so into the hills, the trees and underbrush abruptly disappear. The rambling, three-story stucco house owned by Toni Garrett and her husband, Gene Farb, straddles that border. The firestorm leveled their detached garage, destroyed their landscaping, and tossed burning embers onto their slate roof, but the house itself survived.

Even as construction began all around them, the Farbs put off their own rebuilding. They were busy shoring up their financially troubled business, Whole Earth Access, a chain of stores imbued with the Zen-ish philosophy of Stewart Brand's *Whole Earth Catalog*. Besides, their house was intact, and so they didn't feel the same urgencies as those who had been burned out. Although they had been among the last families to move into the neighborhood, they were glad to serve as nurturers to the newly dispossessed. After the fire, a once and future neighbor was often on the premises, sharing an impromptu meal, swapping notes about children, discussing plans for rebuilding.

It was natural, Toni Garrett told me as we sat in her reinvented garden, that she and her husband would take on "deep feelings for everyone else's losses." In a world suddenly fissured between those whose houses were destroyed and those whose houses still stood, all attention flowed to the victims of fate.

"It was strange, being here when all your friends had lost everything," Toni Garrett said. She felt a little guilty—why me? she wondered—and a little envious as well. "I need a fire," she caught herself thinking. "I need an excuse to start over." Confronted with neighbors' decisions about the new homes that she regarded as mistaken and damaging, she felt silenced, fearful of rebuke. What did she, scarcely singed herself, know about life after fire?

Before the conflagration, the Farbs' comfortable home had been the biggest in the neighborhood. No longer. Across the street the residence of Michael and Deborah Lesser grew, story by story, over two long years of construction, a Berlin Wall shutting off the old from the new. The neighbors mostly despise it, and even architect Stanley Saitowitz has scarcely a good word for the result of his own design. "The idea in the beginning was to build something modest," he said when I spoke with him in his modernist San Francisco office, "but Michael kept wanting to add more—an extra room on the side of the house, a couple of rooms downstairs, places that could be rented out. Though his old house was generic Arts and Crafts, nothing remarkable architecturally, he convinced the insurance company it was the Parthenon, and so he had the money to do what he wanted."

The Lessers' house is the most obvious but not the only disturbance in the neighborhood. A few doors down on the other side of Vicente Road, where before the fire a rambling 1924 masonry and wood-trimmed home once stood, an outsize stucco and copper-clad ship's prow now looms over the street. Sharon Drager's new residence, 4,500 square feet on three levels, with six bathrooms and a separate suite for the housekeeper, carries the trademark tics of the late, quintessentially L.A. architect Frank Israel, and bears no relation to the northern California terrain.

Drager, a New York émigré, a vascular surgeon, and the mother of two teenagers, saw the building of a house as her one chance to be "a patroness of architecture." The media granted her wish: the architectural magazines piled on her living-room coffee table contain an anthology of adulatory articles, chief among them Paul Goldberger's 1995 *New York Times Sunday Magazine* essay, "The Masterpieces They Call Home," which canonizes "the Drager House" as if it were Frank Lloyd Wright's "Fallingwater."

"The house looks like me," Sharon Drager said as we walked from room to room, the walls as deliberately out of plumb as those in a Halloween house of horrors. "It's an edgy house for an edgy owner." Seen in the architectural magazines, the Drager House appears to stand alone, as if in a sculpture garden. But the photographs effectively eliminate the rest of the neighborhood. Across the street there's a standard-issue suburban residence, built on spec by a contractor. Next door another house has now been built, so close to the Drager home that the distinctive side view of Frank Israel's design, the one celebrated in the architecture magazines, has disappeared.

WHEN the Farbs had been asked to approve their neighbors' designs for rebuilding, they never once raised an objection. The Lessers' house, across the street, was too big, they felt; the tower on the new Tuscan-style home of their next-door neighbors, the Walrods, too imposing. But those people had suffered enough. Whatever they wanted to do was fine. Yet when it was the Farbs' turn to seek the approval of their neighbors for their own modest rebuilding of a garage and game room, Michael Lesser vetoed the design. It was bad enough from his point of view that someday the pine trees, planted at the suggestion of a *feng shui* practitioner, would intrude on the Lessers' newly attained view. But it was definitely unacceptable that the Farbs' plans called for a structure six feet higher than the old garage.

Michael Lesser makes a dogged and unpleasant adversary. A few years before the fire, he had complained that his then-neighbor had built an extension to his home a few feet beyond the legal setback and demanded, noisily if fruitlessly, that it be torn down. Lesser's objections to the Farbs' garage, coming at the last possible moment after nine months of planning, presented a major inconvenience. At first Toni Garrett

43

was "angry enough to slug it out," but after a few weeks of reflection, she and her husband decided that they "weren't inclined to pursue struggles."

Construction was postponed, and the architect went back to the drawing board. Several months and several thousand dollars later, a new design emerged. Toni Garrett wrote to the Lessers, asking them to help defray the added cost, but they never responded, and the Farbs were unwilling to press the matter further. Too much trouble, they believed, too much bad karma. Besides, the Lessers' daughter had grown up with their son. They didn't want adults' arguments to complicate their children's lives.

Not long after the Lessers moved into their new home, Toni Garrett organized a fiftieth-birthday party for Deborah Lesser. She'd settled into her new home, Deborah told her neighbors, even though its austere geometries didn't offer a single quiet corner where late at night she could curl up with a book. She wanted to stay there forever. She'd had a garden before the fire, Deborah reminded her friends, and it was time to start a new one. She'd really appreciate the gift of a tree, something that would grow with the new house, and so the neighbors gave her gift certificates to pay for landscaping.

The months slip into years, and the landscaping still isn't done. The Lessers' property remains unkempt. They can't see the ugliness from their own house, so acutely angled are their windows. But Toni Garrett and Gene Farb see it and recoil every time they look across the street, and so does everyone else who passes by.

WHEN so much that was once neighborly has been commercialized—when even the Welcome Wagon, once a simple gesture of community goodwill, now trades on that goodwill to shill for local merchants— only the terminally naive will be shocked by the turn of events in the Berkeley hills. At the outset, the residents who survived the fire of 1991 believed that they could do better—believed that they could *be* better— than this. "It could have been a real utopia," writer Jeremy Larner ruefully told me as we walked this misbegotten terrain. But over time they have demonstrated that this aspiration was sheer hubris—that, beyond raiding the public treasury for welfare assistance by another name, the idea of the public interest was meaningless and civic virtue beyond their lines of sight.

Eighteen months after the firestorm, a local contractor became embroiled in a venomous dispute with four families, refugees from the fire who had rebuilt and now are irate that the $849,000 house the contractor was building on spec would destroy their views. (In the hills, views affect property values. Local realtors calculate the value of a bay view at $25,000 per bridge.)

"This is more than a legal issue," one resident on his way to the courthouse told a *Phoenix Journal* reporter. "It's a community issue."

"We're living in America," the contractor responded. "I can build what I want."

Fire-damaged people, struggling to take care of themselves after a great loss, have in the process done even greater damage to themselves as well as to others. "I'm entitled to get everything that's coming to me," the survivors of the fire typically said, and the rest of this thought, although usually left unspoken, was implicit in their deeds. "Neighbors, planners, government officials: don't get in my way while I'm getting what's mine."

Much of what has happened since 1991 bears witness to the triumph of selfishness: immense and ugly structures designed without a care for context or consanguinity, neighbors who coexist amid smoldering resentments, neighborhoods that combine the most outmoded features of the old with the grotesqueries of the new, a twice-scarred hillside, and a polity missing in action. The Phoenix neighborhood groups and their good intentions faded away, as did the secessionist fantasy of a new enclave called Tuscany. People concentrated instead on building up the walls that surround their gated private lives.

Some houses still stand in a state of perpetual incompletion, their missing windows and walls mute testimony to the miscalculations of contractors who overbuilt in hopes of making fast and easy money. There are, as well, occupied houses whose unbuilt steps, unlandscaped yards, and unfinished exterior surfaces suggest an insurance settlement not quite rich enough for the blueprints in hand. In the burn zone, although the views are wondrous, "for sale" signs are almost as plentiful as trees.

Talk, Not Guns, in a
San Francisco Neighborhood

THE SETTING is pleasant enough, a comfortably scruffy church meeting room in a quiet San Francisco neighborhood, but the tone of the gathering is tense. On one side of the room sits the extended Gonzales family, immigrants from Nicaragua, while across from them sit the Jordans, an African-American family. In between are four neighbors who are acting as mediators, as well as translators for several of the Gonzaleses.

This meeting, taking place under the auspices of an organization called Community Boards, is supposed to settle the quarrels that plague the two-unit building in which these households live. A man's home is his castle, or so the saying goes, but in this instance, the Gonzaleses' six-room castle is situated directly above the Jordans' six room castle, and this is how the troubles began.

A few months after the Gonzaleses moved into their apartment, the Jordans began to complain about the ceaseless noise from upstairs: children bouncing on trampolines, T.V.'s and stereos blaring, wives and husbands yelling. The Gonzaleses insisted that they

This chapter was coauthored with Elliot Marseille. For reasons of privacy, the names of the disputants have been changed, as have certain other pertinent identifying data.

47

couldn't understand what was upsetting the Jordans. "In our culture, we would never bother our neighbors about something like this," says Maria Gonzales, the main spokesperson for her family at this meeting. Out of frustration, the Jordans would bang on the ceiling with a broom handle, which only infuriated the Gonzaleses and prompted them to retaliate.

As these charges are voiced at the meeting, emotions start to escalate. The Jordans insist that the Gonzaleses, who help support themselves by selling odds and ends, confine their possessions to their allotted half of the garage. Maria Gonzales complains that Lamond Kidd, boyfriend of one of the Jordan daughters, called her names and made her afraid to do her laundry in the garage. The Gonzaleses had phoned the police when Hector Gonzales, the grandfather, discovered that his tires had been slashed while his car was parked in front of the house. In turn, the Jordans called the police when Maria Gonzales screamed "nigger" and "bitch" from her front window. Soon enough, the neighbors were regularly calling the police, and rumors were flying that one household, maybe both, had guns.

All this history is overwhelming the peacemakers. Community Boards sets up such sessions with the intention of getting these stories out, then encouraging people to talk honestly to one another, but instead the room feels like a boiler about to explode.

Suddenly, Lamond Kidd stands up. "This is bullshit, man! I knew they would come here and lie and that is just what they're doing. . . . I work for my money, I pay taxes! Why don't they get a job? . . . Why does Isabel gotta speak Spanish? . . . I'm sick of their damn lying, so I am outta here!"

The room grows instantly quiet. If Kidd walks out, that will probably mean the end of things, a waste of all the time spent in bringing these families face to face. John Doggett, a soft-spoken black man in his fifties, one of the mediators, turns to Lamond. "So you feel disrespected when Maria speaks in Spanish?" Kidd nods. "I understand you feel that way," Doggett goes on, "but it is their right to have a translator. The other family members do not speak good English, and Maria didn't want to be concerned about having to translate." Kidd shakes his head once again, almost as if he were listening to an uncle he admires, and then sits back down.

Slowly, guided by panel members' interjections, the Jordans and Gonzaleses begin speaking to one another in a more civil tone. Still, their stories remain as different from one another as the versions of *Rashomon*, with no one making concessions to the truth as the other family sees it. Ninety minutes into the session, the heads of the two households finally speak up. "Let us try to respect one another," says the matriarch of the Jordan family, and this modest and sensible suggestion seems to draw out the chivalrous side of Hector Gonzales. "*Acuerdo*," he says through a translator. "Agreed. . . . If they respect us, we will respect them. We do not understand each other's language. But let us live in peace and we will leave them in peace."

1

More than two decades ago, San Francisco attorney Ray Shonholtz became disillusioned with the impact of the law on daily life. Even though he was running the Legal Clinic at the University of San Francisco Law School, which provided lawyers for the poor, he felt that more law, with all its awesome formality and impersonalism, solemn strangers deciding the fates of strangers, wasn't needed. Instead, people had to learn how to talk things out, settling quarrels with the help of neighbors trained in mediation. "Community conflict resolution mechanisms," he wrote, "are among the few effective tools for . . . the reduction of anger . . . between people who know each other."

With $150,000 contributed by local foundations—a budget that has since grown to $750,000 annually—Shonholz started testing out his idea. The heart of the enterprise has always been the volunteers who serve on conciliation panels, recruited from all the different neighborhoods that make up San Francisco. Now Community Boards is one of the city's biggest multiracial community groups and also one of its most popular. At a time when many organizations are hunting for volunteers, 500 people are on the waiting list for the next mediators' training session. The caseload has grown steadily—1,400 people with their problems, 300 full hearings in a single year, more cases than are tried annually before a jury in the city's municipal courts.

Nearly one dispute in five involves adolescents in potentially serious trouble with the law. Recently, for instance, a fourteen-year-old Filipino teenager named Matt Priolo encountered three Anglo boys he believed were giving him "hard looks." He waved a pistol at them to scare them off, and as they gunned their car, Priolo, fearful that they were going to back into him, fired off a round from a .25-caliber automatic pistol, shattering the rear window. "We're gonna kill you," Matt Priolo was told—a real possibility in a city where each year nearly 600 violent crimes are committed by juveniles. His worried family sought the help of Community Boards.

As the mediation session progressed and personal feelings came out, the youths realized that despite the gang insignias and the message of us-versus-them that the insignias symbolize, they were just teenagers, scarred and scared by the violence on the streets. Matt Priolo promised to pay for the damage he had done to the car, and word went out to leave him alone.

It would be naive to imagine that every conflict can have such a sweet ending, that every dispute can be talked through this peaceably, for only in romance novels and soap operas do things invariably get resolved so tidily. Yet mediation not only resolves disputes, much as a court does; it also offers an element of catharsis, as individuals realize that they are actually being taken seriously.

Neighborhood conciliation combines an inexpensive alternative to going to court with a form of therapy, an approach whose usefulness reaches beyond disagreements among neighbors. Since 1981, the organization has been training "conflict managers" for San Francisco's public schools—nine-year-olds who mediate playground fist fights and help settle whose turn it is to use the computer, and high school students who sit in on matters ranging from "he said, she said" tiffs to racially charged conflicts. In the neighborhoods, volunteers are hearing cases that pit social workers against families with clashing ideas about how to raise children.

When California embarked on a massive "stop smoking" campaign several years ago, it enlisted Community

Boards. The organization was unwilling to persuade people to quit smoking, since taking sides is antithetical to its go-between mission, but it did offer a forum where smokers and nonsmokers working in unhappy proximity could talk through their grievances. More recently, the U.S. Department of Justice asked Community Boards to design a process for settling disputes under laws protecting the rights of the disabled. As one might anticipate, the model the organization came up with involves conciliation, with at least one disabled person among the mediators.

2

The atmosphere in the Gonzales-Jordan hearing improves when the panel members abandon their attempts to sort out the past, and instead ask each family to describe what it wants for the future. "Just two things, keep the noise down and do not damage the property," says Lamond Kidd, who, since his eruption, has become a voice of reason. "No name calling," Janelle Jordan adds. "The two families can pass each other and not talk," Hector Gonzales replies. From this modest start, other understandings follow. Hector volunteers to clean out the back yard, and Janelle responds: "Our kids will help. We'll all have a barbecue." The families decide who will represent them if a crisis erupts. At five o'clock, nearly four hours after it began, the session ends with an agreement signed by everyone, and the scheduling of a future meeting.

Critics of neighborhood mediation contend that this approach emphasizes amity over vindication, sliding past matters of right and wrong. "The ideology of harmony," writes anthropologist Laura Nader, "the rhetoric of personal therapized harmony which pushes anger and intimacy back into the household have relegated massive outpourings of discontent into buckshot complaints." In fact, a fundamental premise of the Community Boards approach is that conflict is a wound that can be healed by the community, rather than a battle that individual adversaries win or lose, and the sessions are designed to invite the kind of insight associated with therapy.

Peace sometimes comes at the expense of justice, as a therapeutic fog envelops the proceedings. But in more legalistic, justice-driven confrontations between private parties, such as divorce or landlord-tenant cases, the process itself is often punitive. And in most matters brought to Community Boards, the ideology of mediation is exactly right—peace and justice aren't conflicting aspirations, and there is no "right" answer.

THE real power in this system doesn't come from law—no court enforces what the disputants decide— but from the moral authority invested by the parties in these proceedings. Not long ago, AIDS Care, a San Francisco nonprofit group whose mission is to connect people with AIDS with a wide array of health and social-service providers, turned to Community Boards to save itself from internal chaos. The conflict revolved around a volunteer named Jesse Nordstrom and the business manager, Carl Jacoby. Nordstrom, who had made the center the focus of his life, believed he knew how things should be run. But when he made suggestions to business manager Carl Jacoby, he got no satis-faction. For his part, the business manager regarded Nordstrom as a busybody.

Nordstrom started voicing dissatisfaction with Jac-oby's work, then became so outspoken about what was going wrong that he was said to be telling the press terrible tales of managerial incompetence. At this juncture, Reid Cushing, the center's director, who had tried unsuccessfully to settle the conflict, proposed bringing the matter to Community Boards.

During the mediation session, Cushing sat between Nordstrom and Jacoby, much as a father might sit be-tween two quarreling children. Jacoby was tense, and when he talked, he studiously avoided eye contact with Nordstrom. While he was diplomatic, his dismay at having to sit through another round of accusations was evident. Nordstrom came across as sharp-witted and articulate; it was easy enough to imagine him try-ing to order others around.

Cushing initially dominated the discussion, thank-ing Nordstrom for his hard work while defending Jac-oby from Nordstrom's accusations. Though this was a nice enough gesture, it did not penetrate to the heart of things. Even when Nordstrom said he never in-tended to air his grievances in the press, Jacoby, who was unassuaged, made it plain that he didn't trust Nordstrom and complained that he found Nord-strom's constant carping really hurtful.

While wounded feelings are the coin of the realm in San Francisco, Jacoby was a numbers man who rarely talked about such things. Coming from him, this plain statement made Nordstrom stop and reflect, for he had not perceived the impact of his actions in such simple human terms. Yet as the talk continued to cover the same territory, the mediators realized nothing useful would happen unless the terms of the conversation changed. They called a brief time-out.

During the break, the panelists realized that director Reid Cushing, for all his fine intentions, was really getting in the way. The only way out is through, or so Community Boards contends, and Cushing was preventing the disputants from getting through the hard part on their own. Cushing was asked to step back, letting Jacoby and Nordstrom speak directly to one another, and he readily agreed.

Nordstrom had also done some rethinking during the break. When the conciliation resumed, he apologized to Jacoby for the pain he had caused. "I know I can be overly moralistic and controlling. I was talking with my mother about the problems I was having with you guys, and you know what she said? 'There you go again!'" When Jacoby heard that story, more personal and intimate than anything he had known about Nordstrom before, he was able to see Nordstrom not simply as a nuisance and a threat but as a person. He accepted the apology and warmly thanked Nordstrom for all his hard work.

"Those moments are like walking," says panel member Paul Van de Carr, "one leg can move forward only after the other has first taken a step." Soon, the participants had broken into a run, re-learning that they cared more about seeing AIDS Care succeed than about besting one another. An ecstatic Cushing was in tears as he embraced his two colleagues. "In my experience," says panelist Melissa Burke, "people are often talking to one another again at the end of a session, there is friendship and good will. Here there was more—people were displaying the presence of healing, even love."

Whether the issue is as narrowly focused as a spouse's unhappiness about out-of-control drinking or as broad as the litany of neighborhood teenagers' grievances with the patrolling police, as simple as a barking dog or as complex as restructuring a financial agreement, most people are not accustomed to having a real chance to say their piece or to listen so intently. Instead, their instinct is to turn their apparent antagonist into an enemy, to fight back. Mediation introduces them to a different way.

Many volunteers report that they too have changed. Usually they start out with the hope of helping their neighbors and feeling rejuvenated in the process. Yet the essential skills of democratic citizenship, the talents that Alexis de Tocqueville, in *Democracy in America*, had in mind in his discussion of "self-interest rightly understood"—these also come into play during every mediation. The impact of such psychological and political learning extends leagues beyond any specific dispute.

THE story of the Jordans and the Gonzaleses gets another public airing six weeks after the initial session. This time, though, the Gonzaleses are no-shows. Nonetheless, Janelle Jordan acknowledges that relations between the two households have gotten better since the first session. Lamond Kidd, whose temper placed him at the epicenter of the conflicts, has made his peace with the Gonzaleses. For their part, the Gonzaleses have ceased to shout racist insults out the window. The atmosphere of impending violence is much diminished.

Yet headache-inducing noise levels persist. Hector Gonzales wants to maintain the agreement, Janelle Jordan says, but he cannot control everything that goes on in his own home. Once, when Janelle tried to be her family's ambassador, as the agreement contemplated, the Gonzaleses swore at her and called the police. "The officers told me, 'Don't go up there, whatever Community Boards says. It's dangerous.'"

The Jordans have realized a hard truth: The main source of friction between the two households is not personal, which is why their problems can't be settled by talking things through; it is rooted in the out-of-control lives of the Gonzales household. The mediation itself taught them this lesson: Without those hours of painful public exchanges, says Janelle Jordan, her family would be futilely trying for a peaceable resolution—or, more dangerously, looking to win their feud. Having figured out that the struggle is unwinnable and the price of perpetual fighting too high, they have decided to move.

Several mediators leave the session discouraged. There was too much ingrained racism to sort out, they say, too much outright lying, too much talking at, rather than talking to one another. But in mediation, as in life, there aren't always panaceas.

3

When Community Boards was launched a generation ago, the idea of finding ways to settle disagreements outside the formal legal system was unfamiliar, the prospects uncertain. Now, such mediation is common in both the public and private sectors. About 200 American cities and towns have set up their own versions of Community Boards. Private firms report a success rate of better than 80 percent, as well as substantial financial savings, when they resolve disputes through mediation instead of going to court.

"Community conflict resolution provides people a unique opportunity to perform civic work, reduce community and individual alienation, and prevent violent and potentially violent situations from escalating," Ray Shonholtz, Community Boards' charismatic and indefatigable founder, points out. "It is this very work that serves to build new alliances and relationships at the community level." Shonholtz has taken this strategy to Eastern Europe and Russia. There, his new organization, Partnerships for Peace, has trained more than 7,000 people to handle conflicts ranging from ethnic clashes to environmental disputes. In Czechoslovakia, these conciliators even played a part in brokering the peaceful divorce of the Slovak and Czech republics.

Closer to home, however, organizations like Community Boards face a new crisis. They have done their work so well that they risk being shunted aside by experts. Mediation is increasingly being sponsored by government, not to give back to people some control over their lives but instead to make dispute resolution more efficient. Several states have passed laws requiring cities and towns to set up mediation centers. These ventures are supposed to be citywide, not neighborhood-centered; staffed by licensed mediators, not volunteers; and directly linked to the police and the courts, rather than taking advantage of word-of-mouth referrals.

This approach to mediation is all too consistent with a conception of politics that treats ordinary citizens as moral couch potatoes, unable to settle anything of consequence on their own. But volunteer-based organizations like Community Boards instill a sense of real autonomy, authentic personal power, in those who bring their problems to their neighbors. They produce agreements that often work better than imposed settlements. And they remind the citizen-mediators that they can contribute tangibly to the welfare of their own neighborhood. Less tangible but just as important, the experience seems to encourage and sustain a deep sense of civic competence. That kind of character-building matters, and not only in a particular neighborhood or community, because it promotes the health of the republic.

A Suburb at Odds:
The Epic Battle of
Mount Laurel

THE DAY was unseasonably warm for an autumn Sunday in southern New Jersey. Inside Jacob's Chapel in the town of Mount Laurel, some twenty miles east of Philadelphia, the recently restored stained-glass windows were opened wide to catch the breeze. For the sixty members of the all-black African Methodist Episcopalian congregation who were present, this October 1970 Sunday was a special day. The congregation had invited Mount Laurel's mayor to announce the town's response to a plan to rezone thirty-two acres of land so that thirty-six garden apartments could be built for poor, mostly local, and mostly black families.

The pews were old and worn, salvaged from another church and sawn down to fit the small room, but the parishioners sat alert to what the mayor would say. Prominent among them were Mary Robinson, one of the elders in the congregation, and her daughter, Ethel Lawrence, forty-two years old, who earlier that morning had played the piano, as she always did for

This chapter was coauthored with John Dwyer and Larry Rosenthal.

Sunday services. Both mother and daughter were members of a community group that had written the housing proposal, then secured the funds needed to take an option on those thirty-two acres, and so what the mayor had to say mattered especially to them. All around them new housing developments, with their sprawling ranches and ersatz Taras, were transforming Mount Laurel from a small rural community to a booming suburb and pricing local residents out of their hometown. The new homes were vital if the next generation—Ethel's *children's* generation—were to remain in Mount Laurel.

The mood in Jacob's Chapel was guardedly optimistic. Despite some preliminary setbacks at earlier township council meetings, demands to redraw plans and then redraw them again, the parishioners believed things could be worked out; after all, blacks and whites in Mount Laurel were hardly strangers to one another. Black families had lived in the township since late in the seventeenth century, first as slaves and later as tenant farmers. To the most venerable of the black families, the Gaineses and the Stills, their manumission papers, which dated from the American Revolution, were their most prized possessions.

A third of a millennium is a very long time. Quaker families in Mount Laurel, whose ancestry dated back an equally long time, knew the black community very well. Generation upon generation, blacks and whites had grown up together and worked the white families' farms together; in hard times they had helped each other out with food and firewood. There had been little overt opposition when, soon after World War II, blacks sought an end to racially separate public schools. Blacks and whites regarded one another as friends—though friends who knew, and kept to, their respective places—and surely friends didn't turn one another away.

But if the mayor had this history on his mind, he didn't let on. Nostalgia was irrelevant to, even inconsistent with, suburbanization. The mayor was committed to the kind of growth that spelled prosperity—"good ratables," as New Jersey politicians said, meaning development that generates lots of tax dollars and requires few public outlays—and poor people, even those whose families had lived there for many generations, didn't fit into this picture. The town's zoning ordinance didn't allow garden apartments or any other multifamily housing anywhere in Mount Laurel, and that was exactly how things were going to stay: the township council would never approve the community group's request.

Ethel Lawrence and the others in Jacob's Chapel recall the mayor's words as sharply as a brand that sears the skin. After talking about all the changes that were fast coming to Mount Laurel, the new prosperity that this once sleepy farm town was enjoying, he came to the punch line. *"If you people"*—you poor and black people, that is—*"can't afford to live in our town, then you'll just have to leave."*

You people. The mayor had transformed neighbors and helpmates into insiders and outsiders, those who belonged to "our town" and those who didn't. The bonds of neighborliness and friendship went unmentioned, for they had all become irrelevant in a world where money was the single measure of status and belonging. In that world, the power of law would be used not to promote the idea of community but instead to enshrine exclusivity by walling out the poor.

That fateful moment in Jacob's Chapel marked the beginning of fifteen years of path-breaking litigation. The *Mount Laurel* cases, as they came to be known, affected not just this one township. Those rulings put the concept of "fair share" on the public agenda and forced a wholesale revision of zoning across the state. Their impact reached far beyond New Jersey, affecting policies from Massachusetts to California, as *Mount Laurel* became the *Roe v. Wade* of fair housing, the *Brown v. Board of Education* of exclusionary zoning.

Ethel Lawrence was personally transformed in the process. From being a devoted mother and good neighbor who had lived her life in a small town, she became the symbol of a cause. She put aside the fretfulness of her family and the hostility of onetime friends, refused to be intimidated by threats of violence, and stayed committed to what she believed in perfect faith was the right thing to do. What Ethel Lawrence accomplished is as memorable and brave as, if less well known than, Rosa Parks's refusal to move to the back of the bus for a white man in Montgomery, Alabama.

1

Mount Laurel residents regularly tell a self-deprecating story about their town. Every time they plan a

Fourth of July parade, they say, there's an argument: since there is neither a main street nor a town square, no one can agree on where the parade route should begin or end. This story carries the sting of a deeper truth, for in all respects, not just geographic, Mount Laurel has no center. There is no coffee shop where the locals hang out, not even a real grocery store—for those things, you still have to drive to a neighboring town. Massive housing developments have doubled and redoubled the township's population over the past three decades. Office blocks and high-tech industrial complexes euphemistically described as parks occupy prime real estate near the major highways. Mount Laurel is neither a farming community nor a suburb that sends its breadwinners off to jobs in the nearby cities. It has become an amalgam of city and suburb—not quite so futurist as an "edge city" but rather the kind of place that urban planners, meaning no compliment, call a slurb.

Today this town has acquired an identity, though surely it is not the one the managers of its future had in mind. Mount Laurel is known as the defendant in the zoning case that went on forever—the town where the dug-in resistance of well-off landowners and new homeowners to housing even a tiny number of poor families brought on a famous courtroom battle over the nation's suburban soul.

During the centennial celebrations in 1972, the citizens of Mount Laurel Township tried to recreate its past as a prosperous farm village whose pride was Rancocas Woods, which once attracted summer visitors with games of chance and open-air dancing. At the centennial there were four band concerts and a beard-growing contest, a turkey shoot and a kite-flying contest. But the pageant was as much a reflection of contemporary life as an exercise in nostalgia. Instead of the exhibition of prize farm animals traditional in rural communities, there was a pet show featuring well-coifed and mannerly dogs and cats. By 1972, there were almost no farm animals—almost no farms either—left in Mount Laurel.

For almost three centuries, from the founding of the community until the 1950s, change came exceedingly slowly. But the changes marked since midcentury have been as basic as if someone had pressed the fast-forward button, and every trend, every aspect of the nation's coming of age that had bypassed the town, manifested itself in a single generation. Outside events partly shaped this transformation, because Mount Laurel was not isolated from the surrounding world. Exit 4 off the New Jersey Turnpike opened in 1952, and in the early 1970s came Interstate 295 barely a mile away. While the highways bisected the township, denying it the possibility of physical cohesion, they also gave Mount Laurel a direct link to the northeast corridor. RCA had already opened a major plant nearby, and the interchanges offered a logical site for the offices, the hygienic-looking manufacturing plants, and the hotel chains that were to come.

Meanwhile, a Levittown, that quintessential suburban venture of the postwar era, was built a few miles to the northeast, and in short order forty-five thousand people, many of them soldiers assigned to nearby Fort Dix and their young families, moved in. Developers who had earlier dismissed the region as too remote began to eye Mount Laurel as a giant in-fill, virgin land that was a manageable commute to Camden and Philadelphia.

But the way in which Mount Laurel was remade was no act of submission to the gods of development. The community willed the changes upon itself and made them happen. It got exactly what it wanted: tract housing, economic growth—and nothing for the poor.

As early as the mid-1950s, well before suburban development had reached the town, a Philadelphia developer took an option on two thousand acres of prime agricultural land. Although nothing came of that venture because the builder went broke, it shows that, from the first signs of development, practical-minded Mount Laurel farm owners would not let sentiment intrude on the new economics that made housing tracts a more valuable cash crop than tomatoes. Soon thereafter, Mount Laurel's first development opened on the easternmost fringe of the township in Rancocas Woods, which at one time had been the town's recreation spot. This was hardly another Levittown—most of the new homes were log cabins, and their owners were dubbed "woodies"—but it marked the beginning of an influx of newcomers.

Commercial development was also on the minds of local officials. At a township council meeting in 1963, the mayor boasted of "several hot business prospects" that were considering building offices near Exit 4. Just a few years later, as housing projects much more ambitious than Rancocas Woods were being launched, his successor, Bill Haines, whose ancestors arrived in Laurel in the eighteenth century, became an advocate for something that was new then, even visionary, called planned unit developments (PUDs). Patterned after Reston, Virginia—more grandiosely, after Italian hill villages and New England towns—PUDs are large-scale, self-contained communities within a community. When Larchmont opened in Mount Laurel in 1970, it was only the second such complex to be built in the state.

This tendency to embrace the new, with all of its ambiguous blessings, already apparent at the time of the centennial celebration, has accelerated since. Mount Laurel's business directory boasts health spas, a tanning salon, and a bar where upscale corporate employees meet for "food, drink, and great times," all located near the turnpike exit. The township's population increased at a faster rate than that of any other community in this rapidly suburbanizing state. It nearly doubled between 1950 and 1960, to 5,249, then doubled again in the next decade. By 1980, the population had grown to more than 17,000, as nearly three thousand new housing units, many in the new planned unit development, were built; in the next decade the population doubled yet again, to 34,000.

The demand for public services similarly mushroomed. The township outgrew its two prewar schools —one became a senior center, the other an administration building—and built six elementary and middle schools. The continuing pursuit of "good ratables" has provided an ever-increasing stream of tax revenues. Three industrial parks in Mount Laurel house twenty companies, including Honda, Bell Atlantic, and National Football League Films. A Holiday Inn, a Quality Court, an Executive Motor Lodge, and a Hilton accommodate visiting corporate executives.

All the familiar problems of growth have accompanied this prosperity. Traffic jams, once unknown, are twice-daily occurrences, and the number of car accidents has climbed too, to more than a thousand in 1990, a 20 percent increase in just five years. Drugs, once thought to be a city vice, are used by teenagers who complain that they're living in Dullsville. Crime has increased as well, and the much-expanded police force in Mount Laurel now carries automatics rather than revolvers. In place of the farms there are only pastoral names like Apple Way, Quail Run, and Orchard Court that developers, hoping to evoke nostalgia, assign to their brand-new streets.

Mount Laurel's history bears some resemblance to the story of Grover's Corners, the mythical New Hampshire community close by the Massachusetts border, pop. 3,149, where Thornton Wilder set the American classic *Our Town*. Both were settled in the late 1600s, and at the beginning of the present century both were sleepy villages, neither growing nor shrinking much in size, surrounded by farms, overwhelmingly Republican in their politics. All the change comes later, in our time— it's as if, instead of looking backward, the all-knowing stage manager who narrates the play is gazing into the future, not at all sure that he likes what he sees.

Grover's Corners is by and large a really nice place, as the stage manager tells the audience. Dr. Gibbs makes house calls; bashful boys treat their high school sweethearts to strawberry sodas; everyone looks after the town drunk, for "he'd seen a peck of trouble," and almost none of the residents lock their doors at night (though even at the turn of the century this trusting practice is beginning to disappear as the town starts to "citify").

Yet one of the first things the stage manager says about Grover's Corners is that there's a bad neighborhood "across the tracks . . . Polish Town's across the tracks, and some Canuck families," and these ethnic families are stand-ins for blacks on the bottom rung of the social status ladder. Grover's Corners is also a place where money talks, though in muted tones. As a child, Rebecca, whose life history is traced out in the play, is forever saving. When her mother tells her "it's a good thing to spend some every now and then," she answers, "Mama, do you know what I love most in the world—do you?—Money."

An actor planted in the audience pesters the town's newspaper editor, Mr. Webb, to address "social injustice and industrial inequality," and he responds in a jokey way. "Oh, yes, everybody is [aware]—somethin' terrible. Seems like they spend most of their time talking about who's rich and who's poor." But the heckler is in no mood to be fobbed off with jokes. "Then why don't they do something about it?" he persists.

"Well, I dunno," Mr. Webb answers, "I guess we're all hunting like everybody else for a way the diligent and sensible can rise to the top and the lazy and quarrelsome can sink to the bottom. But it ain't easy to find. Meanwhile, *we do all that we can to help those that can't help themselves and those that can we leave alone.*"

That answer—Thornton Wilder's answer—mixes an appreciation for the vicissitudes of life, which don't always reward the deserving, with a lively social conscience. Among the well-off families in Mount Laurel, however, no similar sense of social obligation is apparent. By the time the mayor of Mount Laurel stands up to address the black congregation in Jacob's Chapel, money and exclusivity are all that matter. *"If you people can't afford to live in our town, then you'll just have to leave."*

2

From the outset, the Quaker settlers in the Mount Laurel region depended on the help of nonwhites, initially Native Americans and later blacks, for their survival. Quakers brought the first African Americans to Burlington County as slaves as early as 1664; a county court judgment in 1685 enforced a verbal contract in which two slaves were traded for "6500 good well-burnt bricks." Although the Quakers were morally opposed to slavery, their sense of economic necessity came first. While the slaves were emancipated a century or so later, after the American Revolutionary War, most stayed on as tenet farmers, re-creating their economic dependency in a relationship that lasted for well over a century. The freedmen and freedwomen formed their first congregation in 1811 and later named their African Methodist Episcopalian church Jacob's Chapel, after Quaker farmer Albert Jacobs, who paid three dollars for the land on which the church presently sits and then contributed the property to the congregation.

By the 1840s, Mount Laurel had become a haven for freed blacks, as each new settler was given a quarter of an acre by the Quakers. It was also a stopping point on the Underground Railroad. Traces of that hiding place remain underneath the floorboards in the vestibule of Jacob's Chapel.

In the graveyard alongside the church, a dozen tombstones are inscribed with testimonials to the men who fought during the Civil War in the Colored Infantry, and alongside each of these stones rests the star of the Grand Army of the Republic. So many bodies have been buried in that graveyard that the precise location of all the grave sites is no longer known, and when a member of the congregation dies the grave digger has to tap out an unused plot.

Ethel Lawrence, who became the pivotal figure in the struggle for affordable housing in the town, traces her own roots in Mount Laurel back six generations, to a white Virginia woman who came in the 1850s on the Underground Railroad to have her half-black baby. Born in 1926, the second of Leslie and Mary Robinson's eight children, Ethel Lawrence remembers growing up in the 1930s mostly as an idyll. "We were poor but it didn't matter so much. There was always food on the table, vegetables and fruits we canned for the winter. We chopped down firewood to keep warm. We took the feed out of those old muslin bags and bleached them to make sheets and tablecloths. If there was a hog killing, three or four families would join in. Since black families like the innards . . . when [white] farmers killed pigs, they'd give them to you. Everyone knew everybody else and if you were in trouble, everybody helped. We got along beautifully."

The same kind of story is told by old-time Quakers like Buddy Rudderow, who remembers "rubbing shoulders with the black families of the community. . . . We all knew each other." Yet when Ethel Lawrence pauses to reflect on precisely how blacks and whites in Mount Laurel lived side by side, it is not as equals but rather as people who knew in their bones their assigned stations in life. "We got along together, just as long as I remembered who I was and they remembered who they were—as long as I remembered to stay in my place and they remembered to stay in their place, then we got along fine."

The ownership of property was one thing that defined a person's status in the community: it was the white farmers who owned the land and the black farm workers who depended on the farmers' largesse for a place to live. Law and custom were place definers as well. Although New Jersey is conventionally considered a northern state, North Jersey, which clusters around New York City, is in this respect very different from South Jersey. In its geographic location, no farther north than Maryland, and in its social etiquette as well, South Jersey has not been much removed from Dixie. The Ku Klux Klan was active there in its several incarnations, and the identities of local Klansmen are known to the black families: during the 1980s, a high school classmate of Ethel Lawrence's youngest daughter, Renee, a girl whose father is an ex-Klansman, fled from an abusive home to live for two years with the

Lawrences. While skinheads have supplanted the Klan among today's teenagers, they pose a similar menace, getting their kicks from beating up black and Jewish children and planting crosses on black families' lawns. Until World War II, blacks were obliged to sit in the last rows of the Moorestown movie theater, and Riley's, the local drugstore, wouldn't let blacks sit at the soda fountain. Mount Laurel's schools were officially segregated until the late 1940s. This was what the blacks wanted, some whites claim, but that is wishful remembering. Quaker patriarch Buddy Rudderow recalls that one family sent its blond daughter to the white school, but when the teachers found out that one of her parents was black, the girl was forced to attend the colored school. South Jersey was nothing like South Carolina, however—it didn't take sit-ins or fire hoses to change some of the folkways in Mount Laurel. Well before the swellings of the civil rights movement, the black community got the simple justice it asked for. The schools were integrated, Riley's opened its lunch counter, the movie theater let blacks sit where they wished, and all the while a semblance of civility was maintained.

Economics, not Jim Crow, took the hardest toll on the black families, whose lives began to unravel with the opening of the Mount Laurel exit off the New Jersey Turnpike in 1952. The state claimed some farmland to build the highway, and although the surveyors were careful to protect the old farmhouses, some of the tenant houses were plowed under for the roadway. The white farmers didn't complain because they were compensated for their losses, but they began to let the tenant farmers go. When the Interstate highway was constructed a few years later, the state took more land and more tenant farmers were displaced. There was no place in the township for them to move—no place, that is, except a handful of shacks in a shabby neighborhood known as Springville. Eventually those shacks would become the springboard for the *Mount Laurel* lawsuit.

Ask old-time Mount Laurel residents where Springville is and you'll likely draw a blank stare, then a flash of recognition. "You mean Jewtown," they say, entirely unselfconsciously, providing yet another insight into the social consciousness of the community.

Springville was originally farmed by homesteaders, but they couldn't make a living because of the high water table on which these 422 acres mostly sit. In the early 1900s, most of them sold their land to Jewish families who had emigrated from Russia and were living in the slums of Philadelphia—hence "Jewtown." Later, the year-round residents were joined by other Jewish families fleeing the heat of Philadelphia summers. They lived in modest cottages, hastily cobbled together and not suited for winter use.

Those were the halcyon days in Springville, but the neighborhood began to slip after the Second World War. The chicken business, the economic mainstay, became unprofitable because of automation. The children and grandchildren of the families who used to spend their summers in Mount Laurel were now grown up with their own families, and they wanted someplace nicer. The synagogue shut its doors, and over time the building found new uses as a storehouse, a window shop, and a mosque. The end of the war also brought an influx of GIs to nearby Fort Dix, and, with housing in the area extremely tight, the abandoned chicken coops were converted into residences. These were tiny, just a couple of rooms that had rudimentary plumbing or no plumbing at all, a single door perilously close to the kerosene heater, but they were cheap and also filled a need. The GIs moved in, transients with no ties to the town. Poor families, white and black, mostly migrant workers, moved in as well. The neighborhood bar attracted a rowdy crowd. People in town started seeing Springville as a slum and an embarrassment. Although a single Jewish landlord and a few poor Jewish families stayed on, the era of "Jewtown" was fading. Locals began referring to Springville as "Tobacco Road."

Cleaning up Springville became, in the mid-1960s, a crusade for local health officials and politicians alike. It was a way to improve Mount Laurel's image and in the process alter the character of its population. Much of the housing in Springville was substandard: a survey showed that half of the eighty-eight homes were, by the state's building-code standards, either deteriorated or dilapidated. The wells used for drinking water were contaminated with human sewage. Several of the converted chicken coops had burned down, killing some of the people who lived in them. Town officials felt these places should not be rehabilitated. The only thing to do was to tear them down. *"A mission of mercy"* is how Joe Alvarez, who was then the town's zoning officer and later was elected to the township council, characterizes this campaign. But those whose lives were directly touched felt otherwise. According to state law, local officials had to ensure that the housing was made fit for people to live in or else make other arrangements for displaced residents. Because they were unwilling to do either, local officials usually waited until a family moved out before conducting their inspection. Then, with no tenants whom they were legally obliged to relocate, they plastered the dwelling with yellow stickers that read "Unfit for Habitation" and tore down the condemned homes.

"I know we had a very effective program," says Alvarez. "It may have resulted in eliminating a few homes, but then it was a good reflection on the town."

3

Mary Robinson and her daughter Ethel Lawrence kept watch on these developments. Both mother and daughter had sought to secure their own futures against the changes taking place in Mount Laurel.

By the standards of Mount Laurel, Mary Robinson, then nearly sixty years old, a widow whose children were all grown, was an activist. Two decades earlier, she had spoken out against racial segregation in the schools and the refusal of Riley's daughter to serve blacks; she had sent her daughter, then just sixteen, to protest a movie house in Burlington that required blacks to sit in the very front rows. She owned her own home, which she and her late husband, Leslie, bought in 1935 for a thousand dollars.

In 1954, Ethel Lawrence and her husband, Thomas, a welder who worked for United States Pipe and Foundry

Company, rented a bungalow on an acre of land on Elbo Lane, in a neighborhood known as Little Texas. They dressed up the outside of their home with flowers and shade trees, raised a few rabbits and some chickens, planted squash, collard greens, tomatoes, cabbage, string beans, and strawberries in the backyard. Within a few years they had saved up enough to make the down payment on the six-thousand-dollar purchase price.

With farms shrinking and Springville gradually being razed, though, it didn't take a seer to realize that none of these families, not even those whose ancestors are listed in the Jacob's Chapel Bible, would be able to remain there. Unless something was done to bend the economic forces that were turning farms into subdivisions for the rising middle class, there would be no home they could afford—no place in Mount Laurel for the next generation, the eight children Ethel and Thomas Lawrence were raising on Elbo Lane. It was the thought of what might happen to those children that stirred Ethel Lawrence to do something. The formation of the Springville Action Council—the federal community-action program come to Mount Laurel—gave her the chance. As she remembers that era, "Reverend Wood, a white man who was on the council's board, told me that 'all these do-gooders really mean well but they can't know what it means to be poor or to be black, because they have never been poor or black.' That reverend was exactly what you would think a Christian would be. He saw no color. He just saw human need."

Stuart Wood had been sent to Mount Laurel in 1966 with an unusual assignment, to create a ministry without a church. He rented a house in Ramblewood, the development that was filling up with young executives' families, and set about looking for a mission. The day he was taken through Springville, he knew he had found his calling.

"Right away I thought, 'Something needs to be done here,'" and during the coming months Stuart Wood knocked on every door in Springville. "Here were poor Jews, Cubans, poor whites, blacks. The chicken coops they lived in were like places where you cage an animal." Later he would tell reporters that Springville was "a festering cancer, worse than the worst slums in New York City," where living conditions "made me puke." The minister usually spent his days in Springville, or else with the liberal Quakers from the neighboring town, or in seething Camden, fifteen miles and a light year away. At night he returned to Ramblewood, where the lawns were perfectly cropped, gin and tonic flowed at endless cocktail parties, and the talk was about steadily rising property values.

The members of the Springville Action Council knew that decent shelter for the town's poor families was a prime need; the critical question was how to make this happen. Town officials played along, believing that the group was harmless, until it received a six-thousand-dollar grant from the state's activist Department of Community Affairs for the state's first low-cost rural housing development. This was only seed money: the ultimate aim was to tap into federal subsidies for low-income rental housing to build two- and three-bedroom garden apartments. Planners volunteered their time to design the complex, and the state funds were used to take out an option on a thirty-two-acre parcel in Springville, then on the market at a thousand dollars an acre.

"The landowner told me I was next to God for wanting to help the people of Springville," Reverend Wood recalls. Yet before the apartments could be built, Mount Laurel would have to amend its master plan, because the zoning law on the books allowed for only single-family residences. Ethel Lawrence and Mary Robinson were sure that the township council would go along. After all, Mount Laurel was their town too and had been for generations. Surely the unarticulated sense of community revealed in the painless desegregation of the schools two decades earlier would bring Mount Laurel's officials to accede to the reasonable wishes of the town's black citizens. But this perception proved highly romanticized.

The first sign of trouble came when the Department of Community Affairs announced the seed-money grant. The press release got the facts all wrong: the projected Mount Laurel apartments would be rented for next to nothing, it said, and people on welfare would be recruited to live in them. Although this was untrue—the housing was actually intended for the working poor who were being pushed out of Mount Laurel—the story made page one in the local press.

The firestorm it ignited set the tone for all the controversies to come. From 1968, when the state grant was announced, until today, when middle-class residents in Mount Laurel hear "affordable housing," they don't think about Ethel Lawrence and her generation of ancestors from Mount Laurel. Most of the people who have moved into the new, middle-class developments have no sense that their adopted town has any history—they would be dumbfounded to learn that free black families were living in Mount Laurel before there was a United States of America. Nor do they have in mind people like Ethel Lawrence's oldest daughter, Thomasene, a medical assistant who during the late 1960s was struggling to raise her children in one of Springville's converted chicken coops.

What the suburbanites *do* think goes something like this. Very poor people are coming . . . very poor outsiders . . . very poor outsiders on welfare . . . *lots of very poor and black outsiders on welfare are coming to Mount Laurel from places like Camden, and they will bring violence and drugs, and they will wreck our schools. They will destroy our way of life.* This mixture of paranoia and urban reality explains why so many homeowners in Rancocas Woods and Ramblewood, the woodies and the strivers who were otherwise so different, were united on this one issue. Housing for the poor should not—at all costs *must* not—be built in Mount Laurel.

4

The Springville Action Council was slated to make its case before the township council in November 1969. The bad news was that Richard Goodwin, the developer of Ramblewood and a powerful influence in local politics, was also on the docket.

What Goodwin had in mind was a new town, which ultimately would become the ten-thousand-unit PUD called Larchmont. To the Mount Laurel politicians, the pitch was irresistible: the new residents will have money in their pockets, they'll give a boost to the economy. It was very hard to follow this performance with a plea for a change in the zoning rules—a modest change, as well, in the direction the town was heading—put forward mainly by a liberal white minister and black women with neither money nor the influence that money can buy. Their only argument, really, was that this was the right thing to do, and that was hardly enough to sway popular sentiment.

From the outset, zoning in Mount Laurel was a way to exclude people regarded by the residents as undesirable. Until 1952, a $2.50 permit was all that was legally required to build a house in Mount Laurel. There was no zoning ordinance on the books then, no planning of any kind, no building inspection carried out. The clerk who handled the building permits lived in a falling-down house that wouldn't have passed even the most cursory inspection. But this attitude shifted when townspeople got wind of a proposed labor camp for migrant workers. Overnight, the township drafted a zoning law—a crude text that ran only a couple of pages—meant less to guide the township's future than to keep out the migrant laborers. The Rancocas Woods development, built a few years later on the site of what had once been an amusement park, was a planner's nightmare. The developers did not install sewers, and, because there wasn't enough drainage, flooding followed every rainstorm. Water pressure from the fire hydrants was so pitifully weak that the volunteer fire department had to pump in water from Rancocas Creek. Not until the mid-1960s, after Ramblewood as well as Rancocas Woods had been approved and the shortcomings of a laissez-faire approach to planning were very apparent, did the town draft a real master plan. Town officials said frankly that they wanted Mount Laurel to be transformed into an "executive-type town," and apartments for the working poor were as out of place in this vision as dandelions in the well-tended suburban garden.

While small-town politics is often a somnambulant affair, Mount Laurel has been notable for the partisan ferocity of its public life. Planning and zoning have figured centrally in this political warfare. Beginning in the late 1950s with the construction of new homes in Rancocas Woods and the first influx of newcomers, a community that had been solidly Republican for generations became the setting for bloody partisan battles. Democrats took control for the first time in 1958, Republicans regained power in 1966, there was a Democratic sweep in 1970, and five years later the GOP was again in command, as the political pendulum continued to swing. These party labels, although regularly used in Mount Laurel, are misleading. The contests in Mount Laurel were not reprises of the great national campaigns of the era—Kennedy versus Nixon or, later, Vietnam and Watergate played out in South Jersey. Mount Laurel's elections confirmed the adage that all politics is local, for the dominant questions, the preoccupying questions, concerned property values, tax rates and assessments, allegations of overdevelopment, claims that incumbents were in the developers' pockets. Behind these issues lay deeper questions of political identity—how can we control our destiny?

Both Democrats and Republicans cast themselves as progressives and their opponents as dinosaurs in matters of development. The Republicans, whose core strength came from the old landowners, described themselves as the promoters of intelligent growth who believed that the way to woo industry was straightforward. Their message was: "We need you and we won't give you flak."

It was the Democrats, mostly newcomers living in the new developments, who wanted to slow the pace of growth. They were concerned about what the proposed planned unit developments would bring— "wall-to-wall housing," as one town council member put it.

The Republicans dismissed the Democrats as arrivistes who had purchased their own small piece of the suburban dream and selfishly wanted to fence out everybody else. The Democrats countered that their opponents, who when in office approved almost every new housing and commercial complex that the builders proposed, were not selfless purveyors of progress, for their financial self-interest was closely tied to their vision of the public interest. A number of prominent Republicans, including Bill Haines, who proudly referred to himself as the father of PUDs, owned hundreds of acres of farmland that developers coveted. They stood to become millionaires if their vision was realized.

"Our town was on the edge of a major development explosion," a Democrat on the council recalls, "and it

just didn't seem to me that the people who were potentially able to profit from that were the best people
to have the role of decision makers." But the Democrats who personally placed great value on Mount
Laurel's small town atmosphere, newcomers who
were eager to lift the drawbridge the moment they arrived, faced a similar conflict when they opposed a
new development. Each side was able to equate the
public interest with personal interest.

All politics is local in another sense: it is a mutual
back-scratching enterprise that thrives on contributions from citizens who expect to be rewarded in kind
by those they help elect. Democrat Alvarez recalls getting fifteen dollars for his campaign from a man for
whom he had found work as the town's truck driver;
Republican Haines remembers that developers contributed the liquor to hold cocktail-party fund-raisers
and "we'd get to keep the leftover half bottles."

The influence of the leading developers on township
politics was bluntly expressed. "We had a marketing
study done as to which direction we should go from
the center of Philadelphia," says Richard Goodwin, developer of Ramblewood and later of another PUD,
"and the line cut right through Mount Laurel. It
wasn't too difficult to get permission from the town
fathers in those days. The leadership was Quaker
farmers. They knew in the back of their minds that
when they sold their land their pot of gold had arrived—payback for the struggles the farmers had all
their lives to scrape out a living." Other tangible rewards accompanied development. One member of the
planning board made a tidy living by selling fences to

Goodwin, and one of the council members drilled all of the developer's wells.

Such partisan antagonisms did not translate into opposing positions on whether the township should change its zoning law to authorize new housing for the poor. Not once did a voice in the political mainstream ever have a kind word to say on that topic. In the late 1960s, the members of a Republican-dominated council turned down the Springville Action Council's plans, one after the other. The Democrats who succeeded them, and the Republicans who followed the Democrats, eventually spent more than a million dollars in lawyers' and experts' fees to fight the proposition, propounded in the *Mount Laurel* New Jersey Supreme Court decisions, that the township had a legal duty to a "fair share" of the region's poor.

5

The Mount Laurel politicians' words and acts carry the sharp scent of race prejudice. When council members talked about Camden, they were talking in a code everyone understood—the meaning was "black." In the Springville neighborhood, discrimination based on race was old news. The area badly needed sewers, streetlights, and roads. "When we asked for something, it might have been wells, it doesn't matter, it was always the same," recalls a longtime resident. "When the mayor found out we were from Springville we met a stone wall. . . . They couldn't wait to get rid of what was already there. Why should they want more?"

Still, Bill Haines believes that "we would have worked things out," referring to the proposed housing for Springville, "because we understood each other." Perhaps his claque, the Quaker farmers with deep roots in Mount Laurel, would eventually have struck a deal. Ethel Lawrence would like to believe that "the old farmers would have had enough foresight to spend money in building homes for these people than spending the money to pay lawyers to keep them out." But the Quaker farmers were no longer in charge, the new suburbanites were running the town, and that altered the equation. "Things changed as the newcomers settled in the community. The old-timers turned against us. All our support died as the old-timers stayed in the background, for they did not want to risk losing the support of the newcomers."

The generation of GOP politicians who came of age in the 1960s wasn't much interested in negotiating. One Republican councilman who lived in Rancocas Woods talks about campaigning in Springville as if the experience had left the taste of ashes perpetually in his mouth. "The conditions there turned my stomach. I remember each time I shook someone's hand and asked for his vote, he'd ask for some favor in return." Although this was par for the course in Mount Laurel politics, he drew back. "I thought it was awful. I told them they could keep their votes and walked out on them." A Ramblewood resident who became mayor of the town speaks sarcastically about the Springville Action Council as people who expected "a million dollars and an El Dorado Cadillac" for the asking.

The Democrats on the council held similar views, even though they came differently to their positions. One councilmember, putting on his planner's hat, believed that building subsidized housing meant "instant slums . . . those people knew damn well we weren't prejudiced." Particularly pointed, and poignant, was the stance of councilman, and later mayor, Joe Alvarez: "I come from a culture of helping people. But the township didn't create the problem, and the township has no responsibility to alleviate the problem."

"I moved to Mount Laurel on November 27, 1954," recounts Alvarez, a native of Puerto Rico, and he savors the exact date. "It was because of fate," he adds, but the facts are somewhat more mundane. He was working for Philco-Ford at the time, living with his family in a rented house in Philadelphia, and he didn't have the cash to make a down payment on a home. An old-time Mount Laurel resident named Earl Bartling was willing to donate construction materials and give advice to this self-described pencil pusher; all Alvarez had to contribute was sweat equity and the $350 cost of a half-acre lot. Alvarez is not the only person whom Bartling helped this way—at least ten houses were built in Mount Laurel because of his remarkable generosity—but Alvarez sees no connection between these private good deeds and any public responsibility. And although he has financed a condominium in Mount Laurel for his son, who otherwise couldn't have afforded to stay, he has no empathy for people like Ethel Lawrence's children who lack the family money to bankroll their own homes.

During the years he has lived in Mount Laurel, there have been occasional racist jibes about Joe Alvarez's ancestry, antagonists who asked him, "Why don't you go back to Puerto Rico?" Yet he regards himself as an American who made it, not as an outsider—in Mount Laurel he insists on being Joe, not José. For six months in 1964, the family moved to Puerto Rico, but they returned when they realized that the New Jersey suburb had become their real home. On the day of their return, says Alvarez, the Holiday Inn's billboard read: "Welcome Back, Joe and Anna."

Like other ethnic Americans, Alvarez assimilated in ways that the descendants of slaves, whatever their wishes, never have been able to. But none of this personal history surfaces when Alvarez talks about people who were seeking affordable housing, like Ethel Lawrence and Mary Robinson. He relies instead on the language of disease and disorder. "It's like grafting a good healthy skin so you can graft in cancer skin and blend it in. Here you have a healthy area. Bringing these people in here, you don't know who they are," he says, with all the ominous implications of the unknown.

Sometimes the politicians spoke about the community's willingness to "take care of our own" but not "having to take care of the world." This is a morally plausible position, the philosophy attributed to the residents of *Our Town*, but the politicians' perpetual antagonism to housing the poor—*any* poor, local or otherwise—unmasks this commitment as a pietism. At one township council meeting, Reverend Stuart Wood remembers, when Springville housing was on the table, "the local health officer poked me black and blue in the chest while pinning me to the wall. He screamed at me, 'Why don't you just sit tight like everyone else until I can condemn all those places and get the people there out?'" The only principles that drove the propertied classes, whom the politicians represented, were efficiency and security, a desire to "keep taxes down and to keep them out," part of their "relentless quest for material benefit along with the promise of freedom— that is, the lack of encumbrances—to improvise fresh identities."

The engineers and planners who worked for the planning board and the township council lodged one objection after another, twenty-two in all, to the proposed housing. The community group received sound advice from able professionals who contributed their time; four separate sets of plans were prepared, and each was rejected. "We were beaten by other professionals," says Stuart Wood, "planners, architects, and PR men selling the dream of a new suburban community of newly upwardly mobile people. They bought that dream—and in the process they killed ours." Politics hid behind the mask of expertise to exclude unwanted neighbors.

"There was no political base in Springville, no voters there. There were just poor, ignorant people," says Dick Goodwin. "The newcomers in Ramblewood didn't want poor people in Mount Laurel."

Meeting after meeting, the township council dominated by Ramblewood and Rancocas homeowners

89

kept stonewalling the community contingent, hoping it would tire and go away. The people who showed up got "very personal—it was better than a TV soap opera," recalls Quaker matriarch Alice Rudderow, who in 1967 sold almost all of her family's 220-acre farm to developers. "Stuart Wood was like a small salmon swimming upstream," observes Goodwin. "He couldn't see that failure was the handwriting on the wall."

Meanwhile, the housing controversy was moving into a new forum. No longer was this a matter for the citizens of Mount Laurel to settle entirely among themselves. The problem was about to be placed in the hands of the judges, who played by entirely different rules.

6

Lawyers and nonlawyers inhabit different worlds. Attorneys think about a lawsuit as a way to get what their clients want while they flex their professional legal muscles; the more novel the legal claim the more muscle flexing, and hence, if they win, the more gratification. But to the laity, lawsuits are fearful and alien events, prolonged battles over arcane territory fought by proxies who, expressing themselves in the obscurantisms of legalese, pitch their pleadings and their pleas to stern, black-sheathed judges. Better to work things out, people generally believe, better not to raise the stakes by invoking the majesty of the law. So it was in Mount Laurel—before a case could be filed on behalf of those who were being driven out, the Legal Services lawyers first had to win the trust of their new clients. The go-between in that enterprise was Reverend Stuart Wood.

Mount Laurel's tactics frustrated the minister and made him question whether he was being of service to anyone. Town council members regarded him as weird, a hippie child of the sixties living in a community that carried on as if Dwight Eisenhower were still in the White House. His outspokenness made him a pariah in the Ramblewood development where he lived, and, although that didn't bother him, it put a strain on his wife. At one cocktail party, Wood recalls, she had been talking intensely with a couple who had just moved in down the block, but the moment they realized that she was Reverend Wood's wife, *that man's* wife, they turned away.

Wood had raised unrealistic hopes within the black community, he thought guiltily. Camden Regional Legal Services' enterprising young attorneys, Peter O'Connor and Carl Bisgaier, had read newspaper accounts of the community group's abortive attempt to get affordable housing. When they met with Wood, he was delighted to hand over responsibility for Springville's future. "I had nothing left," he recalls.

The lawyers came away impressed when they talked with a contingent from the Springville Action Council at Ethel Lawrence's home. Many suburbs had zoning ordinances that walled out poor outsiders, and ultimately the reformers hoped to end this practice. But here was a community that seemed bent on growing faster than anyplace else, while simultaneously ridding itself of the poor families who were already there. Because the town was forcing its own poor residents to move, the attorneys felt that their cause might arouse more sympathy than a lawsuit designed mainly to let in poor and black outsiders.

But the local black community held decidedly mixed views. The older generation of Mount Laurel's black residents didn't want to push matters too hard. "I know the civic leaders [like Mary Robinson and Ethel Lawrence] worked very hard to get housing for the poor in Springville and eventually to be integrated in the new developing areas," said the octagenarian matriarch of that community. But one could not expect low-cost housing to be placed in the big-homes area.

"They wanted a decent place, a convenient place and a nice place to live. But if you don't have the money," she adds, sounding not so very different from politicians like Joe Alvarez or Bill Haines, "one should expect to stay in one's own area."

Some members of the Jacob's Chapel congregation weren't eager to get involved either. One Sunday, the minister delivered a sermon doubting the wisdom of congregation members' devoting so much time to the housing fight. Even members of Ethel Lawrence's own family grumbled at her involvement; but when her children complained that she was foolish to get involved, since she already had her own house, she replied that she was doing it for them, and that stopped the criticism. Ethel's husband, Thomas, chewed out the lawyers for what he regarded as their trouble making, yet he was proud of what his wife was doing. "While he never told me so to my face," she says, "Thomas would brag about me when he went to see his brothers."

Throughout the lengthy struggle, the handful of black professional families who had moved into Rancocas Woods and Ramblewood remained mute. "Secretly they support the cause of housing for the poor," says Ethel Lawrence, "but they were afraid of ruffling the feathers of their neighbors, afraid of risking their positions." Perhaps so, though it is also possible that these successful black families had no wish to invite the ghetto back into their lives and so were entirely comfortable with the strategy that town officials were pursuing.

Blacks who lived in the Springville chicken coops potentially had the most to gain from legal action, but they were scared that their landlords would evict them if they complained; and so they endured, in places like the shanty on which Ethel Lawrence's oldest daughter, Thomasene, spent eighty-eight dollars a month for rent. "Everything leaked," she says, "everything got mildewed, the shower was corroded. The open sewer ran right in back, polluting our drinking water. I was lucky because I had real wood floors and heat in the winter. Others had dirt floors and nearly froze."

These families needed housing, not lawsuits. Suing the township on their behalf meant breaking new legal ground, but not necessarily new ground for housing. A final court decision was probably years away. It would surely be better to win something tangible, Peter O'Connor thought, than to risk everything on the receptivity of New Jersey judges. He hoped he could strike a deal with developer Richard Goodwin to get the units built, and so make a lawsuit unnecessary; though Goodwin was intrigued, he ultimately rejected O'Connor's proposal as politically suicidal.

Over the next few months, Peter O'Connor and Carl Bisgaier came frequently to Mount Laurel. They walked around Springville and attended church services at Jacob's Chapel a Sunday or two. The lawyers were received politely but skeptically. What finally gave them credibility was a lawsuit they brought on behalf of Ethel Lawrence's aunt, Catherine Still. She had gotten weary of making do in a house with no toilet and no running water, and when her landlord refused to make improvements, she brought her grievance to Carl Bisgaier. The lawyer put her rent money in escrow, then took her case to court to test the state's new tenants' rights law. In 1971, Bisgaier won the case: the judge permitted Catherine Still to withhold her rent until the landlord brought her home up to code.

Word quickly went out in Springville that these attorneys weren't empty vests, that they could accomplish something with their legal arguments. Catherine Still's complaint was infinitely less ambitious than the township zoning challenge the lawyers were preparing. But for many years it was the only housing litigation that made any tangible impact on the town. The case known as *Southern Burlington County NAACP et al. v. Township of Mount Laurel*, filed in May 1971, would continue not just for a few years but seemingly forever. It became a Dickensian *Jarndyce v. Jarndyce* of land-use justice, a lawsuit that tested the mettle of the state courts—tested, as well, the character of those communities, black and white, well-off and poor, that together made up Mount Laurel.

7

For the better part of two decades, the Mount Laurel litigation was on the docket of the New Jersey judiciary. Back and forth the dispute went to the state Supreme Court. There were scores of hearings in lower courts, and twice the township tried unsuccessfully to convince the U.S. Supreme Court to review the case.

There were moments of seeming triumph during those long years, notably the 1975 state Supreme Court decision, which Ethel Lawrence's attorney Carl Bisgaier likened to winning the lottery. "Developing municipalities," declared the justices, "must make *realistically possible* the opportunity for an appropriate variety and choice of housing for all categories of people who may desire to live there." But there were also times when the case seemed doomed. In 1978, a trial court judge effectively nullified the Supreme Court's ruling, approving a sham affordable housing ordinance that maintained the status quo in Mount Laurel.

Even after that legal debacle, Ethel Lawrence's confidence never flagged. "It's okay," she told them, "we're going to win."

"Ethel actually cheered *us* up," recalls Carl Bisgaier, shaking his head at the memory.

Then, on January 20, 1983, came the Supreme Court's 120-page opus known as *Mount Laurel II*—and with it complete vindication for the advocates of affordable housing. No other leading judicial opinion in modern times speaks so harshly and so personally about the public officials whose conduct the justices are reviewing. "The ordinance at its core is true to nothing but Mount Laurel's determination to exclude the poor. . . . Mount Laurel's lower income housing effort has been either a total failure or a total success—depending on its intention."

The Supreme Court's 1975 opinion had laid out few specific requirements, instead relying—naively, as it happened—on local communities' willingness to do the right thing. This time, the justices were determined to "put some steel" in their ruling. This time there would be no easy way out for towns like Mount Laurel that were fixated on "good ratables."

Across the state, builders came before local planning boards with proposals for developments that included subsidized units. In Mount Laurel, Peter O'Connor, who had been co-counsel throughout the years of litigation, founded Fair Share Housing, a nonprofit housing organization.

In March 1985, it looked as though the push for genuine affordable housing was finally coming to a successful end. Nearly twenty years after Ethel Lawrence and her mother, Mary Robinson, Reverend Stuart Wood, and the Springville Action Council first proposed building garden apartments for thirty-six poor families in the wrong-side-of-the-tracks part of town, two trials and two Supreme Court opinions later, township officials signed an agreement with Peter

O'Connor, the founder, and Ethel Lawrence, the president of Fair Share Housing.

The New Jersey Supreme Court's 1983 decision in *Mount Laurel II* made a settlement in the township possible; a change in the local political climate made it happen. The politicians who carried on the fight against affordable housing were long gone, and the current generation of elected officials was more inclined to bargain than to fight. But for Peter O'Connor, seeing Ethel Lawrence's dream through to completion had grown into an obsession. The two of them, lawyer and client, spent lots of time together, as O'Connor became almost a member of the family, and when Ethel Lawrence showed up in Jacob's Chapel with Peter O'Connor in tow, members of the congregation twittered that she had found herself a young beau.

The particulars of the deal involved complicated swaps of land claims in the existing developments for $3.3 million paid to Fair Share Housing, as well as a rewritten zoning ordinance to allow for low- and moderate-income homes. Although, under the agreement, 950 new units of affordable housing could potentially be built throughout the township, Mount Laurel officials contemplated that the money O'Connor was getting would pay for just 40 units—only four more than the Springville Action Council had sought a generation earlier.

Characteristically, though, Peter O'Connor wasn't satisfied with such modest prospects; he had something much more ambitious in mind. Equally in character, Ethel Lawrence also hoped that all the years of waiting could produce more housing. O'Connor borrowed from the commercial developer's bag of tricks, spending the cash settlement to buy up parcels, using front men to conceal the purchases, while the township displayed the behavior of a sitting duck. By the time Mount Laurel figured out what was happening, O'Connor has assembled 122 acres—enough property, he figured, to build 255 rental units, more than six times what the township contemplated in the 1985 settlement agreement.

Even with this deal, new pitfalls kept opening up. The financial plans, always seat-of-the-pants, at times resembled an improvisational con game. In 1990, two local landowners, including the Quaker matriarch of the town, took Fair Share Housing to court, questioning the adequacy of the proposed drainage system.

8

The next-to-last chapter in this saga was written in the chilly early spring days of 1997. At long last, Peter O'Connor had solved all the financial puzzles and cleared all the legal hurdles as well. The only remaining step was ratification, by the Mount Laurel Planning Commission, of a plan to build 140 rental apartments for low- and moderate-income families. The Ethel R. Lawrence Homes, they are to be called, and they are designed to blend into the landscape so well that, unless someone points them out, there is no way to know they are "affordable" to non-yuppies.

As a legal matter, the session was a formality, for the terms of the deal had already been approved by the court. Still, the citizens of Mount Laurel refused to abandon the fight. Like Rip Van Winkle—or the San Andreas fault, depending on one's perspective—a long-dormant controversy was reawakened at the prospect of actual construction. "We need this," complained one resident, faced with the prospect of having poor and black families living next door, "like Custer needed more Indians."

Two hundred irate residents showed up at the Commission's first meeting and twice as many turned out for a second hearing. Mount Laurel hadn't seen such citizen activism since its politicians swore defiance of the state Supreme Court a generation earlier. As the initial meeting dragged on past midnight, opponents morphed into environmentalists, worried about potentially endangered plants, and archaeologists, fretful about the burial grounds of the long-vanished Leni Lenape Indians. These were sham issues, since the impact studies had long since been done, the questions laid to rest, but they got the crowd going.

The developer will make millions in "obscene profits" from federal tax credits, claimed a lawyer who represented the newly formed Concerned Citizens of Holiday Village East, a retirement community situated across the street from the site—a proposition that is as untrue as it is incendiary, since the nonprofit corporation is plowing those tax credits back into the project. "Build condos instead of rentals," the attorney urged, as if a family of four earning less than $25,000 (the project's definition of "poor") could afford the down payment.

The police department weighed in with a study of "crime prevention through environmental design," the first such study in Mount Laurel. Plainly, the police were keen to keep a watchful eye on these new neighbors. Vandalism-resistant surveillance cameras should be installed, they insisted; playing fields should be moved to the roadside for easier drive-by police surveillance; and plans for a handball court should be abandoned, replaced by a street hockey court, since "hockey is a popular juvenile activity in the township."

Concern was voiced for the families who would be moving in—forced, as one resident observed with unintended irony, to live "on a plantation." Amid the yelling and jeering, though, the neighbors' truer feelings emerged. Change the name of the apartments, residents demanded, to something that sounded less like a project. "When are you going to stop shoving Ethel down our throats?"

"It's reverse discrimination" against rich homeowners, claimed the denizens of neighboring Heather Glen, where the mini-mansions sell for upward of half a million dollars. "Mr. Court-Man," the court-appointed master in the case was told when he tried to calm the gathering, "you haven't made many friends here. If I were you, I wouldn't start my car."

The citizens professed to be shocked at the mere mention of race, but racial fears were thick in the air. "We lived with this in South Philly and Newark," angry homeowners shouted. This housing will be a "breeding ground for violent crime and drug abuse."

"What are you going to do about the woman with three kids who moves in and then has a baby year after year after year?" one neighbor asked, apparently having forgotten that he was at a planning, rather than a family planning, meeting. After the first meeting, Ethel Lawrence's daughters were assaulted by anonymous phone calls. "Uppity niggers," the callers muttered, then hung up.

"I have three small children," Thomasene Lawrence Paynter, Ethel Lawrence's oldest daughter, told the crowd. "I was one of the people who lived in a chicken house" when the court case was originally filed in 1970. "Now I am a divorcee and I still have a desire to live in Mount Laurel, but I am what's known as one of the working poor. I have worked every day for the last fourteen years as a medical assistant. . . . I have never in my life done drugs or been in jail. I'm the kind of person who is going to be your neighbor, and if this is the kind of person you have an objection to, then God bless you." That message apparently didn't make much of a dent. Thomasene Paynter was hissed when she tried, at the second gathering, to explain why poor working families would want to live in Mount Laurel. When one of her hecklers got in her face, the normally tranquil Ms. Paynter blew up. "So this is what you look like without your sheet on."

Several of Ethel Lawrence's teenage grandchildren were sitting in the auditorium that night, and they left shaken. "I thought we'd won the fight for our civil rights," said one of them. "I thought that was grandma's fight." Ethel Lawrence Halley, another of Ethel Lawrence's daughters, who has devoted the past several years to making her mother's dream come true, wasn't so surprised. With the state's clock for final project approval ticking and no decision forthcoming from an intimidated planning board, "I guess we'll have to go back to court," she said matter-of-factly.

Despite the state Supreme Court ruling—despite a statute on the books and a state agency whose mission is boosting the stock of affordable housing—the Mount Laurel story has been told again and again. Faced with a legal edict, one New Jersey township managed to stall for seven years before allowing poor people to move in, and those apartments were to be occupied by seniors, while in another town it took even longer to open fifty units of affordable rental housing. Nor is this beggar-thy-neighbor attitude unique to New Jersey. In the aptly named Los Angeles enclave of Hidden Hills, residents fought a plan to build forty-eight apartments for seniors. The elderly, they claimed, "will attract gangs and dope." The facts are irrelevant in these instances, for prejudice rules.

In Mount Laurel, however, the Planning Commission did what it was supposed to do: after listening to all the anger that spewed forth during two marathon sessions, it unanimously approved the project. The last chapter, the construction of the new homes, would begin soon afterward.

At the end of the marathon meeting, the Commission's chairman crossed the room to Ethel Lawrence Halley. "Welcome to Mount Laurel," he said. Ethel Halley decided not to tell him that he was the newcomer, that her family had been living in Mount Laurel for a century and a half.

9

Ethel Gertrude Robinson Lawrence would not live to see the new housing spring up on the landscape. On July 19, 1994, at the age of sixty-eight, she died of cancer at her home on Elbo Lane. Just six months later, Ethel's mother and fellow community activist, Mary Robinson, passed away.

Ethel Lawrence never became nearly so famous as Rosa Parks; but like Rosa Parks she lived in an exemplary way that others would describe in the language of politics. It was a life defined by values that Americans, when surveyed, say are what really counts—a sense of personal responsibility, faith in God, respect for others, love for her family, commitment to community and country.

After the first *Mount Laurel* trial court decision in 1972, reporters began coming around to interview her, first from the local papers, then from the big-city dailies and TV stations. "I was her bodyguard, her Rock of Gibraltar," Mary Robinson proudly said of her daughter, "she was educated, she was the spokesman." That attention won her new respect from skeptical members of the Jacob's Chapel congregation. Yet when some of her old associates in the local Democratic Party were named as defendants in the lawsuit, they sniped at her, called her an egotist and a troublemaker, wrote cranky letters in the local paper. This was hardly the worst of it. There were hate mail and obscene calls, and one time a whispery caller threatened that her house would be burned down—after that she kept her porch light turned on through the night. Sometimes people would drive by and shout "nigger"; sometimes they splattered eggs on her front door. Once they fired a shot at her bedroom window. She carried on.

The Jacob's Chapel congregation has shrunk from nearly a hundred members a quarter of a century ago to about half that size, as old parishioners have died off and no one has replaced them. Years ago, simple economics pushed three of Ethel Lawrence's church sisters, her aunts Emma and Laura and her cousin Betty, out of Mount Laurel and into Camden. They had always wanted to return, but they are all dead. Her mother, Mary Robinson, used to say: "I was born here and I want to die here. They can bury me in Jacob's Chapel cemetery." For the last several years of her life Mary suffered from Alzheimer's disease and lived in a nursing home, largely unaware of her surroundings. A few years ago, on Mother's Day, Ethel Lawrence took her mother to church, and although Mary didn't recognize most of the people, she remembered all the words to all the hymns.

There was always a crisis in Ethel Lawrence's extended family to claim her attention—one of her children was diagnosed with lupus, another was out of work—and always a neighbor or friend's kin who needed her help. Those nine children are all grown, and she was a grandmother twenty-five times over when she died.

Her daughter Ruth, after serving in the army, returned home for a while, to work nights in the local hospital and live next door to her mother. Clayton

Lawrence, a marine sergeant on the front lines during the fighting in Kuwait, will be the first, he says, to sign up for affordable housing in Mount Laurel. Renee, Ethel's youngest child, was the first member of the family to finish college and became an officer with a title company. Some of Ethel's children, like Frances and Renee, are settled into their own suburban lives. Others, like Frances's twin brother, Frank, a salesman for a company that sells technical equipment, want to come home. Mary Smith, Ethel Lawrence's niece and a plaintiff in the 1971 lawsuit, was living in Springville with her infant daughter in an unheated chicken coop when the case was filed. Long ago she gave up her own hopes of moving back to Mount Laurel. Maybe there will be some place in Mount Laurel for her daughter, who is fast approaching thirty.

"They're tough, that generation," says Mary Smith, talking about her aunt. "I watched her bury her husband and then, in the space of little more than a year, put three brothers in the ground. 'She's not going to make it,' I thought, yet somehow she kept going."

"I got a little stronger as I went along," said Ethel Lawrence, and she never complained through all the twists and turns of a case that most of the time seemed to be a lost cause. The event that disturbed her most occurred in 1990, when the lawsuit alleging drainage problems was filed. It wasn't the case itself that troubled her so much as the fact that Alice Rudderow, the Quaker matron, was a plaintiff. "What she did to our housing shocked me," Ethel Lawrence said. "She had saved a little piece of property she hadn't sold [to the developers, which is what gave her grounds to litigate]. She's fighting the hardest battle against us. I went over there to explain the project, but it didn't do any good. That hurt me personally more than anything." It represented a betrayal of the unwritten codes that whites and blacks in Mount Laurel had lived by in years past. "When we were children, her children used to play with us," she added, believing that such a fact from half a century ago should still carry moral weight.

Ethel Lawrence never knew what it meant to feel sorry for herself. "The people that I feel sorry for are the powers-that-be in Mount Laurel. They tell you they're Christian people, but they don't want to deal with poor people on earth. They're going to have a hard time in the hereafter. There's poor people in heaven and poor people in hell. God meant for us to live in harmony on earth, or else he'd have made rich and poor communities in the hereafter." Perhaps she's right, although a sadder reading of the account of how long, how fiercely, and how successfully the Township of Mount Laurel fought against housing the poor would conclude that there must be Heather Glens and Ramblewoods for the souls of the rich, Springville chicken coops for the souls of the poor, gated communities even in heaven.

Houses Divided:
A Gay Man,
His Teenage Neighbor,
and a Murder

I⊤ IS ONE OF the quieter blocks of Brussels Street, in an obscure residential corner of San Francisco. A few blocks down the hill, highway 101 edges out of the city and into Brisbane on its way to the airport, and the sound of jets flying directly overhead shocks the senses. When the fog blows clear, though, the views are fine: There is Candlestick Park, visible from the rise at the top of the street, and the Bay beyond.

Not so long ago, workingmen could afford to buy homes on Brussels Street. And fifteen or twenty years back, most of the people who still live here, house painters and rug cleaners, longshoremen and lithographers and government office workers, saved up the couple of thousand dollars they needed for a down payment. They moved out of downtown apartments, where people didn't even know the family living down the hall, to make a neighborhood that seemed a little utopia. Everybody got along, the old

Italian families and the new black families, the Chinese families and the racially mixed families.

As the people who bought those homes grew older, their kids moved away, but the convivial feelings endured. Newcomers were welcomed with block parties, and all the generations celebrated Halloween in Esther and Archie Brown's big backyard. People here are decent, the residents of Brussels Street said, they are good neighbors.

At approximately 7:30 P.M. on the night of Saturday, November 28, 1987, two days after Thanksgiving, George Smoot, 52, was stabbed to death with a kitchen knife on the front deck of his home.

There was no mystery about who had done the stabbing. The killer confessed within the hour: He was seventeen-year-old Darrell Johnson (not his real name), who lived two houses down. The mystery was why the teenager had violently assaulted his neighbor. The people of Brussels Street, who thought they knew one another, had no answers, and the uncertainty settled in like a fog that separated houses on the block. As pro-Smoot and pro-Johnson factions formed, conversations grew fewer and more strained.

George Smoot was a gay white man; Darrell Johnson is black. And even in a neighborhood where people imagined that they didn't think in the categories of color or sexual preference, these facts soon acquired far more than demographic significance. To the people of Brussels Street, George Smoot's stabbing was an inexplicable act. It was also a test of survival for a little community whose members had suddenly become strangers.

1

The night of the killing, George Smoot's neighbors had settled into their after-dinner lives, listening to music or watching TV or talking around the kitchen table, when a number of them heard a desperate-sounding scream. "*Help . . . Help . . . Help!*" went the cry, three or four times over as many seconds, followed by silence.

Two doors down from George Smoot's house, Larry Tom, the oldest son of Sue and Dick Tom, was working in the family's basement workshop. One house farther along, Mark Fournier, Jan Fournier's son, who was home for the long Thanksgiving weekend from his job at the McDonnell Douglas plant in Long Beach, was in the attic. Each of them, hearing the cry, could tell that it came from Smoot's house. They ran out into the street.

On a block where almost all the houses are yesterday's suburban dreams, George Smoot's was an anachronism, a tiny bungalow hidden from plain sight, perched at the crest of a narrow lot 37 steps up from the street. Mark Fournier and Larry Tom took those steps two at a time. Blood was already staining the wooden deck, and there was blood on the door. The two men pushed the door, but it wouldn't budge. Smoot had fallen on the kitchen floor, and his body was jammed against the doorway.

When Smoot heard the familiar voices, he slowly edged across the floor, away from the door. Blood was spurting from a deep wound in his chest. "Get my mother!" Fournier shouted, and Tom ran off. Moments later, Jan Fournier was on the scene. Because she works as a hospital lab technician, Jan Fournier knew something about medical emergencies. Together, she and her son applied pressure to the wound, and their arms and hands became covered with Smoot's blood. "Who did it?" she asked, and Smoot answered, "The boy from next door."

Apparently, Smoot had already crawled to the telephone—there was a trail of blood leading from the kitchen to the living room carpet, where the phone sat—and called 911. Several neighbors, alerted by Larry Tom to what was happening, had also called 911. Within five minutes, a patrol car from the nearby Ingleside Station was on the scene, and soon an ambulance arrived.

The police car and the ambulance drew the neighbors out of their houses, and they watched the paramedics carry Smoot down the stairs. He was naked except for shorts and slippers, and his body, held down by restraining straps, was convulsing from shock. His face was as white as alabaster.

At about 10:30 P.M., patrolmen notified the neighbors that Smoot had died on the operating table. Meanwhile, the policemen went from neighbor to neighbor, learning in snatched interviews the little that people knew about the events of the night. "The boy from next door": That's what George Smoot had said, but the houses on either side were occupied by adults who had no children. Two doors down, though, lived the Johnsons, Fred and Lisa, and their two children, Darrell, age seventeen, and Velma, age twelve (the names of the family have been changed). When the police appeared, no one was home, but about an hour later, while the detectives were questioning the Toms, they received word that the Johnsons had returned.

Police inspectors Frank McCoy and Marvin Dean discussed some of the events with people on the block the week after the knifing, when they came to a neighborhood meeting. The two men shared further details of their investigation when they spoke privately with Bettie Campbell, George Smoot's older sister, and Larry Zabo, who twenty years earlier had been his lover and who remained his closest friend. The Johnsons themselves recounted the boy's story to some of their neighbors, and Darrell Johnson confided in Chris Rivers (not his real name), a buddy since kindergarten. Those accounts, gleaned through interviews, are remarkably consistent. From them, one version of that evening—Darrell Johnson's version—can be pieced together.

George Smoot and Darrell Johnson knew one another, though not well. Darrell had worked for Smoot a couple of times during the previous year, doing heavy yard work and hauling. Smoot had complained to neighbors and friends that Darrell couldn't follow even the simplest instructions. But he needed help digging out a cellar that was eventually going to be a darkroom, and the afternoon of the stabbing the teenager was working at Smoot's house.

While he was there, Darrell reportedly told the police, Smoot had followed him into the bathroom and unzipped his fly—"He came on to me" is what he said when we talked. A few minutes before seven o'clock, Darrell's account continues, an agitated George Smoot showed up at the Johnsons' front door, asking for Darrell.

Fred and Lisa Johnson, Darrell's parents, had gone off to an early movie, and Velma, Darrell's sister, reportedly answered the door. When she told Smoot that Darrell wasn't home, he allegedly grabbed her, putting his hands around her neck as if to choke her. Just then, the secondhand reports continue, Darrell appeared. He fought with Smoot, who released Velma. The girl sprinted to the kitchen, where she grabbed a carving knife, and ran back to her brother. The boy pushed Smoot out the door. But, as Darrell tells it, as Smoot headed up the street to his own house, he shouted, "I'll get you!"

Darrell, now holding the knife in his hand, dashed after Smoot and followed him up the 37 steps to his house—or so the accounts continue. He caught up with him on the deck and plunged the knife deep into the right side of Smoot's chest. It is unclear whether he followed Smoot into the house: Bettie Campbell, Smoot's sister, was told by police that traces of blood had been found on the Soloflex machine in the living room. What is known is that Darrell tossed the knife into the neighbor's backyard, where the police found it. Darrell and Velma then ran to their aunt and uncle's house in the next block. About an hour later, according to neighbors, the two Johnson youngsters came back.

Some of George Smoot's friends will tell you that this story is a fantasy, that something else—drugs or sex or money—must explain what happened. For one thing, on a quiet street, where everyone hears everything, why did no one hear the alleged scuffle between Smoot and Darrell? The story sounds more incredible in light of the reports from those who knew George Smoot. It's not that these accounts are uniformly flattering, for Smoot was no saint, but the man who emerges from these recountings seems incapable of the violence that, both Darrell and Velma Johnson insist, directly led to the stabbing.

And yet this is only a part of the mystery. If you look inside the Johnsons' household, listening to what they have to say, listening to the people who know them well, the events of November 18, 1987, become even harder to comprehend. Darrell Johnson is no hoodlum, but a boy trying to keep his life in order. What provocation would be required, or what memory of some past provocation would have to be triggered, for him to take the life of another?

2

George Smoot was a man of many parts, and no one was ever allowed close enough to know all of them. He grew up in Wichita Falls, Texas, son of a none-too-prosperous lawyer, a man fifteen years older than his wife and who was in his 50s by the time Smoot was born. Smoot's childhood held stretches of solitude as broad as the plains.

He studied English in college and enrolled in the Air Force ROTC. The Air Force shipped him to Syracuse, New York, where, while finishing up his military obligation in the reserves, he returned to his first academic love and began working on his Ph.D. in English in the fall of 1962.

George Smoot had figured out very early on that he was homosexual. When he arrived in Syracuse, he met a psychology graduate student named Larry Zabo, and from the first, Zabo was smitten with the slender, angular man he saw as romantic and enigmatic, brilliant and wildly sexy. It was Zabo who pushed to make a relationship happen; Zabo who worked hard to make himself indispensable; Zabo who became the settling, domesticating influence in Smoot's life.

The two of them, and a coterie of friends, played ceaselessly with ideas. "George always had an opinion on everything," remembers a one-time fellow graduate student. In 1969, with his Ph.D. dissertation on Dylan Thomas still unfinished, Smoot moved with Zabo from Syracuse to take a teaching job at Sacramento State University. "Sacramento was heaven at first," Zabo recalls. "We both had great jobs, and California was so new, so exciting." Yet soon enough, things became bumpier, both professionally and personally. Smoot, his Ph.D. still not completed, was denied tenure. He took a frustrating job teaching English at the local community college. And he started venturing further afield in the realms of sex.

Back in their Syracuse days, Smoot and Zabo used to go out, at Smoot's instigation, in search of men to have sex with. When they traveled to New York or Mexico City, they would head for the bars and bring someone home, someone young and muscular and maybe a bit tough. Eventually, Smoot left the relatively tame world of three-ways and headed off into the gamier reaches of gay life, the world of leather and S and M. In the process, he left behind his romance with Larry Zabo, too.

After the breakup of another love affair, Smoot slipped into a prolonged depression in the mid 1970s. He would lament the circumstances of his life, while feeling powerless to change them. Then, in 1979, a technical writing job at Lockheed's Silicon Valley plant opened up. Smoot doubted whether he could manage the change. "You've got to go," a psychologist friend told him. "You really have no choice."

Several years later, Smoot moved from tech writer to computer programmer and, in time, he became a research engineer, doing classified work on the Trident missile system. In the world of computers, a young person's world, George Smoot, a made-over English professor approaching the half-century mark, was one of a kind. He was "steadfast . . . thoroughly professional," says his onetime supervisor Jan Wallace. With most of his colleagues, Smoot kept his distance—he was helpful when they needed advice, but he seldom sought them out, and never talked with them about his life.

The exception was John Rumelhart, a 25-year-old free spirit from Texas. "Maybe we became friends because I was half his age, and he felt younger when he hung around me," Rumelhart muses. Over fast-food lunches—"rant and rave sessions," Rumelhart called them—Smoot would tell of his belief that his bosses were gunning for him. "Lockheed tends to stamp out differentness," Rumelhart says. And Smoot was bitterly convinced that, because of what he called "my lifestyle," he had been denied the higher security clearance he needed to advance in Lockheed.

"When George told me that he was gay, I was kind of grossed out. I told him the idea of two men having sex together repulsed me," says Rumelhart. But eventually they could joke about sex: at lunch, Smoot would point out all the hot-looking busboys while Rumelhart pointed out the foxy waitresses. And Rumelhart, who knew about remodeling houses because his father had built the family's home himself, helped Smoot build his deck.

"We'd work four or five hours," Rumelhart remembers, "then George would cook up some elaborate Mexican meal, and we'd sit and talk, and talk and talk about gardening and photography and politics and our past histories and the meaning of life. I'd say that when you die, that's it, but George thought that something, not God, but something, linked it all together."

Smoot had only a handful of companions. The most significant was Larry Zabo, his old boyfriend, who remained his one best friend. In the age of AIDS, Smoot had cut way down on his tricking, but for several years he maintained a sexual relationship with a younger man of Chinese-Hawaiian descent.

The sexual liaison, like the friendship with Rumelhart, kept Smoot young, and that was important to a man who worried about aging. He complained about his aches and pains, and wondered how, eventually, he would manage the 37 steps to his house. He fretted about the beginning of a paunch; just before Thanksgiving, he had bought the Soloflex machine that dominated his small living room. Though he looked ten years younger than his age, Smoot was obsessed with his appearance. "A couple of years ago, we were in the brightly lighted lobby of a movie theater," Larry Zabo remembers. "I looked at George, he stared back at me in terror, as if I had exposed all the lines and wrinkles, all the signs of age."

Once George Smoot bought an eyesore of a house in 1984, it became the driving force of his life. From books he learned about carpentry and wiring, stained glass and plumbing. The place reveals his sweat and his caring in every corner, from the inlaid tile and wood kitchen floor to the clean-edged deck and the intricate herringbone pattern on the handcrafted wooden door. "My little monstrosity on Brussels Street," he described the house in his will, a typically backhanded way for Smoot to express his love.

It was directly because of the house that Smoot came to know Darrell Johnson, and that relationship with the seventeen-year-old who lived two doors down ended in his death.

3

If you were looking for a real-life version of Bill Cosby's TV family, the Johnsons would be prime candidates. Lisa, Darrell's mother, is a petite woman who can still turn heads. She is a technical expert at a downtown bank. Fred, Darrell's father, an easygoing man with a quick smile, works in the local media. Lisa is the quiet one, the emotional bedrock of the home, the lioness always on guard for her cubs. Few people on the block knew her. "She drives in with her electric garage door opener, that's it," said neighbor Virgilio Razzo.

Fred Johnson is the outgoing one, always checking in with the people on the block, swapping jazz records with his next-door neighbor Manuel Floyd, and talking job possibilities with Cliff Bloom, an old neighbor who lives a block down the street. "I wouldn't want a better neighbor," says John Harlin, who lives across the street. Fred Johnson is the kind of father who managed his son's Little League team when the boy was younger, who shows up for all the sports banquets his son goes to, all the plays both children have appeared in.

Velma, Darrell's twelve-year-old sister, is very much a little girl just beginning to come to terms with adolescence. She is the family prodigy, a good student with hopes for college, who is serious about dance ("ballet, tap, jazz, and modern," she proudly recites during our conversation), who plays piano and acts in school plays. In a production of *The Wizard of Oz* a few years earlier, Velma was a Munchkin. Darrell was the Tin Man.

At age seventeen, Darrell Johnson retains the adolescent's characteristic suspicion of most adults. He has the rubbery face of a natural comedian, and as I spoke with him and his family, his expression shifted with his transient emotions. Sometimes he withdrew behind a veil of sullenness. Yet as he watched his sister talking about how, unable to sleep for many nights after the stabbing, she would crawl into her parents' bed, his face revealed something that looked like love.

One neighbor, who happens to be black, describes Darrell as "a teenager who wanted to be super-black, to hang around with super-black kids . . . That means he has to be tough"; another neighbor, who happens to be white, calls him "the nicest kid in the world." Darrell has gotten into his share of scrapes, including taking a joyride in the family's brand new car, but until the stabbing he had stayed out of trouble with the law.

At McAteer High School, where he is a senior, Darrell has a reputation as a cut-up, a jock of middling talent who pushed hard to earn playing time on the football team, a student slipping through school with passable grades, a guy who likes spending time with his buddies.

"He's a real character," says his friend Chris Rivers. "He looks like a character, and he knows how to make people laugh. Like at school, he'd start flirting with the ugliest girls around, or he'd start imitating girls."

The Johnsons' story is a modern version of the classic American family tale: the parents who save up to buy a home, who put off thinking about themselves so they can do what's best for their children (though they are not Catholic, the Johnsons sent their children to parochial school for several years, thinking that they would get a better education there). The family relies on their kin for emotional support, and they trust in God for the ultimate meaning of things.

Even before Darrell stabbed George Smoot, the fall of 1987 had been a miserable time for the Johnsons. Lisa's best friend died of leukemia. And on September 24, Darrell was initiated in the game of "Violation."

Darrell tells the story in a voice stripped of feeling. "After football practice, the guys were joking around. They said they were going to 'violate' me. I thought

119

they were going to do something like dump dirt in my helmet. In the locker room, six guys grabbed me and threw me down on the floor. I was on my knees. One of the guys got a broom and started twisting it. He was trying to stick it in my butt. He missed, and he pinched my testicle to the ground. I was screaming, it hurt so, but they said, 'Take it like a man.'"

After several minutes, Darrell's teammates left. The teenager remained on the locker room floor, unable to move. When the coach walked in, he saw the ripped testicle and called an ambulance. At the University of California Medical Center, the boy's testicle was opened up to check for internal damage, then stitched back with some 50 dissolving stitches. The next day, he went home.

As soon as it happened, Darrell says, he wanted to put the hazing incident behind him. Four days later, though in intense pain, he was back in school, bandaged and using a cane and telling jokes on himself. There was talk about expelling Darrell's teammates, and about forfeiting the football season, but Darrell didn't want anyone to get in trouble.

All they wanted, Fred and Lisa Johnson told Mc-Ateer's principal, Ted Moore, was an apology from the teammates, and that they received. Moore issued minor suspensions to students involved and a mild rebuke to the coach. (When the newspaper ran a front-page story about the locker room incident on January 28—four months after it happened—San Francisco schools superintendent Ramon Cortines expressed anger and surprise, and launched an official investigation.)

What nobody seemed to realize early on was that Darrell, in all but the technical legal sense, had been raped. His teammates had named the "game" exactly right: Violation. And afterward, there was no one Darrell could vent his anger on—no one until his encounter with George Smoot nine weeks later.

This is the kind of incident that can spark the syndrome called homosexual panic. "Young men, whose sexual identities are not yet entirely formed, are at greatest risk of panicking when someone else tries to 'feminize' them," notes Dr. John Rouse, assistant clinical professor of psychiatry at the University of California, San Francisco. "An act of violence is a way of dealing with that panic, because it both gets rid of the offending stimulus and reasserts one's status as a man."

Darrell had had passing encounters with gay men before he met George Smoot. His daily trip home from school took him through the Castro, and Chris Rivers says that gay men would "whisper" at them: once, Chris says, Darrell was asked if he was "into oral sex." Darrell was angered by these men—"faggots," he called them—but he told Chris that "I won't do anything as long as they don't bother me."

Nobody in the Johnson family understood the possible link between the locker room incident, these uncomfortable encounters with gay men, and Darrell's subsequent assault on George Smoot. Fred saw the culmination of events in Biblical terms. "When the stabbing happened, I reread the passage about Job. I kept asking God, 'Why are we being put to this test?' Job was a good person and he was good to his family. I feel we are the same way. Is this a test for later?"

When I asked Darrell to tell me how he felt about the stabbing, he struggled to maintain a mask of impassivity, and when he spoke, it was as if he were in a trance. "I feel like something you'd see on TV. If it can happen to me . . ." His voice trailed off, the thought left unfinished.

"I don't want to let it affect me," Darrell added—the fantasy of an adolescent who still doesn't realize that all acts have consequences, and that certain acts have the power to transform entire lives.

4

"What did you know about George Smoot?" the police asked Lisa Johnson, standing in front of her house on the night of November 28. "He was a fag," she answered. It was a response that, widely repeated, would contribute to the fissioning of a neighborhood.

On the night after the stabbing, though, there was only shock and sadness on Brussels Street. Small stories about George Smoot's neighborliness were passed along—about the orchid that he had given to the Toms to add to their collection, about how he took care of the Floyds' cats when they were away, about the open house he had held the previous Christmas to celebrate the restoration of his home. And concern was felt over what was happening in a neighborhood that no longer resembled a little utopia.

A month before George Smoot was stabbed, a 56-year-old woman named Virginia Lowery, who lived only a block away on Brussels, had been brutally murdered, in what the police told neighbors was a hate murder, probably committed by an intimate who despised her. The house itself was untouched, and a safe that reportedly contained $400,000 worth of jewelry was left unopened. That case remained unsolved. Now there was the stabbing, and while there was no logical reason to link the two killings, the juxtaposition caused some sleepless nights up and down the block.

What happened during the days immediately following the stabbing increased neighbors' anxieties. Smoot's body had been tagged a "John Doe" when it was taken away in the ambulance, and while that wasn't extraordinary, the corpse remained at the morgue, unidentified, well into the following week. When Esther Brown learned that the coroner's office needed someone to identify the body before it would notify anyone, she called her neighbor Dick Tom, and convinced him to go with her to the morgue. Only then was Smoot's sister, Bettie Campbell, contacted, and it was a week after the murder before Smoot's closest friends had been informed.

The night of the stabbing, Darrell Johnson was taken to police headquarters for questioning. He was released a few hours later. Neighbors said they were angry and offended because while the police were searching George Smoot's house the night of the murder, their laughter had echoed across the street.

Manuel and Nancy Floyd, who live in the house between George Smoot's and the Johnsons', had heard that laughter. They regarded the stabbing as a macho act by a boy who was proving his toughness by killing a gay man—a fag, as Lisa Johnson had called him— and with that in mind they contacted Community United Against Violence, a gay group whose efforts focus on preventing violent crimes against homosexuals. "I've never seen a community-based response quite so intense as this, gay or straight," says CUAV's Randy Schell, commenting on the neighborhood's reaction. At Schell's suggestion, Floyd phoned the police department's homicide division.

Neighbor Bruce Grosjean and his wife, Emy, were troubled that the police didn't seem to be doing much investigating, and that all their questions had to do with Smoot's character, not his assailant's.

Joined by his wife and seven of their neighbors, Grosjean wrote to police inspector Frank McCoy on December 4, a week after the stabbing. The letter bristled with questions about the credibility of the tale that the Johnson youngsters were reportedly telling, and pointed out George Smoot's "nest making and open-door attitude." It concluded with a plea that police talk to the residents of the neighborhood. "The people on this block will have to live with the consequences of this investigation for many years, and a tragedy of this magnitude, if not properly addressed, could be the seed of more tragedy. We cannot believe that because someone has accused George of possible molestation that police think his death is somehow justified."

Two days later, inspectors McCoy and Marvin Dean came to the Grosjeans' home and reported to a gathering of neighbors on their investigation. According to neighbors who attended, McCoy said he believed Velma Johnson's version of the events leading up to the stabbing. He had questioned the twelve-year-old twice, and his eighteen years of experience as a detective had persuaded him that if a child didn't change

124

her story—and Velma hadn't—she was telling the truth. McCoy flatly denied that George Smoot's being gay had anything to do with the investigation. As he told a reporter later, "I respect each victim, regardless of his beliefs. Every victim is a sad tragedy, without exception. The question itself is insulting."

Several people on the block left that session unsatisfied. They felt the police were dragging their feet, and they were angry at Lisa and Fred Johnson for what one resident, who knew the Johnsons well, called "the arrogance of thinking 'we can lie and get out of this.'" Some neighbors chose discreet silence. Jan Fournier, known on Brussels Street as a sensitive and caring person, had been covered in Smoot's blood after the stabbing, and she was badly shaken up by the event, several neighbors said. Fournier wondered whether she or her son Mark had been exposed to AIDS—for after all, she thought, Smoot was a gay man, and so at particular risk.

Ellie and Cliff Bloom were outraged at Bruce Grosjean's letter. "When I saw it, I wanted to rip it up," says Cliff, an Englishman who came to San Francisco a dozen years ago and who has lived in the neighborhood most of that time. "All compassion had been thrown out the window." Those who signed that letter were "hysterical," he thought. They were letting their emotions run wild, turning Darrell Johnson "into a serial killer"; they had taken on the mentality of a "lynch mob."

"I liked George—we both did," Bloom says. Several days after the stabbing, Ellie Bloom, weeping, had left a bouquet of wildflowers on Smoot's doorstep. But "we have so much more history with the Johnson family," Cliff says, and Ellie adds, "if ever I was in trouble, those people would come to my aid." Now Smoot was dead and the Johnsons were alive; "My concern," says Bloom, "is for the living."

Cliff Bloom believed that Darrell Johnson was telling the truth, at least about the sexual advance. Several years earlier, when Bloom was helping Smoot paint his house, "George flirted with me, came on to me. It was subtle. I dealt with it immediately, it was easily handled. But I'm a grown man, and come-ons go with the territory in San Francisco. What if I were seventeen?"

Esther Brown regarded Darrell Johnson very differently: He was a difficult teenager. She recalled the time when he borrowed ten dollars from her, then had to be chased down to return the loan; and she remembered how little effort he had made when a neighbor hired him to do yard work. Esther the peacemaker didn't want to talk publicly about the stabbing; what she had to say to the Johnsons she would say privately. But while the Blooms and the Browns had been close friends—close enough that, for a time, the Blooms had stayed in the Browns' house—in the aftermath of the stabbing, without ever announcing the fact, the two couples stopped talking with one another.

This was not the only rupture on the block. The Johnsons, fearful of their neighbors' reactions, fearful even of the possibility of some act of retribution, stayed isolated inside their home. Gone were the usual neighborly waves from cars and curbside conversations.

Race isn't an issue in the neighborhood, Cliff Bloom insisted. "Otherwise, we"—he is white, his wife Ellie is black—"wouldn't have felt so much a part of the neighborhood." But then Bloom added that the bigotry was "concealed," and recalled that, decades back, blacks had a hard time buying homes in the area. To Dick Tom, the tensions only confirmed a split between the black families and the rest of the neighborhood; he wouldn't pop into the house of a black family the way he regularly ventured into Jan Fournier's home, Tom said. "This isn't a racial thing," says Fred Johnson, but although a half-dozen neighbors stopped by to see the Johnsons in the days after the stabbing, there was just one white neighbor, Cliff Bloom, among them.

"I used to think this was such a great neighborhood. Now I'm not so sure," says Esther Brown, whom neighbors called "the glue" of Brussels Street—who for more than 30 years has put so much energy into organizing the block parties and the Halloween gatherings and the neighborhood watch. Other people started paying more attention to the not-so-petty crimes in the neighborhood, the drug busts and the purse-snatchings, and felt less safe than they had before.

The people of Brussels Street were truly good neighbors, who swapped recipes and looked out for one another's houses. But they were not intimates, they had never been tested in times of trouble, and that made all the difference. The stabbing of George Smoot, for reasons that remained wholly mysterious, was so primal and so threatening an act that people were forced back behind their own double-locked doors, to confide only in those they knew they could trust. That stabbing was really all there was for neighbors to talk about, yet it was too painful to talk about. Though there was hope that a memorial service for Smoot, planned by Esther Brown and the Floyds, would help heal the wounds, people wondered whether the Johnsons would come, and what such a ceremony would mean if they didn't.

5

"Our job is to gather facts, not make judgments," says police inspector Frank McCoy. "The facts speak for themselves."

On January 7, 1988, Darrell Johnson was charged with voluntary manslaughter in the death of George Smoot. Neither the detectives nor Walter Aldridge, the DA handling the case, would discuss what lay behind the decision to file charges.

When John Burris, the Johnsons' attorney, brought the family into his office and told them the news, Darrell began crying, then Velma and Lisa and Fred. "I won't be home for Christmas," Darrell kept saying, a child in a grown-up world. Burris is a veteran criminal and civil rights lawyer who has worked with many black families in trouble, but this was a moment so highly charged that he had to leave the office before he broke down himself.

Larry Zabo, whom George Smoot referred to in his will as "my friend and lover and brother from the beginning," was relieved that charges had been brought against Darrell Johnson. He, like some of the neighbors, had feared that the criminal justice system wasn't taking the case seriously, that the death of a remarkable man would go officially unnoticed because he was gay.

Zabo kept thinking about a poem titled "Prajna" (the Sanskrit word for wisdom) that Smoot had written to him for his birthday. Here was a rarely seen side of Smoot, hinting at sense of exhilaration at having accomplished something in his life:

Some people in the village
Said the mountain was impossible
To climb.
An inestimable number
Neglected to take notice of its being there.
While one faction declared
It was purely an illusion.

Because of which, he
(pausing for breath at its dizzy top)
Speculated upon the
Enormous improbability
Of explaining how he got there

IN THE spring of 1998, Johnson was tried and convicted of manslaughter. His short sentence—five years—angered gay activists, who charged that the judge had given the teenager "time off" for killing a gay man.

Places

||||||||||||||||||||||||||||||||

What School Choice
Really Means: Fact and
PR in East Harlem

O<small>N STANDARD-ISSUE</small> maps of Manhattan, Ninety-sixth Street on the Upper East Side is shown slightly thicker than the lines representing neighboring streets, to signify that traffic on it runs both east and west. There is no hint of a border on these maps, no intimation that Ninety-sixth Street marks a division between two dramatically different worlds.

South of Ninety-sixth Street lie some of New York City's most fashionable addresses. The brass doorknobs of the brownstones gleam; a one-million dollar condo is a steal. Nannies push strollers along Fifth Avenue and in Central Park, and adolescents stream forth from private schools. Lawyers and investment bankers look as if they had stepped straight out of the display windows at Talbot's or Brooks Brothers. Almost the only nonwhite faces to be seen belong to the help.

To the north of Ninety-sixth Street lies East Harlem. On its two hundred square blocks many of the brownstones are empty, boarded up, covered with barbed wire and jagged bits of glass to keep out the vagrants and drug addicts. Half of East Harlem's population of 120,000 is Hispanic, and almost all the rest is African-American. New arrivals come mostly from dirt-poor Caribbean and Central American countries. By all the standard social measures, East Harlem is among the worst-off neighborhoods in the city.

Yet every school-day morning brings a rare sight, as a thousand or so children from elsewhere in the city, many of them from families that could easily afford private academies, negotiate the buses and subways with practiced cool to join the 14,000 Hispanic and black children who attend East Harlem's elementary and junior high schools. These students come to East Harlem not because some official issued an integration order or redrew a school-district boundary but because their families have chosen to send them here. Remarkably, in some of the battered school buildings of the neighborhood, where these children attend classes with the children of the barrio, an exemplary education can be had. East Harlem's schools have, in fact, become famous, at least among educators, for their quality—relative to that of other inner-city schools, anyway—and the story of the transformation of these schools has by now acquired the status of an oft-told legend.

In 1970, when each of New York City's elementary and junior high schools was assigned to one of thirty-two community school districts, with powerful elected school boards that had the right to pick the local superintendent, East Harlem's schools, which make up District Four, were widely regarded as the city's worst.

In 1974 the children scored thirty-second—dead last—on standardized reading tests. Absenteeism was chronic among teachers as well as students. Gangs had turned junior high corridors into battlegrounds, school bathrooms into drug bazaars. And yet scarcely a decade later this prototypical blackboard jungle had come to be hailed as something of a model for urban education. The most widely cited measure of its accomplishment is the reported improvement in reading achievement: by the mid-1980s East Harlem's scores had risen from the very worst citywide to a level approximating the citywide average.

Behind this change, East Harlem's boosters say, lies the simple but revolutionary fact that parents in East Harlem are now allowed to choose their children's schools—thereby introducing the salutary effects of competition into institutions dispirited by inertia, red tape, and the chaos of the surrounding community. These changes are not unique to East Harlem. Across the country, public school choice has been one of the most widely adopted reforms of the past decade, and enthusiasts for one or another version of school choice span the political spectrum. But what does make East Harlem special, and why I spent weeks there in 1992 and 1993, is that it came first—and that New York has decided to extend its school-choice program citywide. In District Four choice has been sustained as a guiding philosophy for over two decades—a geological epoch in the faddish world of education policy. Moreover, the system of choice has been implemented in a city where the difficulties of making *anything* happen are well known, and in a neighborhood characterized by deep social pathology. It is undeniable that much of the education in East Harlem is better than what was available a quarter century ago. But did choice make the difference? And how much difference has actually been made?

These are important questions, the answers to which have implications for schools around the country. Even as legions of defenders hold up East Harlem as a national model, contending that this kind of choice within school districts is preferable to charter schools or vouchers, critics assail some of what has happened there as a triumph of public relations. Yes, they say, many East Harlem mini-schools may get a silk-stocking trade, and may offer instruction that is as good as in the better private schools, but just a few corridors away are classrooms with no middle-class students and all the familiar woes of inner-city education. And, they say, the way the system labeled "choice" works in practice makes such disparities inevitable.

1

During the mid-1950s the novelist Dan Wakefield, then a young reporter, lived in Spanish Harlem for six months and delivered a savage indictment of official neglect, especially in the public schools. "[The schools] have been of little help to the children of Spanish Harlem in escaping the realities of its streets, or . . . changing those realities to something like the promise of the posters that smile from the classrooms," Wakefield wrote in *Island in the City*. "The schools, in fact, have blocked out the possibilities of the world beyond even more profoundly than the tenement buildings around them." The situation only deteriorated in 1968, when black and radical white parents and teachers throughout the city fought the teachers' union and the education bureaucracy for greater local control over schools. They got it in 1970, after several bitter teachers' strikes, but the aftermath brought infighting of every kind among the board members of the thirty-two newly created school districts.

Things began to improve in District Four in 1973, when an insurgent slate was elected to the school board. Robert Rodriguez, an East Harlem native who headed the slate and directed the East Harlem Neighborhood Manpower Service Center, was only twenty-one at the time. The new board chairman was committed to running a clean enterprise, in which educational priorities didn't get confused with personal agendas and board members didn't push pet programs or hand out patronage jobs to friends. Keeping fellow board members and local leaders from meddling in the details of personnel and programs didn't prove easy, however, and tensions ran so high that police officers were sometimes present at board meetings to assure order.

When Rodriguez came to power, the district superintendent was seen by many in the community as symbolizing the old, unresponsive regime. The superintendent was quickly forced out, and the board chose as his successor Anthony Alvarado, a charismatic thirty-year-old Puerto Rican from East Harlem. His fast-track career had taken him from Fordham University to half a dozen jobs in education, including running an experimental preschool and heading up a bilingual elementary school.

As the District Four superintendent, Alvarado brought in new black and Hispanic principals—a good idea in itself, and certainly also a way of fending off potential local critics. He also pushed an agenda that included alternative schools, bilingual schools (which now enroll 2,000 of the district's students), a districtwide reading program, and major infusions of federal and state dollars.

The alternative schools have gotten the most attention, yet they began almost accidentally. In 1974 Alvarado approached Deborah Meier, a longtime teacher on Manhattan's Upper West Side and a pedagogical reformer committed to bringing open classrooms to city schools, and asked if she would be interested in running her own elementary school. Meier jumped at the chance. In the school she had in mind, classrooms would have places to build things, quiet spaces for reading, and corners for painting. Teachers would move around, offering individual help. Classes would be small by city standards, and teachers would come to know their students well, because they would spend two years with the same children. The new school would depend for its survival on parents' willingness to accept the risks of an unfamiliar kind of education for their children, and also on teachers' willingness to surrender their lunch hours to students and their after-school hours to meetings that ran as long as in socialist heaven. The school had to start small, Meier argued, one grade at a time, with no set curriculum—"If the teacher cared a lot [about a topic] and the kids cared a lot, that was a good topic"—and no guaranteed results.

Although classes like this have been routine for half a century in the best progressive private academies, the school Meier and Alvarado proposed to create was a deviant institution in New York City public schools, where teachers typically stood at the front of the classroom talking at rows of nodding heads and covering a prescribed curriculum. Central Park East, as Meier's elementary school was called, started out in the fall of 1974 on two floors of P.S. 171, a run-down elementary school with which it would be competing for students and resources. Many of the Puerto Rican parents living in the neighborhood, whose memories of their own education led them to equate quality with order, were suspicious of a white Jewish woman and her permissive ideas. Some community activists wanted a school rooted more in the language and struggles of the barrio than in the theories of John Dewey and Jean Piaget. But the school attracted students, and after a troubled first few years its reputation as a good place to learn began to spread. Soon there were more applicants than spaces, with many of the applications coming from outside East Harlem.

The same year that Central Park East opened its doors, two other alternative schools opened, to serve grades five through nine: the East Harlem Performing Arts School and the BETA ("better education through alternatives") School, which took rejects from other schools, where they had made teachers' lives hell (the BETA School would close in 1990).

In 1976 Alvarado hired Seymour Fliegel, who had been a teacher and administrator in Harlem for two decades, to oversee the existing alternative schools and help create many new ones. By 1982 two new primary schools, Central Park East II and River East, were launched to meet a rising demand for open classrooms. Though they began as spinoffs to Central Park East, and took students from a common pool of applicants, the new academies gradually developed their own identities. From the outset, places in these schools were much sought-after, and soon educators with other dreams appeared at Fliegel's doorstep. Alan Sofferman, who had taught fifth and sixth grades at P.S. 96, and who eventually became its assistant principal, imagined a School of Science and Humanities, as tradition-oriented as any parochial school. Students would wear uniforms, and silence would be observed as orderly ranks of pupils passed by one another in the corridors. Leonard Bernstein, a science teacher, designed the Isaac Newton School with the intention of exposing the brightest youngsters from the ghetto to state-of-the-art instruction in science and math. Beryl Epton, who had taught at the BETA School, wanted a chance to work with younger children who had troubled histories. She started the Children's Workshop, the smallest of East Harlem's alternative schools, a one-room second-through-fourth-grade class for children who had been or were likely to be held back because of behavioral problems. New schools opened almost every year, each one trying to find its special niche. Their names reveal the range of aspirations: the Academy of Environmental Science, the Maritime

School, the East Harlem Career Academy, the Talented and Gifted School.

While every other district in the city was pleading poverty, East Harlem usually found the money to do what it wanted. For one thing, its administrators came to realize that because the notion of choice pushed the right buttons at Ronald Reagan's Department of Education, Washington after 1980 would be forthcoming with cash. At one point during the 1980s District Four received more federal money per student than any other school district in the country. The Republicans from Washington and the liberal Democrats from Spanish Harlem have made strange bedfellows, and there are those who say that the district was manipulated. Yet in the cutthroat world of New York City school politics, Washington's support bought East Harlem a measure of protection.

District Four was also prepared to fend for itself. For years it engaged heavily in the risky business of deficit financing, and it outmaneuvered the dozing downtown bureaucrats. The alternative schools, with their tiny staffs, could not live with the seniority system that reigned in every other city district. So the principals (called directors) of the alternative schools recruited teachers mainly by word of mouth, and turned to Fliegel to slip the new teachers onto the payroll regardless of seniority.

The teachers' unions initially protested about all the rules East Harlem was breaking. But they backed off when they saw members volunteering to swap protections won through collective bargaining for the rewards of professionalism. (Today the New York City teachers' contract specifies that with a three-quarters-majority vote the teachers at any school can waive rules about class size and teachers' schedules.)

"I could say, 'We had a long-range plan: we envisioned a choice program ten years down the line.'" Fliegel says, "But things don't work that way. It developed organically." Slowly, if haphazardly, with a sizable dose of what Fliegel calls "creative noncompliance" with the rules, an alternative system parallel to the regular schools emerged, with a handful of alternative elementary schools and a somewhat larger number of junior highs—twenty-two alternative schools in all by 1982, offering a wide range of options. But then there were enough options to enable every sixth-grade student in East Harlem to have at least *some* choice, although competition for places at the most popular schools was sufficiently intense that the schools, not the parents and students, ended up doing most of the picking. Still, by 1982 half of East Harlem's junior high students were attending one of the alternative schools, and by that year East Harlem had moved from thirty-second to fifteenth in the city in reading scores. District Four began getting national attention.

2

East Harlem officials focus on District Four's dramatically improved test scores when trumpeting their success. In 1974, they note, only 15.3 percent of the district's students could read at or above grade level; by 1988 the proportion had quadrupled, to 62.5 percent.

This fact is always seized on by those who would commend the East Harlem experience to other school systems. Yet those statistics, while technically correct, are somewhat misleading, and a close look at them begins to reveal some other realities of the East Harlem experience. The biggest improvements in reading scores occurred in 1975 (13 percentage points), when the choice program was just getting started, and in 1986 (9.5 percentage points), when New York City switched to a different test. In those two years reading levels improved substantially all across the city.

Moreover, in 1988 the city was using a test whose norms—the criteria for what should be expected by way of performance—had been set a decade earlier. But in the interim there had been a marked increase in basic-skills levels, and so the norms were out-of-date. It's as if a high-jump bar had remained at a certain height even as the jumpers had grown taller. After new national norms were established, in 1989, the proportion of youngsters performing at grade level dropped to 42 percent in East Harlem (as against 48 percent citywide). This doesn't mean that things weren't getting better in East Harlem, but it does mean that the statistical gain is not as fantastically large as is commonly claimed. Nor have matters changed much since then. Last year 43 percent of students in East Harlem (as compared with 49 percent of students citywide) were doing grade-level work.

Comparisons with other districts do show that from 1978, when norms were previously established, to 1989

District Four's reading scores rose by 14.2 percent, as compared with 2.3 percent for the city as a whole. That was the second-biggest improvement recorded in all of the city's districts. (The biggest improvement, 14.5 percent occurred in Bedford-Stuyvesant, a Brooklyn district that is 98 percent black and Hispanic, whose school system combines choice at the junior high level with a strong emphasis on scholastic drills and testing.) Performance on the mathematics test has been far weaker. Between 1986 and 1994, when the citywide test for mathematics was adopted, District Four fell from twentieth to twenty-seventh place.

It is hard to know how much of the improvement in reading scores to attribute to choice. For one thing, much of the gain has been recorded in neighborhood elementary schools, where choice has not been as widely available as in the junior highs. For another, the districtwide data conceal variations as great as can be found among public schools anywhere in America. In 1991 at least 75 percent of the students at the most elite East Harlem schools, including the Talented and Gifted School (TAG) for elementary students and Manhattan East and Isaac Newton for junior high students, scored at or above grade level. At Central Park East Secondary School, with a more diverse student body, more than half of the junior high school students read at grade level. Until recently these schools received special funding from the federal magnet-schools program, and they have attracted most of the students who come from outside East Harlem. TAG, for example, is 40 percent white.

The question of who is attending which East Harlem schools goes to the heart of the system of choice. In its publicity brochures, District Four describes its schools as "Schools That Dare to Compete," but the fact is that in many cases it is not the schools but the students that are competing—competing for the schools. A mother visiting New York Prep while I was there was eager to persuade its director at the time, Brian Spears, that her daughter, who was shyly tagging along, should be admitted.

"Why do you want to send your daughter here?" Spears asked.

"You've got computers and a good reading program," the mother said. "It's a safe school. I've got a younger daughter downstairs in the elementary school, and the principal there says it's good."

"There are two hundred and fifty applicants for seventy places," Spears replied, and then added, "The fact that you've come down, shown an interest, that's very important."

Sometimes parents treat the selection process as casually as if they were selecting a brand of cereal. Other parents—ones considering elementary schools in particular—base their decisions on factors like proximity and the safety of the neighborhood, which are important but only indirectly related to the quality of the education their children will receive. And for the many youngsters who are characterized by district officials as "at risk"—including children with young mothers strung out on crack, children who have worn thin the patience of their grandmothers, children living in group homes or on the streets—there is no responsible adult to make a choice.

Choice is a tool wielded less decisively by parents than by the school directors, the most adept of whom, like Spears, seek out students they think will succeed in their schools. Five alternative junior highs recruit many of their best students from elementary schools located in the same building that they themselves occupy. Until the past few years others ran their own early-admissions programs, effectively picking students before most parents had a chance to apply. It is largely because of this hidden selection process—which screens both for levels of skill and for traits of character—that some very good schools have been created in East Harlem.

A hierarchy has emerged, reflecting the extent to which schools can be selective. At the top are the so-called elite schools, which the ablest East Harlem children and most of the youngsters from outside neighborhoods attend. The highly selective sixth-through-eighth-grade school Manhattan East, which offers what it calls "a rigorous classical academic program," attracts as many as eighty of its 215 students from the world outside District Four; this integration would be less likely to occur if the school had less say over who gets in from the world *inside* District Four. The junior high school New York Prep, in the middle of the academic pecking order but with four applicants for every place, can also fill up with good children and reject all likely troublemakers. At the bottom of the heap are schools that virtually none of each year's 1,400 prospective seventh-graders in District Four would choose. These get the hundreds of children who are left over after the more successful schools have made their picks.

In theory, unsuccessful schools in a competitive system would be shut down and replaced with more-popular alternatives. That can be hard to arrange, though, when one reason that a school is unsuccessful is that it has been saddled with the least-promising and most-disruptive students—a change of name, director, and educational philosophy can accomplish only so much. It's also hard to arrange in the real world, where a teachers'-union contract guarantees job security and where many among the poor are possessive even of terrible schools, because these happen to be *their* schools. In nearly two decades only three alternative schools have been shut down in East Harlem. For all these reasons, a substantial proportion of elementary and junior high students wind up in schools that remain largely unaffected by the improvements in District Four.

3

Diversity is just an abstraction until you walk into the East 109th Street building that in the 1980s was a conventional junior high for 1,300 students. At that time it was a school with a reputation for student violence and dead-end teaching. Now the building houses four alternative elementary and junior high schools: the Harbor Performing Arts School, the Talented and Gifted School, the East Harlem Career Academy, and the Key School. Pedagogically these places are worlds apart, though they are separated physically by no more than a staircase or a fire door.

A visitor must sign in at a guard's desk before entering—a reminder that trouble is always possible from the crack dealers or the bullying high schoolers who hang around. When I visited the building, the guard was a young woman from the neighborhood, a recent high school graduate who returned to a book of word puzzles when no visitors were in sight. She carried no weapon and would have scared no one, but she offered at least the illusion of protection.

The Talented and Gifted School's name is no mere euphemism. Prospective TAG students take a battery of intelligence and psychological tests, and submit to interviews. The school rejects six children for every one it accepts. In one classroom I saw, pre-kindergartners age four were already beginning to write. A first-grade classroom was filled with stuffed dolls, likenesses of themselves that the children had crafted. "I'm Leslie," the writing on one doll proclaimed. "My puppy sleeps in my bed." "I'm Jenna," said the words on another. "I went to Florida." There was an "Artists' Touch" corner and an "Our Pets" corner. On the wall were cartoon figures demonstrating "angry," "afraid," and "frustrated." I asked the teacher's aide whether "frustrated" wasn't too sophisticated a concept for these six-year-olds, but she assured me that they get it. One of the kids volunteered, "It's the feeling I have when I can't do what I want."

Two floors away, at the Harbor Performing Arts School, with 210 seventh- through ninth-graders, a dance teacher led a dozen girls through a routine. The girls stood poised at the bar. "First position and stop and step back and step forward—don't use your arm, use your entire body . . . first position three, down on four. . . . Please stop fidgeting. Don't give me third,

Ebony—we're in fifth." A sign hanging in the room read, IF YOU'RE NOT WORKING ON YOURSELF, YOU'RE NOT WORKING, and intensity was sketched on the girls' straining faces. From down the hall came the sounds of a choir practicing a medley of songs. In a month the Harbor School's singers and dancers would begin rehearsing their major school production, a Broadway musical. The director at the time, Leslie Moore, told me that these classes build self-esteem. "If teenagers who are having trouble in math or English can succeed in singing or dancing," she said, "with all the discipline that that demands, they don't walk away defeated; they'll stay in school, maybe catch on to academic work. There's also some direct carry-over, since students in music or drama have to make sense of words."

Four hundred students apply for the seventy openings in the seventh grade at Harbor. Some will go on to La Guardia High School of Music and Art and Performing Arts—in 1990 ten of the twelve who applied there were admitted—and more will attend prep schools or the city's selective high schools. A handful of alumni are celebrated, among them Amani A. W.-Murray, who has released a saxophone album to bravo reviews, and Carlos Guity, a boy from the slums of the southeast Bronx who became an acrobat with the Big Apple Circus.

A typical junior high teacher with 150 students to teach over five periods can't be expected to remember all the students' names, let alone know very much about them. The intimate scale of some of the East Harlem junior high schools invites teachers to invest themselves, much like coaches, in their students' futures. On my initial visit to New York Prep, which occupies the fifth floor of an old elementary school, a boy whom I will call Jaime Morelia, home on vacation after his first term at a Connecticut prep school, came in to check up on his former teachers and see his friends. Jaime's natural ease made him seem more like a college freshman than a fifteen-year-old. He appeared to have made the transition from Harlem to an elite private academy without difficulty. His grades were decent and his confidence was intact. "It's different there," he said. "The work isn't so easy. And it's quiet. I'm used to noise. But we had good preparation for it, and the school is small enough so you can become close to everybody."

Christina Giammalva, who until recently divided her time between teaching history at New York Prep and placing her students at prep schools, believed that Jaime would make it at prep school. Although there were students with stronger academic records and better test scores, Jaime was clear-headed, a survivor. When his father disappeared from the family picture, Jaime, then thirteen, became the man of the house. All during his time at New York Prep he had to juggle the heavy and sometimes conflicting demands of home and school.

In terms of overall reading scores, New York Prep isn't impressive: in 1991 only 35 percent of the students there were reading at or above grade level. But typically eight or nine of the seventy ninth-graders at New York Prep, many of whom have lived lives at least as hard as Jaime's, will go on to private schools. Student programs involving Scarsdale High and

Princeton University, and field trips to places like Boston and Washington, D.C., show New York Prep's students something of the world beyond the ghetto. One or two afternoons after school every week, 120 of the 210 students spend nearly an hour getting to Columbia University, where they are tutored by law-school and business-school students. Those accepted by private schools take an intensive summer course to hone their academic skills and prepare them psychologically for what's ahead. Almost all will go on to college. Don't pay too much attention to the test scores, the teachers at New York Prep write in their recommendation letters, because we know this student. We won't hide the weaknesses, but we will tell you why they're manageable. In ordinary junior highs in inner cities this degree of involvement in the lives of students is largely unheard of.

The teachers' predictions cannot be infallible, of course, because few among us live perfectly mapped-out and predictable lives. Certainly not most fifteen-year-olds—they believe in their own immortality, and their eyes are on many prizes all at once.

We know how treacherous the passage from ghetto to private school can be from stories like that of Edmund Perry, whose journey from Harlem to Phillips Exeter Academy ended in robbery and death. Jaime's story is not so tragic, only shadowed and human. During his first year at prep school he was caught cheating—in Spanish, of all subjects—and placed on probation. This past spring, at the end of his junior year, he used a teacher's telephone calling card to phone his mother and his friends in East Harlem. He was found

151

out—how could it have been otherwise?—and expelled. Now he is enrolled in a New York City public high school.

What Jaime Morelia did was plainly wrong, and his moral compass was calibrated finely enough for him to know that. The deeper puzzle is why he behaved as he did. Christina Giammalva speculates that for Jaime the psychological distance may have been too great, the demands to conform to prep-school mores too imposing. Perhaps, Giammalva says, he made those phone calls to invite rejection, rather than be forced to do the rejecting.

Jaime's failure cannot be chalked up entirely to adolescent acting-out, because the school's insensitivity is pertinent too. When Jaime first got into trouble, his prep-school mentors never called his mother to enlist her support, and the first she heard of her son's expulsion was after the fact. Nor is the school's attitude unusual—and this makes the success stories even more special. Another graduate of New York Prep, a boy I'll call Jamail Robinson, was almost kept from returning to a private school where he had spent two years because his mother, a security guard raising two children, owed the school $1,000. School officials were ready to bounce Jamail without even talking to his mother; it took several anxious phone calls from Giammalva to get him reinstated. When Jamail went on to graduate from a private school (one of half a dozen or so New York Prep alumni to do so), he was picked by both the faculty and the students as the senior who best embodied their school's ideals.

THE Key School, which occupies the basement of the same building that houses the Talented and Gifted School and the Harbor School for the Performing Arts, is a school that reflects the underside of reform in East Harlem. None of the Key School's 120 seventh- through ninth-graders chose to be there. The places in this school are filled by youngsters who can't make it elsewhere, and enrollment at Key keeps climbing. Desperate administrators of other alternative schools plead with its director, Iris Novak, to take one more hard-to-handle adolescent, one more kid that nobody else wants. The last arrival had stolen $600 collected for a school dinner from a teacher's handbag at his old school. There are almost no other schools in the district for problem students. Those who can't make it here may be sent to special-education classes for the emotionally disabled, where about one East Harlem child in fifteen winds up.

The Key School is a dark place, out of sight, with none of the amenities of the more elite schools. Its ceilings vibrate whenever students from the Harbor School are playing basketball or practicing their ballet movements in the gym upstairs. Its name could be a metaphor for opening up new opportunities or, perhaps more fittingly, for locking a jail cell.

As I talked with Novak, students came and went, pleading for the key to the bathroom, a privilege granted at the absolute discretion of the director. It's an emergency, each of them insisted. A burly ninth-grader stormed in, demanding the return of his hat, which Novak had confiscated earlier in the day. "Gimme back my fuckin' hat," he screamed at Novak. "You think I'm a nice kid but I'm not. I'm mean." Novak wrote it all down, and then silenced the kid with a look and a rumbling voice that comes from having trained for the stage. "I'm not your mother or sister or girlfriend or grandmother. I'm the director of this school. I demand to be treated with respect. There will be no 'fuck, fuck' here. You are suspended." The day before, after one student had held up another at gunpoint on the sidewalk, security guards were called in; they put the suspect up against the wall and frisked him.

Only nine percent of the students at the Key School are reading at grade level. This isn't surprising, given the composition of the school. Even among East Harlem schools that are not designated as repositories for problem children, more than a few have only one youngster in five—if that—making the grade, and have experienced a decline in performance levels during the past decade. The worst of these schools was Music 13, which until June of 1990 (when it was shut down) coped with seventh- through ninth-graders.

"If you're interested in music, a strong academic background, and high standards," the brochure given to parents bravely announced, "Music 13 is the place to be." The name of Music 13 was intended to reveal its special focus, and there was an able music teacher, Luis Rosa, on the premises. But nobody really chose to attend Music 13, and by the end few at the school cared much about music anymore. The "13" in its name turned out to be more significant than the "Music."

The building that housed it was formerly Junior High School 13, and when two of Deborah Meier's schools were moved there in 1985, some neighborhood parents rebelled. We want to keep our *own* school, they insisted—even though the junior high had been such a misery that most parents had stopped sending their children there years before. A number of teachers also wanted to stay on, and a grandfather clause in the union contract entitled them to do so. Some of the half dozen who remained—"the grandfathers"—epitomized much of what has gone wrong with many big-city schools. During my visit to the school one teacher read the *New York Times* while students chattered, another shouted desperately for order, and a third delivered a by-the-book lesson to a class of uninterested ninth-graders. Often the teachers didn't bother to show up, or else let the director know a day ahead of time that they felt "a sickness coming on." Music 13 had become a school in name but not intention, a place of last resort.

Students like an eighth-grader I'll call Kevin Jones were stuck. "Kevin is intelligent and articulate, with a real talent for science and basketball," Ira Lyons, the third director at Music 13 in five years, told me. "He has more brains than I do." Kevin first attended Isaac Newton, but was kicked out after being accused of smashing the headlights of the director's car. He has had fights with other students at Music 13. Family conferences came to nothing when the boy's elderly and deeply religious grandmother insisted that he was no trouble at home. "High-ability kickouts don't mesh

155

with low-ability kids," Lyons said. "He belongs in a school that would challenge him." But no other school was interested.

Every urban school district has its Kevin Joneses, and they're probably no worse off at a place like Music 13 than at some run-down junior high in the Bronx. That reality points to the expedient bargain that has in effect been struck in East Harlem among those who have worked for reform. The deal is essentially this: Through the mechanism called choice—a mechanism that gives some options to parents and students but at the same time is rigged to give even more options to school directors—we can greatly improve the situation for about a third of our students, offering them a far better education than they could otherwise have had in one of the most battered neighborhoods in America. Perhaps we can even offer something useful to another third of our students. But the bottom third will be virtually abandoned—as they would have been anyway.

4

Confronted with crumbling buildings and daily episodes of violence, with splintered families and refractory bureaucrats—problems that elsewhere might in themselves suck up all the energy of school leaders— East Harlem has transformed a number of its schools. Elsewhere, initiatives are frequently abandoned when their champions leave, but the alternative schools in East Harlem have survived the departure of Alvarado and Fliegel, the entrepreneurs who launched the plan. They have survived a procession of chancellors at 110 Livingston Street, most of whom have been cool to what the district is doing. They weathered a 1988 financial scandal that brought down Alvarado's successor, cast suspicion on Fliegel's successor as director of alternative schools (who was later exonerated), and for a while left East Harlem's schools in the hands of an acting superintendent who made no secret of her dislike for the alternative-schools programs. Whether any further progress is possible in District Four—and whether other New York City districts will be able to proceed with plans for similar restructuring—depends on the level of funding in the New York City schools.

East Harlem, with all its problems, has built a far better school system than I have seen in any comparable neighborhood. For all the hype about reading-test scores, what's more impressive is the students' generally clearer writing and focused thinking, their greater self-confidence and understanding, and their willingness and ability to enter the world beyond the ghetto in high school and afterward. Graduates from junior highs in East Harlem *are* making it out of the barrio. In the intensely competitive environment of New York City's elite high schools, sorting is nearly as rigid as it was under the old British eleven-plus exam system. The four examination schools—Bronx High School of Science, Stuyvesant High, La Guardia High School, and Brooklyn Technical High School—are among the very best high schools in the nation. Another handful, including Aviation High and East Harlem's Manhattan Center for Science and Mathematics, enroll the next

157

tier of students. The nonselective schools get the left-
overs. In the mid 1970s fewer than ten of East Harlem's junior high graduates were accepted by the examination high schools. By 1987 things had radically
changed. East Harlem sent 139 youngsters, or 10 percent of the district's graduating class that year, to
those elite high schools—double the citywide average.
An additional 13 percent enrolled at four other high
schools that also screen their students—a rate four
times as high as the city average. That same year at
least thirty-six students from East Harlem received
scholarships to private schools, including some of the
best ones in the country.

Some of the students who travel to East Harlem
from other parts of the city volunteered to me that for
the first time in their lives they are being treated with
respect by teachers. Teachers reported that the small-
ness and autonomy of the alternative schools enable
them to identify a distinctive voice in each of their
children and to respond in kind. In the corridors and
directors' offices where teachers congregate, the talk is
mainly about what works in the classroom and what
doesn't, not about Macy's sales and last night's Knicks
game. Not all the schools are as innovative as those
that Deborah Meier founded, for there are, after all,
only a handful of such educators. But as the history of
good urban parochial schools suggests, educational innovation isn't essential to success. What *is* essential is
that the school take the time to shape an identity that
seems right to those who inhabit the premises, and
that this effort be sustained by teachers and administrators who have a measure of independence, a feeling

of being driven, and a capacity to know each of their charges. If the idea of intimate enclaves in factory-like city schools is going to take hold, it must happen not by treating East Harlem as a model to be mechanically applied, and certainly not by taking literally the misleading metaphor of the schools as a marketplace. Instead, it must happen as an approach adapted to the particularities of place.

Schools like those in East Harlem are being asked to accomplish the impossible—to challenge the highly achieving and rescue those who otherwise would drop out, to ease racial separation and reduce inequity in schooling, and all the while to function as the cutting edge of educational innovation. In truth, there are no easy paths even to modest progress. What's needed can be as time-consuming and undramatic as meticulous planning, into-the-wee-hours sessions with anxious school-board members, months of meetings with teachers and school directors to give content to the dreams, and then endless reassurances to parents troubled by what is new and untried. And even then, as District Four shows, there may well remain a large portion of the student population for whom reform might just as well never have occurred.

It is essential to risk the mistakes that so often accompany newness and to resist overpromising. Each school will have to find its own way, because everywhere the talents and the possibilities are different, but out of the process something of real value can emerge. This much, at least, East Harlem has to teach the rest of America, as the nation quietly but unmistakably embarks on the great experiment of remaking its schools, one by one.

Good Schools in Bad Times:
Reading, Writing—and Hustling
for Support—in LA

Noxember 1991 was unseasonably warm. In thousands of Los Angeles classrooms decorated with paper
cutout turkeys, children sweated it out in classrooms
that, by noontime, felt like furnaces. With the Los Angeles Unified School District dealing with budget cuts
of more than a quarter of a billion dollars, air condi-
tioning, like adequate supplies of chalk and textbooks,
had become a luxury.

Around the Coke machines in their lounges, teachers
were talking about another strike, the second in two
years. They were angry at the just-announced 3 percent pay cut and the two unpaid days off, a Christ-
mastime bag of coal from a school board that, having
cut back everything else—$276 million was chopped
from this year's budget—now demanded sacrifices
from those who are expected to make literate citizens
out of the thirty or more kids who crowd into each
L.A. classroom. Generally the new students are young
immigrants from homes where, if children are read to
by their parents, it's in Spanish or Tagalog or Russian,
not English.

But, despite the sorry plight of most L.A. schools, there are some elementary schools scattered across the city that manage to offer their pupils a true education. Measured by the standard metric of California's reading and math tests, these schools are doing at least decently—and certainly better than they have in the past. Their real successes, though, are measured by subtler criteria: students' growing self-confidence, their evident pleasure in being in school, their engagement with ideas in real books—"Charlotte's Web," even Shakespeare in fourth grade—and in writing that clears a pathway to their imaginations. At a time when negotiating the trip to school may mean finding a corridor free from gang warfare, when being a twelve-year-old can mean taking over as the head of the family, many of the children in these schools are, astonishingly, flourishing.

The hope in public education is always to identify the magic bullet—"the one best system," as turn-of-the-century pedagogues called it. That's why the surf's *always* up in the schools, as waves of reform roll in, only to crash against the far shore as new waves appear. In fact, while there are some good ideas worth sharing among lots of schools, deep and enduring reform doesn't happen wholesale. Los Angeles school district headquarters, Sacramento, Washington: All could help by trimming rules that bury innovations in paper, more good counsel, challenging textbooks and better benchmarks of progress, and more dollars, too. Some of this is happening. In California, for instance, former Supt. of Public Instruction Bill Honig pushed through stiffer intellectual standards and

161

demanded more challenging texts. But what makes a good school is mostly the special alchemy of its principal and teachers, students and parents. Particularly in elementary schools—where I spent time crouching in classrooms to get a child's-eye view of things, then talked with the grownups who work there—the specifics of what's taught really matter less than children's intuition that they are known and valued and loved.

1

Consider the Open School, a public school for 385 first- through sixth-graders housed in bungalows adjoining Crescent Heights Elementary School, in affluent Westside L.A. Students volunteer for this magnet school, one of eighty-six in Los Angeles, from every corner of the 708-square-mile district, some spending as long as two hours each way to get there and home again. The waiting list numbers in the hundreds, and by the district's rule no more than 40 percent of the students at any magnet school are white; at the Open School, the rest, selected by a computer, happen to be about evenly divided among blacks, Asians, and Latinos.

Though it was founded in 1977, the heyday of the back-to-basics era, this school has taken a very different approach. The child's own natural curiosity is the centerpiece of the teaching process; everything that goes on in the school is meant to pique, then to focus, that curiosity. At any given moment, there will be students working on the garden that they've built for themselves, while others sit at computer terminals, devising a program to chart the breathing patterns of a whale.

For the visitor who remembers classrooms as places where students sit in fixed rows, facing a teacher who runs the show with unquestioned authority, even an hour spent in Barbara Moreno and Mona Sheppard's combined fifth- and sixth-grade class means sensory overload—like going straight from a silent movie to "Star Wars." Each of the seven classrooms is made up of two trailers that are yoked together. About sixty kids group and un-group themselves, while the two teachers, along with a teacher's aide and often a parent volunteer, meet with small clusters. During the day, the entire class will occasionally come together, perhaps to get instructions on how to start a project. But then it's back to designing a mandala on the computer, or a solitary walk outside.

The idea that this classroom is spinning out of control is just the misconception of a linear-minded adult. When you ask them, these kids explain how the story they're writing and illustrating relates to the experiment they're conducting. They can show you, among other things, how the "taming" of the American West is seen from the perspectives of the frontiersman (and woman) and the Native American, drawing on texts, artwork and narratives spun out by a highly sophisticated computer program developed by Apple Computer, which relies on the school to try out its latest ideas. It's noisy at the Open School, but it's the good noise of people of several generations who have blurred the line between play and work. While the school has its share of problems—among them the lack of teachers to help students whose home language is neither English nor Spanish, and the tendency of some kids to test the limits of freedom—these seem manageable.

Hanging on the wall of principal Roberta Blatt's office are two taped-together sheets of paper, developed collectively, that chart the intellectual flow. There's a rationale for the sequence of subjects, which begins with the children's immediate environment and proceeds, year by year, through the building of a city to the world as a community. Some kids, Blatt tells me, seem to have a magnet in their bellies that hooks them to the computer. There are some natural politicians as well, such as the assistant mayor of the combined fourth- and fifth-grade class (the day I'm visiting, the mayor is out having her tonsils removed), who guides me around the classroom, showing off the city landscape and the charter of the new town.

The Open School's performance on the California reading and math tests is everything that the most anxious parent could hope for. Scores show that the students do better in reading and math than their peers in most Westside schools, despite the school's having a more racially and economically mixed enrollment—and despite its refusal to teach to the tests, shaping the curriculum with an eye on them. While Blatt is pleased with the results, particularly the fact that students in the bottom quarter of the class also score higher than their Westside counterparts, she tells me that she hadn't actually looked at the figures before I inquired. What she *has* paid attention to are the individual children's scores for particular skills, such as word-recognition or fractions, since these results will help classroom teachers work individually with youngsters.

"We have to identify which children aren't making it and develop programs for them," she says.

The open-school philosophy dates back nearly a century to John Dewey, but this is the only public school in Los Angeles that has adopted it. Yet school officials elsewhere in the district are beginning to borrow ideas that have been used for years at the school, such as team teaching, reading real books, involving parents in all aspects of school life. It's not clear, however, how long the district will maintain schools like this one. The extras cost money, of course, and those dollars mostly come from California's desegregation funds—$50 per student per year. But if Sacramento, pleading poverty, doesn't keep contributing so generously to magnet schools, will anyone pick up the slack?

2

While Beth Ojena, principal of the Coeur D'Alene Elementary School in Venice, has known her share of eight-year-old poets and computer whizzes, she also has seen a different side of children's lives. "He was doin' it to my girlfriend," said one eight-year-old girl, explaining to Ojena why she was so angry, as the principal struggled to keep a shocked look off her face.

"Gee, I was only dry-humpin' her," the boy indignantly replied.

As young as they are, Ojena knows, these kids have lived many more years than she has. So have many of the 300 children attending Coeur D'Alene, a school as diverse in its enrollment as any place in America.

About a quarter of the children come from working-class families, who live in the bungalows well away from the Venice beach. Thirty or so live in Marina del Rey, where a starter home can run upward of half a million dollars. A sizable contingent of kids, many bused from the overcrowded Mid-Wilshire/Hollywood area, start out barely able to say "hello" in English. Such children have become a familiar presence in a school system where, in educationese, almost all the public schools are "PHBAO schools"—places whose enrollment is predominantly Latino, black, Asian and other nonwhites.

What's astonishing is that nearly a quarter of the students at Coeur D'Alene are homeless—far more than in any other Los Angeles school. The good life of the Santa Monica and Venice beaches has attracted the very poorest as well as the very richest—and as many as three in ten of the county's homeless are children. The luckier ones sleep on the pine church pews or in the jam-packed apartments of the Bible Tabernacle Shelter, Los Angeles' biggest shelter for homeless families.

When Ojena came to Coeur D'Alene six years earlier, the mix of students was combustible. With the help of a technique called assertive discipline, widely practiced in L.A. schools, but nowhere more fully implemented than here, Ojena began to bring things under control. In every classroom, the do's and don'ts are written out, in a kind of self-determined charter of obligations: "Follow directions," says one class's list, "Be on task; keep hands to self; remember to stop, look, and listen."

Breaking these commandments has consequences, such as being benched during recess or having a note sent home. The emphasis, though, is on rewarding good behavior. First thing every Monday morning, all of the children gather on the playground to cheer as certificates are handed out to each classroom's citizen of the week, as well as to the trash-buster and the most academically improved.

For children who stay awhile, Coeur D'Alene can work small miracles. For the children from Marina del Rey, the school delivers a dose of real Los Angeles. And although kids can be terrible snobs, picking their friends on the basis of who's got the Chanel sweatshirts, here the egalitarianism of the elders seems to have trickled down. Among the haves and the have-lesses, there's a potent mixture of genuine love and discipline, with a social worker and a psychologist there at least one day a week to help the homeless kids unknot the tangles of real life. While instruction is more traditional than at the Open School—orderliness and control matter more, spontaneity counts for less—many of the same elements of instruction are in place.

Literature is being read, imaginations are being prodded in frequent writing assignments, an IBM-developed "Write to Read" computer program coaxes six-year-olds into telling their own stories. When fourth-graders reading "Phantom of the Opera" were asked to write stories about the people living behind their own masks, one black girl wrote in her journal: "People think they can treat me bad because of my color. They don't take the time to see behind the mask, to know me."

These innovations are paying off. Schoolwide reading test scores, though not yet up to the Westside average, have improved markedly over the past few years. Every teacher has a cheering story to tell, such as the tale of Ivonne Henriquez from El Salvador, a shy and engaging second-grader who guided me around her classroom. When she began school, Ivonne spoke just a few words of English. By year's end, she had won a personal computer in a citywide contest for the most improved writer.

It's the uncertain futures of these children that keep teachers awake nights. "Many of these children want so badly to learn," says Agnes Stevens, a former nun and volunteer tutor and mother-confessor for the kids from Bible Tabernacle. They dread the long holidays when they're out of school. Some kids stay for years, then disappear; others leave after just a few days. More than once, a homeless youngster has been selected as citizen of the week on a Friday, only to move on before picking up the award at the Monday ceremony.

With funds so tight, Ojena has to spend a third of her time writing grant proposals to government agencies, local foundations and private corporations. Outside money pays for the social worker, nurse, and psychologist, and the bilingual aides, too. But these grants—which amount to about $70,000 annually—won't be renewed indefinitely, because foundations regard giving away money as akin to planting seeds that someone else will nurture—in this case, supposedly the L.A. school district. Who knows how much longer Coeur D'Alene can remain a model for reaching out to the poorest kids in society?

3

The scene at the 112th Street Elementary School could have been lifted from a nostalgic rendering of the American heartland schoolhouse. As I walk into a first-grade classroom with principal Roberta Benjamin—the Queen, as she jokingly calls herself—twenty children, neatly dressed and attentive, chorus, "Good morning, Mrs. Benjamin."

Yet there's nothing nostalgic about this setting in the heart of Watts. Despite the visible presence of a tough-looking guard, a couple of teachers have been mugged on the playground in broad daylight. While the adjacent street features trim bungalows with lawns manicured almost to Bel-Air standards, the tranquillity is deceptive. One block away sits the Nickerson Gardens housing project, ground zero for the Crips and the Bloods. At night, gunshots are as common as bird song; the odds that a male teenager will make it to adulthood are worse than in Bangladesh.

In 1998, under pressure to settle a long-standing and acrimonious desegregation lawsuit, the school board launched the Ten Schools Program. New money and ideas would be pumped into the ten grade schools with the worst achievement scores, all located in South-Central Los Angeles. The program brought in new leaders and handpicked staffs. At the ten schools, the student-teacher ratio, which in other L.A. elementary schools is 30 to 1, is about 20 to 1. The school year runs longer in these schools, and every Saturday there are optional classes in subjects such as chamber music and Spanish playwriting.

When Benjamin arrived in 1986, the school had the worst test scores in the city. Kids were out of control, and when parents appeared at school, it was usually to heap abuse on the principal. "You're little," one parent told her. "You're not going to last."

Two homemade posters in the school's administration office are the first thing a visitor sees. One shows a tombstone labeled "1989–90 [California basic skills test] scores. Rest in Peace." It memorializes a year when test scores suddenly took a drop. The second, dated 1991, trumpets "Rebirth—the Phoenix Rose from the Ashes!!" The results don't rate unqualified cheers—across the school district, nine out of ten second-graders read better than the average 112th Street kid—but the kindergartners' performance is remarkable. Their reading scores rose 12 percentage points and are now close to the district average. The jump in math is even greater: The children are now performing with the upper third of all L.A. youngsters.

This transformation hasn't come about easily. Restoring order by relying on the assertive discipline strategy came first on Benjamin's agenda. Attention is paid to the minutest details of kids' behavior, producing a level of control that initially seems oppressive to a visitor who longs for the noise of the Open School.

"*Manos atrás* (hands behind your back)," insists teacher John Cook as he pilots his mostly Spanish-speaking kindergartners, looking as solemn as a class of young novitiates, onto the playground. First-grade teacher Noel Parker is finishing up a lesson and the kids are hanging on his every word. "If you're talking and not paying attention, you'll pay one sticker. . . . Those of you who cooperate will have stickers when you come back." Stickers are awarded for almost everything, and on Fridays, kids who have accumulated ten stickers get to pick a prize from the grab bag.

In Robert Pearlman's fifth-grade class, the students are lined up in teams for a math drill. "English, *Español, Español*, English": Pearlman checks off the lineup of students, confirming which language to use for the multiplication questions.

As I walk around the school, teachers point out children who have been sexually abused by foster parents, children whose parents put them to work delivering crack cocaine and children abandoned like yesterday's newspaper. "This stuff would drive adults around the bend," says Benjamin. "Yet we expect the kids to cope. And, mostly, they do."

In such a universe, the school has to do more than educate. It needs to reach out to parents. Parents are asked to sign a pledge to read each day to their children and give them a quiet place to work, and many live up to their promises. Parents also get written reports from the teacher every Tuesday; 70 percent showed up for this fall's parent-teacher conference.

This school also has to heal and comfort children. My sense of the oppressiveness of the discipline fades as I begin to sense the caring that humanizes all the rules. It may be hands behind the back at 112th Street, but there are lots of pats on the back and hugs as well.

From the beginning, the Ten Schools Program has been a political football. With the district's five-year commitment about to run out, Benjamin and her colleagues were nervous. The $15 million that pays for the extras comes mostly from state and federal aid that is beginning to shrink.

Most of the school's graduates stay in the neighborhood, attending Markham Middle School and then Jordan High. Unaccountably, these schools were never linked to the remade elementary schools and, as several elementary principals said, the light of educational innovation has not shone brightly on them. The newly acquired skills and fragile self-confidence of a 112th Street student often disappear in adolescence, in the impersonal corridors of junior high.

SOME things don't change for generations. At the end of Thanksgiving break, the paper Pilgrims are taken down from schoolroom walls, replaced by holly and dreidels.

The real pilgrims, though, are the kids themselves. What they're seeking—what they surely deserve—is a safe and comforting place, interesting things to learn and grownups who believe they can have bright futures—lives played out neither on the streets nor in dead-end jobs. In distinctive ways, the Open School, Coeur D'Alene, and 112th Street deliver all those things. But in these, as in other good public schools, the successes are contingent and problematic, the lion is always waiting just outside the gates.

Tales from the Bright Side: The Surprising Success of America's Biggest Community College

AT 8:30 A.M. on a mid-December morning, the temperature in the heart of downtown Miami is already well into the eighties, and the narrow, potholed streets have come alive. Unboxed Sony TVs are being peddled straight off the back of a truck. Cocaine-filled plastic baggies are flashed and spandex-clad hips unsubtly waggled. A store window promises instant delivery of a license to carry a concealed weapon.

The modern white buildings of the downtown campus of Miami-Dade Community College rise abruptly out of this *danse macrabre* like Alhambra from a junkyard. Palm trees and brilliant green lawns dot the campus. TV screens in the main building report on upcoming basketball games and bookstore best-sellers. Teachers carry stacks of papers to hand back; students gossip about weekend dates as they wait for the elevators.

There is also a mountain of snow at the campus entrance—and therein lies a tale.

It's Snow Day at Miami-Dade, and fifth-graders from the nearby elementary schools, almost all of them Hispanic and black, have been bused in to play in seven tons of crushed ice. Kids briefly freed from the routine of fractions and vocabulary drills overrun the escalators and walkways, and Alhambra is temporarily transformed into an ersatz winter wonderland.

Snow Day, it turns out, is just one of many ways the college acts as the Good Citizen of Miami. Its annual book fair has brought writers such as Isabel Allende, Peter Matthiessen, and Martin Amis to town; its film festival imports cinematic exotica to arid south Florida. Snow Day brings black and Hispanic kids together, sending a signal that the college is neutral territory, an academic Switzerland amid the local ethnic wars. And Snow Day also delivers an educational message: ten-year-olds' eyes are being opened to a world that's mere blocks away physically, but light years away intellectually, from home. In a few years, some of these kids will be back as students.

With more than 125,000 students taking at least one course—more than 79,000 for college credit—this five-campus school is the biggest college in the United States. In addition to the downtown campus, there are the original site just north of riot-torn Liberty City, two campuses in the burgeoning suburbs south of Miami, and a medical center situated at the county's midtown medical complex. Overall, the college enrolls more freshmen and sophomores than the nine Florida state universities combined. More than half the students are Hispanic (nationwide, only Los Angeles

Community College enrolls more Hispanics), 18 percent are black, and there are more foreign students than at any other American institution of higher learning.

Miami-Dade offers 135 separate programs ranging from English and chemistry to air-conditioning technology and mortuary science (half the state's undertakers are trained at the college). For certain vocational programs, including police training and graphics, the school delivers a money-back guarantee that graduates will land good jobs—and well over 90 percent of Miami-Dade's voc ed graduates either have jobs in their fields or have continued their education.

Miami-Dade isn't just a vocational school, though. The students run the gamut from faculty brats heading for professional careers to middle-aged dropouts, many of whom speak primarily Spanish or Haitian Creole and all of whom are determined to disprove the notion that there are no second—or third or fourth —acts in American lives. This variety of often conflicting student needs could well mean that no serious teaching gets done. But what's most remarkable about Miami-Dade—what makes it, according to a 1984 survey conducted by the University of Texas, the best community college in the country—is its commitment to making distinguished teaching the centerpiece of the institution.

The emphasis on teaching permeates every aspect of college life. President Robert McCabe promotes it with a fervor that approaches evangelism. It has led the college to adopt what administrators called the Marriott Plan, in which (just as in the hotel business) a staff member takes responsibility for a whole checklist of

176

niceties—making sure, for example, that the lights work and that every classroom has fresh chalk and clean blackboards. The pedagogical imperative influences core courses, teachers' raises and promotions, faculty retraining, and regular reports to students on their academic progress. It even prompted the recent decision to spend money on new faculty offices—to provide professors with decent places to work, and so tempt them to spend more time on campus—rather than on a fancier student union. "Higher education has failed to take teaching seriously, failed to incorporate what's known about learning," says McCabe. "We're doing things differently."

"If you really want to find out about how a college can make teaching better," says former Harvard president Derek Bok, "go talk to Bob McCabe."

THE invention of the two-year community college, former University of California president Clark Kerr has argued, is the real innovation of American twentieth-century education. Today more than half of all post-secondary students are enrolled in two-year schools. Yet the mission of the community college remains up for grabs. To some, it is meant to be a mini-university, whose essential task is equipping talented but badly schooled students for advanced academic work. Others regard it as a shock absorber that, as former Harvard president A. Lawrence Lowell observed more than half a century ago, could keep "out of college . . . young people who have no taste for higher education." Such schools are supposed to "cool out" students who aren't really suited for academics, redirecting them into increasingly popular vocational programs.

Like most community colleges, Miami-Dade grew too fast for much self-reflection. Founded in 1960, its initial enrollment of 2,025 doubled in the sixties and seventies about as often as the price of IBM stock. Vocational classes were offered alongside general education classes whose contents were uncritically borrowed from the University of Florida. Thousands of exiles from Castro's Cuba learned English at Miami-Dade, as did a later wave of refugees from Baby Doc's Haiti.

The college led a precarious existence in its early years—its classes held in an airplane hangar and converted barracks on a deserted air base, its policies scrutinized by the Dade County school board. But even then one thing was clear: Miami-Dade's leadership chose not to play it safe. At the time, every single one of Florida's public and private schools and colleges was segregated. The nearest college that admitted blacks was 200 miles north in Daytona. But from the outset, Miami-Dade Community College was racially integrated, simply because that seemed the right thing to do. This is the tradition in which McCabe situates himself. "I'm a risk-taker," he says.

1

The voice on the phone-mail message delivered to the nearly 1,000 faculty members and administrators at Miami-Dade was unmistakably President McCabe's, the New Yorkese softened by four decades spent in the South. But the content of the message was less familiar.

"I was wondering whether anyone else was awake this morning," McCabe mused aloud, "to see that beautiful sunrise." It came as news to some that President McCabe could find the time even to notice the sunrise, let alone to concoct such New Age nudgery. Though these were hard personal times for McCabe, who has had to cope with both the death in 1989 of his wife Bonnie (for whom the main building at the downtown campus is named) and his own recovery from painful injuries suffered in a car crash two years later, that private, wistful side isn't often on display. What most people see is his workaholism—endless rounds of money-raising and politicking, speech-making and award-collecting. Among his laurels is the McGraw Education Prize for "having a truly exciting impact on education."

McCabe's top aides refer to him as a visionary, and although that description gilds the lily, he has breathed life into enough interesting ideas to fill the resumes of half a dozen college presidents. Some years ago, for example, a brief item appeared in the press noting that Alex Haley's epic family history, *Roots*, was going to be made into a TV miniseries. In short order, McCabe met with Haley in L.A. to pitch the idea of turning the miniseries into a TV course for college credit. Haley would work with Miami-Dade faculty members to create the curriculum. The author said yes—and the rest, including the $600,000 the college earned by selling the course materials to 500 schools, is history. Lately McCabe has been preoccupied with helping thousands of Miami-based Pan Am workers, from top execs to baggage checkers, who lost their jobs when the airline suddenly folded. McCabe has no doubt this is his school's responsibility. He undertook the same kind of effort when Eastern went broke in 1990. Then, a contribution from Miami's Private Industry Council plus some expert budget-juggling produced a crash course in how to get a job and how to handle the psychological trauma of losing one. Many of the Eastern employees who enrolled have stayed on to pick up the skills for second careers as hotel managers, realtors, or nurse-practitioners.

Money is even tighter this time around. Like most states, Florida has typically treated its community colleges as ugly ducklings. Facing a budget deficit in 1992, the state ordered a cutback; for the first time in its thirty-two year history, Miami-Dade had to turn away eligible students. That didn't stop McCabe, however. Working closely with the Miami business leadership and the state's congressional delegation, he sought—and got—$3 million from the U.S. Department of Labor, a portion of which will go to the college for the retraining of laid-off workers.

McCabe has also waded into some of the toughest fights in this factious city. He tried to mediate a dispute over awarding the key to the city to Nelson Mandela, venerated by blacks but demonized by the city's Cuban population of his embrace of Fidel Castro. (Despite McCabe's best efforts, Mandela never got the key.) In a city where few dare cross the fervently Fidel-loathing Cuban exiles, McCabe has defended the academic freedom of a social sciences professor who is a Castro sympathizer and allowed a pro-Castro Cuban-born playwright to speak on campus, shortly after Dade county officials cancelled a performance of her play.

A resume like McCabe's might suggest natural charisma, but the man is less prepossessing than his reputation. He resembles an aging cherub with graying, pasted-down hair and a slightly rumpled suit. His voice sometimes drones, and his speeches and articles are overly inclined toward phrases like "feedback data" and "self-actualiztion." His list of the twenty-nine attributes of an excellent faculty, to which he proudly refers, is the stuff of parody: excellent faculty spend time with students, excellent faculty display a "genuine sense or humor," and so on. As someone who professes to be an admirer noted, "You sure don't want to get stuck with Bob McCabe at a cocktail party."

But somehow McCabe makes things happen. Other university presidents appoint faculty committees to take up, say, the question of weeding out inept students or designing a new core course, then step aside. McCabe leads by enthusiasm—not just forming those requisite committees but sticking around to see how they run. There may not be a blueprint for change in his back pocket, as some faculty at Miami-Dade suspect, but his presence is felt whenever something of value is being hashed out. "Community colleges are the most important educational institutions in the country," he says. "The public schools are not getting the job done. It's not hard to help someone who will make it anyway. We know how to salvage lives. We're where the people and the problems are."

McCabe's own life story is a testament to the kind of second chances his college trafficks in. In 1947, the year after he graduated from high school, his father was laid off by the Long Island hotel where he had worked for thirty-two years. Bob had to drop out of college and support the family—by plucking chickens, bundling newspapers, and delivering messages at the UN—while his father looked for a new job. After graduating from the University of Miami, McCabe taught high school in Florida for a while, got his master's degree and met his wife, Bonnie, at Appalachian State, then found his way to the University of Texas doctoral program for community college administrators. He headed back to Miami in 1963, just three years after the college opened its doors.

For McCabe, the school's rapid expansion, driven by the Caribbean immigration of the early 1960s, was a gold rush. He had been at Miami-Dade just two years when he took the lead in opening its south campus. After a brief stint as president of a community college in Newark, New Jersey, he returned to Miami in 1969 and in 1980 became president of the college, a post he held for the next decade and a half.

2

As the fall term winds down at Miami-Dade Community College, faculty members are frantic. They are shouldering the usual burdens of writing exams, coping with pleas for last-minute extensions, placing book orders for the spring term. But in 1992, for the first time, they must also prepare self-evaluations. A handful of math teachers at South Campus is threatening to revolt—remarkable at an institution where almost no one ever bad-mouths the administration.

Miami-Dade faculty members work hard. They teach fifteen hours of classes a week, usually without assistants to help critique papers (a Florida law, known as the Gordon Rule, actually mandates that students commit 24,000 words to paper by their junior year). They have long hours of committee work and student counseling and struggle to keep up with their academic fields. But as Mardee Jenrette, a former biology professor who runs Miami-Dade's Teaching/Learning Project, acknowledges, the self-evaluation process has stirred widespread panic. Small wonder: When coupled with colleagues' and department chairs' appraisals, students' reviews, and faculty-prepared portfolios, these self-assessments will determine salary and status. Those judged the ablest pedagogues will be in line for one of a proposed one hundred new teaching chairs. The new posts (sixty of them are available now) are renewable three-year appointments whose donors range from the state funeral directors association to Miami Jai Alai. They carry a $5,000 pay increase and an additional $2,500 for professional activities, from travel to classroom supplies. Professors who don't pass muster fear they'll find a lump of coal in their Christmas stocking—or, for the untenured, a pink slip.

Far from being sprung on an unsuspecting professoriat, this new system of appraisal was in the works for a number of years and was approved by 69 percent of the faculty in a 1989 referendum. Until then, student rather than teacher performance had been the focus of the college's collective thinking. The best students are encouraged to enroll in an honors program (where they can write about the symbolism in *Heart of Darkness* if they so choose) and pushed into elite colleges as upperclassmen. The less well prepared— nearly three quarters of all the entering students— take rudimentary courses in English as a second language and what are euphemistically called developmental classes in reading, writing, and math.

The message to students is "access with excellence," the academic equivalent of tough love. Under the Standards of Academic Progress, the suggestively acronymed SOAP program, postadolescents who hang around for years repeatedly flunking the same subject are shown the door. About 2,000 students are suspended or dismissed for academic reasons each year. A computerized "academic alert" delivers detailed midterm progress reports to all students; those skating on the academic edge face restrictions on the number and difficulty of subjects they can take. "We reversed this idea of 'do your own thing,'" says McCabe.

But, McCabe argues, until teachers have the tools and the incentives to teach better—"not just teaching subject matter but knowing how to reach out to people in trouble"—there's only so much that students can accomplish. Like most community colleges, Miami-Dade borrowed its rules of promotion from the public schools: tenure after three years, very few tenure denials, and promotions as well as pay raises pegged to seniority. Little thought was given to helping professors effectively profess. The first task of the Miami-Dade Teaching/Learning Project, established in 1986, was putting on paper standards of teaching excellence.

Then came the harder work of translating homily into practice. Centers at each campus offer workshops for professors and staff members on everything from preparing LOTUS spreadsheets to finding alternatives to the open-the-skulls-and-pour-in-the-knowledge approach to teaching. Irene Lipoff, who runs the downtown campus's Teaching/Learning Center, sometimes puts in thirteen-hour days. "I've created a monster," she says only half in jest.

Confronted with the extraordinary range of students—the need to be miracle workers, as math professor Paul Dirks says—teachers welcome the help. At the Centers, professors can learn to teach their students how to take notes by using an analytical approach called circular mapping and how to do their homework. So long as the college can afford it, professors and staff can get instruction in anything they want to learn about, including "earth literacy," a kind of Environmentalism 101. The centers also stress writing, not as a ghettoized course but across the entire curriculum.

Instead of being tossed out to sink or swim, newly hired teachers are assigned to mentors who have reputations as good teachers. They're also required to take two pedagogically oriented graduate courses. For professors who have been at the college for three years or more, such exercises in self-improvement are entirely voluntary. But professional development is part of the new evaluation regimen, as are responsiveness to students and innovativeness in shaping of new courses. And so, whether out of professional pride or an interest in resume-padding, an estimated one third of the faculty members regularly use the Teaching/Learning Centers.

Not surprisingly, the most popular workshops have focused on constructing the self-evaluations. Honest appraisals thick with mea culpas are not what's expected. Instead, the hope is that good teachers will toot their own horns, Lee Iacocca-style. Meanwhile professors who have been earning a living off their yellowed notes are being prodded into taking workshops, expanding their office hours, redoing their syllabi. "I've tried to light fires under certain behinds," says Teaching/Learning Center director Lipoff. "Now they're spiffing up."

Reality, however, may fall short of aspiration. Brief self-evaluation forms are swelling to twenty-page essays. Some professors plan to stuff their portfolios with their students' Christmas cards and wedding invitations—presumably to show their own Mr. and Ms. Chips-like qualities—and are asking students to sign in for office hours. Teachers are recording themselves on video, smiling, and the running campus joke is that an entrepreneur could make a bundle building a life-size cardboard cutout of President McCabe, then posing faculty members with it for a photo op. In classic back-scratching fashion, professors are lining up their colleagues to say nice things about them, then agreeing to do the same.

The system is supposed to identify excellent teaching, but it threatens to degenerate into nothing more than a full-employment program for campus administrators, who are struggling under an avalanche of paper. "These days," says Lipoff, "finding a faculty member who admits to having voted for this process is a little like finding someone who'll confess to having voted for George Bush."

But then, assistant professors up for tenure at leading universities have been known to list letters to newspapers as publications on their vitae or solicit mash notes from their friends and pass them off as letters of recommendation. At least Miami-Dade is trying something new, and although this pioneering venture may eventually collapse under its own weight, this is just the first year of a scheduled three-year trial run. The plan's advocates are confident it will work better once professors grasp that the idea is to reward teaching excellence, not paper trails, and in the meantime, the college's track record of innovation entitles it to a patient audience.

3

Like teachers at any other college surrounded by mean streets, Miami-Dade's medical center faculty don't hang around after work. Ever since the 1980s riots in Overtown and Liberty City, the neighborhoods around the medical center have been no-go zones for street-smart Miamians fortunate enough to live elsewhere. Professors typically drive to the campus, teach their classes, then split for their suburban homes. But for Tessa Tagle, dean of the medical campus, these streets are where Miami-Dade Community College has the opportunity to live up to its middle name.

Tagle's sense of community obligation stems from her own experience growing up with two sets of grandparents in two different sections of San Antonio, Texas. In one, families maintained their homes, kept the local *molina*, or tortilla maker, humming, and watched their kids' progress at the public school or the nearby Catholic school. In the other neighborhood, houses and shops had fallen into shambles, boys barely out of their teens spent long stretches in the penitentiary, and drugs were openly dealt on the streets. A couple of years ago, after a long absence, Tagle returned to her old haunts. How had San Antonio tried to rescue the failing neighborhood in the interim? By installing a sidewalk—"as if the sorrows could be paved over," Tagle says bitterly, "and the people could walk out of poverty. We live in a developed country with under-developed cities living inside of it. That has to change."

There was no reason, Tagle believed, why Miami-Dade Community College couldn't push for such change. So Tagle has introduced a summer program, Medical School for Kids, which puts twelve- and thirteen-year-olds into the medical center's labs, as well as a short course, Health Careers for People in Public Housing, which trains uneducated mothers to do simple but decent-paying jobs like drawing blood. She also wants to enlist faculty and students in the life of the Overtown community. That means activities as basic as showing schoolchildren how to wash their hands and teaching young mothers how to care for their infants. Students at the medical center will have to satisfy a public-service requirement that will take them into Overtown.

Most ambitiously, the neighborhood outreach program contemplates helping citizens develop the skills to help themselves by identifying the needs of their communities and lobbying city agencies. Miami-Dade doesn't intend to be the authoritative voice in Overtown but the convener and catalyst—which makes it more reminiscent of 1960s community action programs like Saul Alinsky's famous Woodlawn Project in Chicago than of the contentious experiment in Chelsea, Massachusetts, in which Boston University took over a failing public school system. At a time when money is tight and the prevailing political mood cautious, the college seems on the verge of becoming an institutional Alinsky for the nineties.

4

At the end of the fall term, students in Elaine Ludovici's developmental writing course at North Campus turn in their portfolios. Throughout the semester, Jean-Pierre, a Haitian-born student, has written about his problems in high school. In one early paper, he described a "negative experience" as "sleeping in class, especially if the teacher is boring . . . the way some teachers teach, something with no feelings." By term's end, he is writing more fluently about his biggest personal accomplishment: graduating from high school. "I was very proud to see after all of those years I've been going to school, I was finally getting out. . . . I was down most of the time and sometimes I would feel like dropping out. But I never quit because I used to tell myself if I stopped going to school, what would I be doing?"

There is no end to the procession of students like Jean-Pierre, teetering at the edge of literacy and yet wanting so badly to make it. About one student in five who enters the college seeking a degree graduates within three years, and twice as many are still enrolled or have left college in good standing. Among the students who, at the outset, were academically eligible for one of Florida's public universities, nearly half graduate, a rate that's competitive with these selective-admission state universities. Seventy percent of all graduates transfer directly to one of the state universities, significantly more than in 1980, and they perform only slightly worse than those who start out at the university.

But students who come to Miami-Dade with real deficiencies in reading, writing, or math have a much harder time. Just one in six who arrives needing remedial help graduates in three years or leaves in good standing. Similarly, students who know little English generally fall by the wayside: Only one in six completes the English as a Second Language courses that precede college-level work. The school struggles to get its students through Florida's College Level Academic Skills Test (CLAST), which the state requires for an associate's degree. In 1990, just 40 percent of those who took the entire test at one sitting passed its math, English, reading, and essay components. And Miami-Dade has been unable to solve another vexing problem: By all criteria, U.S.-born black students consistently do the worst. Their CLAST scores are much lower, they are more likely to drop or be pushed out, and those who graduate are less likely to continue their education than Anglos or Hispanics.

This kind of teaching can be frustrating. Humanities professor Thelma Altschuler recalls bringing to class a short article that described the concept of an inherent human nature as illusory, an excuse to do nothing about poverty or crime. "I read it fast, then asked, 'What did the author say?' Five students raised their hands; they all answered exactly the opposite." Walt Tucker, who teaches developmental reading, broods about "the reality that community colleges reproduce the social class system."

"The CLAST scores may show the limits of what even an exemplary community college can accomplish," says Berkeley professor of education Patricia Cross, who spent a term at Miami-Dade, "but no college in the country has given it a better try." In any case, faculty members don't pay too much attention to the statistics. What keeps them going are the individual success stories they all can tell: the high school dropout who became a dentist, the student from Vietnam who started out knowing no English and is now getting his master's degree in business, the ex–baggage handler who couldn't do fractions when he came and wound up manipulating differential equations, the woman with three kids and a patchy education who stuck it out to become a nurse. "I'm having more fun teaching here than I've ever had in my life," says math professor Paul Dirks. "These kids have been shortchanged academically. They want to get ahead—

and they respond to your concern. They want to make something out of their lives." It's "God's work," says another instructor, with no apologies for the missionary sentiment. This college continues to educate its faculty and students in what it means to be the Good Citizen of Miami.

Uncommon Decency:
Pacific Bell Responds
to AIDS

SITTING nervously in the public health clinic that Friday before Labor Day in 1986, awaiting word on his AIDS test, Pacific Bell repairman Dave Goodenough already half knew what he would be told: he had AIDS. He'd suspected as much for seven months, ever since he first noticed the markings on his chest. His doctor dismissed them as bruises picked up at work, but when the purplish markings started showing up all over his body, Goodenough sought another opinion. It had taken the second doctor only moments to identify the symptoms as "KS"—Kaposi's sarcoma, a type of cancer frequently associated with AIDS—and the test results confirmed that diagnosis.

Suspicions of AIDS are one thing, certainty something very different. "I was wiped out," Goodenough recalls. As he began to sort out the implications of the news, one question kept recurring: Would he—could he—go back to work?

Goodenough had been with Pacific for a decade, and working meant a lot to him. He liked what he did and liked the crew he worked with; he appreciated the fact that he didn't have to hide his homosexuality. Back in Ohio, Goodenough had been sacked from a probation officer's job when word leaked out that he was gay. But San Francisco was different. And even though the phone company had a reputation as a bastion of mid-America, operating with a rule book as thick as a phone directory, by the late 1970s Pacific had just begun learning how to cope with the reality that a sizable number of its employees were gay.

To Goodenough, confirmation of AIDS only reinforced how important it was to him to stay on the job. "If I left the job," he recalls thinking, "it would be like putting a limit on the amount of time I have to live." His friend Tim O'Hara, a longtime Communication Workers of America steward and a spokesman for gay concerns in the union, encouraged Goodenough not to quit—and to tell company officials that he had AIDS.

Initially, Goodenough resisted this last bit of advice. "I won't let anybody know," he insisted. But a few days later he changed his mind. "I can't hold something like this inside," he decided. "It'd be like being in the closet all over again."

On Goodenough's behalf, O'Hara went to Chuck Woodman, supervisor of the 750 people in Operations who keep the phone system in San Francisco up and running. Woodman's response was, "We'll do everything we need to do to keep Dave working," and he called Goodenough's immediate superior to enlist his support. Later that week, Goodenough phoned Woodman to thank him. "You could hear in his tone of voice how much Chuck cared," Goodenough remembers. "What he said kept me going. He told me, 'You've always got a job here.'"

Chuck Woodman hadn't always been so concerned about people with AIDS. To his subordinates Woodman had a reputation as a tough guy, a self-described redneck whose heroes included John Wayne and George Patton. A devout Mormon, father of eight, and grandfather of twenty, Woodman's attitude about AIDS began to change in 1985 when he was transferred to San Francisco. He remembers how he was affected by a funeral for a worker who had died of AIDS.

"As I listened to that minister talking about how angry it made him that people with AIDS were shunned, I began to feel some of that anger," Woodman says. "The whole moral question of homosexuality got put aside."

To learn more, Woodman turned to Tim O'Hara, whom he knew and liked. With O'Hara's assistance, Woodman got a thorough education on AIDS. Information brought understanding, and understanding gradually eased the fear. After that first funeral, Woodman started asking questions. "What can we do for the people with AIDS on the job?" he wondered.

"They need to keep working," O'Hara answered. "It gives them a reason to stay alive."

Woodman began talking with supervisors and visiting workers with AIDS when they were too sick to work. Out of those talks with Woodman and Michael Eriksen, the company's director of preventative medicine and health education, came Pacific's first steps toward dealing with AIDS in the workplace: an AIDS Education Task Force, with company nurses and volunteering union members trained by the San Francisco AIDS Foundation giving presentations in offices and company garages all around the city. Woodman's bosses in the Pacific hierarchy were pleased with his AIDS initiatives. But peers who knew him from his earlier days were stunned. "I got maybe half a dozen calls from guys around the state. 'What are you doing, Woodman?' they'd say. 'Do you love those gay guys?' I told them, 'Until you've walked in these tracks, you can't understand. You start buying in when it's someone you know.' And here's something. Each of those guys called me back later to say, 'I've got someone with AIDS. Now what do I do?'"

Chuck Woodman talks about AIDS as a managerial challenge, the toughest in his nearly forty years at Pacific. "When I look at where I was and where I am now, AIDS has had a bigger impact on my thinking about people than anything I've come up against."

THIS comment about the impact of AIDS is no hyperbole; that isn't Woodman's style. And Woodman's remark applies not just to himself, not even just to Pacific, but to business generally. Just as AIDS changed American society, it has also changed American corporations.

That is not the conventional wisdom. To most managers, AIDS is a medical and social epidemic of still-unknown dimensions—the federal Centers for Disease Control conservatively estimate that 1.5 million Americans now carry the AIDS virus and that by 1991 every county in the United States will have at least one AIDS case. Much less common is a managerial awareness that American business must reckon with AIDS. Managers in general regard AIDS as a problem not for workers but for homosexuals and drug users and their promiscuous sexual partners, as a disease that attacks people outside the office and factory walls.

Such denial, however understandable, doesn't fit the facts. Among 273 companies responding to a 1987 American Society for Personnel Administration survey, one-third acknowledged having workers with AIDS. This was more than triple the percentage reported two years earlier and a figure that will steadily grow, if only because of AIDS's long incubation period (it can take seven years or more for symptoms to develop). Furthermore, those numbers represent only the most direct impact of AIDS, and this is not necessarily its most important dimension to the corporation.

AIDS molds behavior in many ways. In the worst, usually hushed-up incidents, employees afraid of AIDS-carrying coworkers have walked off the job. More common are dances of avoidance—workers refusing to share tools or even sit in the cafeteria with a stricken coworker. And then there is a very different reaction—grief at the loss of a friend and colleague. In a society where, for many, the workplace isn't merely the source of a paycheck but also a source of community, where fellow workers are also friends, there is simply no way for business to wall out AIDS.

How does a company respond to something as alien as AIDS? The best answer, as Pacific learned, is to recognize AIDS as a legitimate part of the corporate environment and to tailor a response that is of a piece with all that the company stands for and is doing. Pacific's reaction to AIDS was affected by the fact that the utility is headquartered in San Francisco—with its large gay community—and that telecommunications is a highly regulated industry. Nevertheless, the remarkable turnaround of this unlikely innovator tells an instructive tale for every major U.S. corporation.

1

Three years after AIDS was first identified, in 1984, Pacific's preventative medicine and health education director, Michael Eriksen, began hearing stories about Pacific employees worried about getting AIDS on the job. There was the coin collector who refused to touch the phone booths in the predominantly gay Castro district of San Francisco. One Los Angeles crew balked at installing phones in the offices of the L.A. AIDS Foundation, and another San Francisco crew insisted on being issued head-to-toe covering before installing phones in General Hospital's AIDS ward. And there was the lineman who refused to use the truck of a fellow employee, rumored to have died of AIDS, until it was sterilized.

As the number of crisis phone calls mounted, Eriksen resolved to determine the dimensions of Pacific's AIDS problem, to conscript other activists in shaping a plan—and to act. Later, one colleague recalled, "Eriksen became our AIDS guru." Bearded, mid-thirties, casual, fresh out of a Johns Hopkins Ph.D. program, Eriksen had been hired several years earlier to move the company toward a "wellness" approach. Already he had developed an in-house program to help employees quit smoking and to enable women to spot the first signs of breast cancer. Eriksen brought an activist's impatience to Pacific. In a company where going by the book is the instinctive response of lifetime employees, he equated going through corporate channels with death by memo.

Eriksen's work on AIDS began with the facts. He reviewed the company's 1984 death certificates and turned up twenty employees who had died of the disease. This meant that, after cancer, AIDS was the most frequent cause of death among active Pacific employees. Pacific officials, who hadn't considered AIDS a workplace issue, were startled; but the data made sense, since the nearly 70,000 employees and 250,000 people in Pacific's larger "family" were concentrated in San Francisco and Los Angeles, two cities with a high incidence of AIDS cases.

Moreover, Eriksen knew that the figure of twenty was decidedly conservative, since it excluded workers who had gone on the permanent disability rolls before dying and cases in which the doctor had not specified AIDS on the death certificate as the cause of death. In the general population, the number of AIDS cases was doubling every year; this meant Pacific was seeing just the beginning of the epidemic. Add those deaths among the company's work force to the stories of Pacific workers' fears about encountering AIDS while serving customers, and something had to be done. But what, and by whom?

If AIDS had been a garden-variety disease, tracing the path of corporate response would be easy. Policy would have been designed by the company's human resources division, with the medical director, Ralph Alexander, having the final say. But because AIDS was new and frightening, it demanded the kind of cross-the-boundaries effort that is hard for a company to marshal on any issue, let alone on a subject so loaded with bias, contention, and misinformation.

The corporate medical group needed to sift prevailing medical wisdom—but that was just the start. The human resources division, drawing on corporate-safety and labor-relations experts, had to determine how AIDS would be treated in the workplace—whether prospective employees would be screened for the virus, whether workers with AIDS could continue on the job—and what benefits to offer people with AIDS. Potentially every manager in the company needed help in handling workplace fears, and not just in San Francisco and in Los Angeles. Phone operators in California's decidedly unswinging Central Valley had no personal fears about contracting AIDS, but expressed real concern for their children. And because the AIDS issue was so hot, whatever the company did was potentially news—that made the corporate communications division a player as well.

Urged on by Michael Eriksen, the lawyers and medics and corporate-safety staffers determined that workers with AIDS would be treated like anyone with a life-threatening illness. The culture of the phone company, with its strong emphasis on two-way commitment and loyalty, kept Pacific from seriously considering the option of revoking the medical coverage of employees with AIDS—a policy that some companies followed. Jim Henderson, the company's executive director of human resources policy and services, says bluntly, "People with AIDS are sick. We don't fire sick people."

This policy was not only humane but also affordable, a vital consideration for any business. Reviewing the company's twenty AIDS-related deaths, Michael Eriksen estimated that the lifetime cost of medical treatment for an AIDS patient ran about $30,000, about the same as costs for treating other life-threatening illnesses such as cancer. To Pacific, whose escalating health costs were subject to review by California's Public Utilities Commission, that news was reassuring.

In practice, AIDS forced the company to make much-needed reforms that went beyond this one disease. For example, Pacific was already searching for ways to reduce reliance on hospitalization. The company sought less expensive alternatives, and its sick workers considered less impersonal ones. Both preferred new options, like at-home or hospice care, which offered more personal settings and attention at reduced costs. These quickly became part of corporate health coverage. Pacific's capacity for individual case management also needed strengthening so it could better determine—on a case-by-case basis—which regimen of care made best sense. Moreover, since many drugs used to treat AIDS patients were most readily available by mail, the company extended its health plan to cover mail-order drugs.

None of these innovations applied to AIDS alone. Indeed, business organizations like the Washington Business Group on Health have preached for years that case management is the best way for a company to tame the costs of catastrophic diseases. But AIDS treatment demonstrated the efficacy of the approach. One Southeastern public utility, relying heavily on hospitalization for AIDS patients, reported that its first eight AIDS cases cost the company $1 million—almost four times Pacific's per-patient cost. At Pacific, AIDS was a catalyst for reshaping many employee health benefits. The resulting package offered better treatment at markedly lower costs.

PACIFIC was drawing from its own traditions in defining benefits for employees with AIDS. But in dealing with workers' fears about being exposed to AIDS through casual contact, Pacific had to determine entirely new responses.

The accounts that Eriksen and Jean Taylor, director of employee counseling, had collected—installers shunning customers, workers avoiding AIDS-stricken associates—hinted at a dangerous level of anxiety in the field. And those employees' misgivings mirrored feelings in the society. In 1984, when AIDS fears had first begun to surface at Pacific, far less was known about the disease than today, and uncertainty left ample room for fearfulness and misinformation.

Managers had to wrestle with difficult questions. How would Pacific allay its employees' worries and thereby ensure that an AIDS incident didn't escalate into a fiasco? How could it protect the confidentiality of disclosures about AIDS while attending to the concerns of employees with the disease? What changes were needed in Pacific's detailed rule book to help managers deal with the special needs of employees with AIDS?

The way Pacific handled the 1985 case of the phone installer who refused an assignment in San Francisco's Castro district suggests the delicacy of the issue and the need for new and nonpunitive approaches to win over frightened workers. When the balking phone installer was suspended, he went to shop steward Tim O'Hara. But instead of lodging a grievance, O'Hara struck a deal. The worker would return to the job and a joint union-management AIDS education program would begin immediately at the site. The idea was feasible because Pacific and its union had developed an unusually cooperative and nonadversarial relationship during the last contract talks.

O'Hara's evenhanded approach respected the workers' fears and met the needs of the company's customers. Meanwhile, the shop steward put together a list of thirty volunteering workers, whose lifestyles ran the gamut from the most traditional heterosexual middle American to the openly gay. If other workers were ever unwilling to make an installation where there was an AIDS victim, this squad was ready to handle the job. Here again, preparation and education worked: no supervisor has ever had to turn to O'Hara's list.

But despite early agreement on nondiscrimination as the broad company policy, corporate AIDS education at Pacific did not advance beyond crisis intervention. While several hundred employees did show up in April 1985 at the company's headquarters downtown for a question-and-answer session with Michael Eriksen and a San Francisco AIDS Foundation representative. But that was a one-time occasion. For all the other employees—the San Francisco work crews who wouldn't dream of coming all the way downtown; the 7,200 back-room personnel working in "San Remote," a Pentagon-like fortress thirty-five miles outside the city in suburban San Ramon; the employees in Los

Angeles and throughout California and Nevada— there was essentially no AIDS education.

Within Pacific's medical department, there was disagreement about the adequacy of the company's approach thus far. The dispute reflected deep differences in perspective between the classic medical approach and the newer views of wellness specialists.

For longtime medical director Ralph Alexander—a consistently conservative official who believed that, as an M.D., he should have the last say—what Pacific was doing sufficed. In discussions with other divisions, Alexander regularly stressed the need to keep a sense of proportion when responding to AIDS, which he viewed as a relatively minor health concern for the company. "There's danger of offending a hell of a lot of people," said Alexander. It was better, he argued, for the company to devote more attention to heart disease and cancer, far bigger killers and diseases that wouldn't "raise eyebrows."

Wellness specialist Michael Eriksen saw matters differently. AIDS, he believed, deserved special attention because it was new and unnerving. He began to hook up with other like-minded colleagues, most of them mid-level managers involved in communications both inside and outside the company. These policy entrepreneurs believed that acting decisively on AIDS was the right thing to do; moreover, such a stance would benefit the company. It was these middle managers who took the lead in shaping Pacific's response to AIDS, exercising leadership from below.

One opening salvo was an article on AIDS that slipped into Pacific's newspaper, *Update*, moving the issue higher on the corporate agenda. In early 1985,

Eriksen had suggested to *Update* editor Diane Olberg that she run an AIDS story; coincidentally, the organizers of the company's blood drive made the same request. They were troubled by reports of workers refusing to donate blood for fear that they could get AIDS—reports that showed the workers' generally low level of knowledge about the disease. Higher-ups would balk at the idea of an article on AIDS, Olberg knew, insisting that this was really just a San Francisco issue. But sensing the importance of the topic, Olberg went ahead on her own.

That first article focused entirely on the facts about AIDS in the workplace, avoiding the sensitive matter of company policy. It appeared on July 22, 1985—the same day Rock Hudson went public with the fact that he had AIDS—and demand for that issue of *Update* was unprecedented. The newspaper had to run reprints. To corporate tea-leaf readers, the coverage said that AIDS was something employees cared about, and that paved the way for other AIDS-related stories. The reaction and the increasing demand for AIDS education sessions in the field sent another message up the corporate ladder: informing those who were healthy but worried might be as important to Pacific as ministering to those with the disease.

2

On March 20, 1986, the conference room at Levi Strauss's downtown San Francisco headquarters was packed. More than 230 managers from 100 companies were there for the first-ever conference on "AIDS in the Workplace." The demand so exceeded the organizer's expectations that 100 would-be participants had to be turned away. Reporters from leading daily newspapers were in the audience and TV crews from as far away as France recorded the event.

It came as no surprise to California executives that Levi Strauss had a big part in organizing this conference. The company had a long history of social activism, and CEO Bob Haas had personally acquired a reputation for dealing forthrightly with AIDS. Back in 1982, when several Levi employees told him that they were nervous about distributing AIDS information leaflets on company property, Haas had responded by stationing himself in the headquarters lobby, handing out leaflets to passersby.

But sharing the spotlight with Levi Strauss was Pacific—and this *was* surprising, for here was a company that usually made itself invisible on provocative topics. The corporation's name was prominent among the conference sponsors because the Pacific Telesis Foundation (established by Pacific's parent) had underwritten—and in conjunction with the San Francisco AIDS Foundation, Pacific's corporate TV group had produced—the first AIDS video aimed at U.S. business.

First screened at a breakfast session attended by twenty CEOs and then shown at the conference, "An Epidemic of Fear" pulled no punches: in telling detail it presented the panic, the medical evidence, the emotional tugs. Present on camera was Todd Shuttlesworth, who had been fired from his job by Broward County, Florida, when he was diagnosed with AIDS. Shuttlesworth's case served to remind managers how expensive a wrongheaded AIDS policy could be to a business; after his dismissal Shuttlesworth had taken his employer to court and secured a six-figure settlement.

Outsiders weren't the only ones surprised at Pacific's prominent visibility. Some high-ranking Pacific officials were amazed and decidedly uncomfortable about this unusual corporate position. It was appropriate for the company to treat its AIDS-stricken workers decently, they agreed. But to link AIDS with the corporation in the public mind was entirely different: that would associate Pacific with gays, drugs, and contagion, potentially driving away prospective employees, conceivably scaring creditors and customers who depended on the company's stability. There was every reason for the company to avoid sticking its neck out, said the advocates of a low corporate profile.

Yet, Pacific did stick its neck out with AIDS-related decisions—decisions that in part reflected the company's determination to change its corporate culture to fit its new competitive realities. Gradually but steadily, Pacific went beyond the nondiscrimination policies that suited the old character of the company to real leadership that helped define the company Pacific was becoming.

PACIFIC Telesis Group is a holding company for Pacific Bell, the regional phone company that accounts for more than 90 percent of the entire business's revenue and PacTel Corporation, which manages the company's diversified businesses. When it was launched after the 1984 AT&T breakup, many viewed Pacific as the weakest of the Baby Bells. "Of all the Bell regional holding companies, Pacific Telephone holds the most risk for investors," declared the *New York Times*. "The company's record of poor earnings and its long-running feud with the California Public Utilities Commission make it a risky investment at best."

Like other AT&T offspring, Pacific (later acquired by Southwestern Bell), had to learn how to respond to the marketplace. And in California, the company found itself in the nation's most fiercely competitive telecommunications markets. Other Bell companies, including Nynex and Southwestern Bell, as well as a host of new entrants, were all clamoring for a piece of the action, advertising heavily to an urbanized population with a reputation for buying whatever is new.

To respond to these changed conditions, Pacific had to meet three challenges: to be financially successful where smart investors were betting against Pacific's likely financial performance; to create an innovative and forward-looking organization, where tradition dictated that long-standing employees had to mold themselves until they gradually developed "Bell-shaped heads"; and to adopt corporate positions responsive to new constituencies that were socially conscious, where the company had always been seen as socially and politically backward. Together these challenges called on Pacific to redefine itself. It was under these conditions that AIDS became a measure of the company's transformation—and a vehicle for it. And it did so at a time when the company's efforts at change consistently misfired, reminding managers just how difficult large-scale change really is.

In its enthusiasm to demonstrate its newfound competitive hustle, for example, Pacific launched aggressive marketing campaigns. But what came to light were dubious sales tactics, like selling unneeded phone services to non-English-speaking customers who didn't understand what they were buying. Morale suffered among employees who didn't expect the phone company to behave like a used car dealership.

Pacific's effort at organizational transformation also ran into problems. To become more innovative, top management realized, the company would need to shake up its rigidly hierarchical structure, a steep pyramid with fourteen precisely delineated levels. The problem was, how to change?

Looking for direction, Pacific contracted with an outside consultant for $40 million worth of leadership-development and personal-growth training. The system was called Kroning, after Charles Krone, the consultant who developed the training material. It backfired. Instead of opening up communication, it sharpened divisions between the "in" group, who claimed to fathom Kroning, and everyone else in the company. Instead of easing relations with the Public Utilities Commission, the controversial corporate expenditure triggered a "cease and desist" recommendation from the Commission's advocacy arm. Instead of improving Pacific's public image, the fiasco yielded a harvest of journalistic ridicule.

A big part of becoming competitive was learning about the state's shifting political environment—and that meant becoming more socially conscious. Historically, Pacific's idea of responsiveness was to join all the Rotary Clubs in California. Though that approach might have worked in the 1950s, in the 1980s California's shifting coalitions of interest groups—blacks, Hispanics, consumer-oriented organizations—increasingly wielded political power. Pacific had long treated these groups as if they were the enemy. Now, however, these same groups were major purchasers of telecommunications services, and they had the ear of the most aggressive state Public Utilities Commission in the country. For the phone company to prosper on its own, it somehow had to co-opt these groups—to reach a mutually workable level of understanding and accommodation.

Steve Coulter, Pacific's director of consumer affairs, had the job of handling these troubling concerns. Coulter was a former Nevada legislator in his mid-thirties, a man who had made a political career out of enlisting constituencies to his cause. His collegial style and political savvy enabled him to get away with being a corporate guerrilla warrior. "A 'no' from above isn't necessarily the end of things," Coulter explains. "I'd ask," 'Where's the block?' Then I'd go look for allies."

Working under Jim Moberg, then the vice president for corporate communications, Coulter had been devising company approaches to new issues such as minority procurement and multilingual services. Coulter was also involved in negotiations over minority hiring and procurement with the NAACP and HACER, a consortium of some of California's major Hispanic groups organized by Pacific. To Coulter, a visible Pacific presence on AIDS was appropriate: it was politically astute, operationally important, and morally right. In collaboration with Michael Eriksen and other allies, Coulter became a leading advocate for an AIDS policy inside Pacific.

The politics were particularly interesting. Pacific had long been in open warfare with San Francisco's affluent and influential gay community, and the company badly needed to mend its fences. In the early 1970s, Jim Henderson, executive director of human resources policy and services, had helped draft the company's policy on homosexuals. Back then, Henderson recalls, "some managers were afraid that gay activists would show up to work wearing dresses." In 1973, those fears prompted Pacific to adopt a policy against employing "manifest homosexuals." In practice, this rule meant that anyone who publicly acknowledged his or her homosexuality couldn't get a job with the phone company.

Although Pacific formally revoked its "manifest homosexuals" policy in 1976, it wasn't until 1986 that the then-defunct policy's earlier existence came to light. By then, Pacific had tangled with the City of San Francisco, refusing to subscribe to a city ordinance barring discrimination against homosexuals. In 1979, the company lost an employee-discrimination lawsuit in the California Supreme Court, which ruled that the state's human rights law prohibited public utilities from refusing to hire gays. Shortly before a trial for damages was scheduled to begin, Pacific lawyers produced a previously undisclosed 1973 job application that confirmed the company's former anti-homosexual policy.

In December 1986, the company negotiated a $3 million settlement, the biggest ever in a gay discrimination case.

All this history—the disclosures of shoddy business practices, the troubles with Kroning, the acknowledged need to reach out to outsiders, the mishandling of the gay community—was artfully deployed by those within Pacific who pushed to make AIDS a visible corporate concern.

Eriksen provided the substantive information on AIDS; Coulter spoke mostly of politics and positioning. What Pacific needed, he argued to his bosses, was a winner, an issue on which the company could do well by doing good. AIDS could be the issue. Confronted with considerable internal opposition, it took all of Coulter's political experience and lots of help from other insiders to carry the day.

In March 1985, at a meeting of San Francisco's Business Leadership Task Force, Levi-Strauss CEO Bob Haas raised the AIDS issue for the CEOs to discuss. The group's agenda already covered items like the role of the elderly worker and health-care cost containment. It was time, Haas said, to put AIDS on the list. Everyone else in the room, top officers from Wells Fargo, Chevron, Bank of America, McKesson—and Pacific—said nothing, as if they could make something very embarrassing go away by being quiet.

Yet despite the CEOs' initial unease, AIDS did not disappear from the agenda. Haas continued to push the matter. So did Leslie Luttgens, organizer of the Leadership Task Force, who served on the boards of several important local foundations, and blue-chip corporations, including Pacific. A one-time president of the United Way, Luttgens combined a strong commitment to social causes with a persuasive but diplomatic style. She had learned about AIDS as an overseer of the University of California–San Francisco Medical School; now she was convinced that trouble in the workplace was inevitable if businesses continued to deny the scary reality of the disease. After Haas made his proposal to the CEO group, Luttgens spent the next few months talking up the need to promote AIDS education, imparting a sense of urgency that kept the issue alive.

Making the rounds about this time was a request from the San Francisco AIDS Foundation for corporate financial support for an AIDS education video. Pacific Telesis Foundation officials expressed considerable interest in funding the video; the in-house filmmakers added their enthusiasm for actually producing it. But at the top of corporate communications, Jim Moberg was unpersuaded. For advice, Moberg turned to Pacific's medical director, Ralph Alexander, and what he heard was conservative medical and corporate policy. According to Alexander, Pacific's role on industrial health issues was as a "national weather vane—and that's why we need to be doubly cautious about having a public profile."

Steve Coulter, like Michael Eriksen, equated caution with timidity. An AIDS video was clearly needed by businesses. Moreover, as Coulter argued in a memo to Alexander, getting the phone company publicly involved in AIDS education might just bolster its position in the pending gay discrimination lawsuit. Such a stance might provide some sorely needed good publicity. It was responsive to the AIDS-related concerns of other stakeholder groups including the NAACP, which, as Coulter pointed out, identified AIDS as a top national health priority. It could also improve relations with California's Congressman Henry Waxman, a powerhouse in telecommunications policy who was historically no friend of Pacific's and the congressmember most knowledgeable about AIDS.

As a savvy corporate politician, Coulter knew that he could not realistically expect Moberg to reverse his decision against the video project. The idea had to be repackaged, and that meant reviving the notion of Leadership Task Force involvement. Perhaps if the AIDS video proposal appeared in a different guise from a different sponsor, the answer would be different. Working with Michael Eriksen and the AIDS Foundation, Coulter sharpened the video proposal, waiting for another chance to bring up the matter with Moberg.

The occasion came on the eve of a December 1985 meeting of the Leadership Task Force. Coulter had been designated to sit in for Moberg as Pacific's representative at the session. On the table was a plan put forth by Leslie Luttgens for an "AIDS in the Workplace" conference. Hoping that he could now deliver Pacific's support for the AIDS video, Coulter phoned Moberg in New York, where Pacific had just signed a statement of mutual cooperation with the NAACP. Coulter's pitch to his boss noted the internal support for the AIDS video—from Luttgens, corporate TV, and the Foundation—as well as the endorsement of enterprises like Bank of America, Chevron, and Levi Strauss.

"I need to be able to say, 'We have $25,000 on the table,'" Coulter argued.

Jim Moberg, euphoric after his successful NAACP negotiation, gave his cautious go-ahead—"as long as we don't seek publicity and don't stand alone." Leslie Luttgens's quiet advocacy had reassured him that AIDS activism was not a far-out idea; after all, here was a Pacific board member offering encouragement and a degree of protection if things misfired.

Then Moberg took up the matter with his fellow VPs, who had questions of their own. "Anytime you do something different from what's normal in the business community," Moberg says, "questions will be raised: 'Why only us?'" Some of these officers wondered aloud whether AIDS wasn't just a passing phenomenon, but Moberg set them straight. "In the end, they accepted the proposal on faith . . . it was enough that someone they trusted advocated it." Now AIDS had become something "owned" by corporate Pacific—not just by some of its more enterprising staffers.

With that corporate approval, Coulter's group went to work. In less than three months, they prepared the video and an inch-thick managers' workbook on AIDS and organized and publicized the conference.

The reaction to the March 1986 gathering was more enthusiastic than even Steve Coulter could have hoped for. Pacific, a company that lately had seen little but media brickbats, was now getting raves; a company known for its habit of avoiding social issues had gone out front, to considerable applause. The thank-you letters and the press clips circulated inside the company. At the next meeting of the Pacific board, Leslie Luttgens made a point of noting that the AIDS video that

Pacific had produced was being aired nationally on PBS, as well as in France and Japan.

There was one internal casualty of the struggle to promote AIDS education: Michael Eriksen was abruptly fired by Ralph Alexander immediately after the AIDS conference. "I no longer have any need for you," the medical director had told Eriksen. There had been continuing disagreements between the two men. For his part, Alexander says, "Some programs he was supposed to run didn't work out."

The loss of Eriksen was deeply troubling to his colleagues, who had relied on his expertise. But his loss at this point was sustainable. There was product and momentum. With the video in hand and the AIDS Education Task Force functioning, the internal education efforts began to pick up. Success led to success. Responding to a request from the union that Pacific require AIDS education, Operations vice president Lee Cox sent a letter to all supervisors, not insisting but recommending that they show the video as part of an AIDS education session.

3

Producing the video pushed Pacific into the public arena on AIDS. What came next was even further removed from corporate tradition and even more dangerous: taking a public position on a statewide AIDS ballot proposition.

An organization led by political extremist Lyndon LaRouche, whose motto, "Spread panic, not AIDS," became the rally cry for a cause, had garnered enough signatures to force a statewide vote on a measure—Proposition 64—that, if passed by the electorate in the November 1986 election, would turn panic into law. The implications of the badly drafted measure were that thousands of workers who had AIDS could be fired, hundreds of students who carried the virus could be removed from school and college; moreover, people with AIDS could be quarantined. It appealed to people's emotions and played on their fears, yet had the simple allure of seeming to offer voters their chance to do something to protect themselves from the dread AIDS virus.

Most of California's chief public figures—politicians, church leaders, educators—opposed the measure. Steve Coulter wanted Pacific to add its voice to the opposition. Yet the huge number of signatures—it took nearly half a million to qualify the measure for the ballot—testified to the proposition's popular appeal. And some of the state's leading political conservatives voiced their strong support for the measure.

Like most companies, Pacific seldom took a stand on any ballot measure that did not directly affect its business. This political principle gave the company an easy and clear dividing line and protected it from needlessly making enemies over extraneous issues. Instead, Pacific preferred to exert its political influence through quieter relationships between lobbyists and lawmakers in the state capital. On the ballot measure, Pacific's lobbyists in Sacramento adamantly urged the company to remain mute.

For months, the debate over Proposition 64 continued inside Pacific. The conservatives from government relations and human resources insisted that opposing the measure would only earn Pacific powerful political enemies. The corporate communications activists countered that silence would put Pacific in league with those who proposed quarantining AIDS carriers and would also offend key external stakeholders, who might then "find additional avenues to criticize the company."

The stalemate was finally broken at the officers' level. Art Latno and Gary McBee, the two top external-affairs officials, determined that the company would publicly urge the defeat of Proposition 64. McBee, who had come to know the human cost of AIDS when a member of his staff died from the disease, became a strong voice for taking on LaRouche. "Given our internal position on AIDS," he says, "it would have been unconscionable for us not to oppose Prop. 64." The officers authorized a $5,000 corporate contribution to the campaign, the biggest single donation from any California business.

The stance was different—a decided shift from business as usual. Yet it reflected a fact of life about the shifting relationship between business and politics. In California—and increasingly across the country—voters were deciding more and more significant policy questions, rather than leaving matters to the elected officials. If a company wanted to have a say on those matters, it had to go public.

In the November 1986 election, California's voters resoundingly rejected Proposition 64. Although some Sacramento lawmakers grumbled at Pacific's lobbyists, the feared retaliation never occurred; and when LaRouche put the same measure on the ballot in June

1988, Pacific officials opposed it without thinking twice.

But the real test of how far Pacific had come on the issue took place in November 1988, when Proposition 102 hit the ballot. This was no kooky extremist's handiwork but a proposal authored by GOP congressman William Dannemeyer that would essentially abolish anonymous AIDS testing. While leading public health figures opposed the measure, fearing that its reporting requirements would drive those at risk for AIDS underground, the proposition did not threaten quarantining. It had modest support among doctors—and, more important, an endorsement from the popular Republican governor, George Deukmejian. Pacific risked political wrath—facing down a barrage of appeals from Dannemeyer—by opposing the measure. McBee again championed that position. The proposition was defeated.

Now there were other constituencies enlisting Pacific in their efforts to combat AIDS. Prompted by Lynn Jiménez in corporate communications, Pacific spent nearly $100,000 in 1987 to promote a Spanish-language AIDS *videonovela*. This venture too had its risks, for the story line dealt candidly with homosexuality and drug use, two topics anathema to the conservative Hispanic community. But HACER, the coalition of Hispanic groups, urged the company to go ahead—despite the opposition of religious and political leaders in the community. The *videonovela* was yet another success story, with local TV stations reporting larger than usual audiences. Pacific Telesis Foundation proceeded with its plans to underwrite a dubbed-into-English version.

In 1988, Pacific and the Foundation received a presidential citation for their AIDS initiative. And there was more recognition: the *Wall Street Journal, Newsweek,* and *Business Week* lauded the company as enlightened; Sam Puckett and Allan Emery's book, *Managing AIDS in the Workplace,* called it a "role model for the rest of the nation" (along with other companies, including Dayton-Hudson, Bank of America, Digital Equipment Corporation, and Westinghouse). AIDS policy had become a winner inside Pacific. And more begat more, with new corporate enthusiasts for AIDS education emerging. "People love favorable recognition," points out Terry Mulready, Moberg's successor as corporate communications vice president. The company produced a video aimed at families, "Talking to Your Family about AIDS," as well as a video for the black community. The making of AIDS policy had taken on a life of its own.

4

On a sunny Wednesday afternoon in July 1988, eleven Pacific employees with the AIDS virus gather in the medical department's conference room for their weekly support group session. Three-piece suits sit amicably alongside flannel shirts. Janice Dragotta, a counselor who spends about a quarter of her company time on AIDS, encourages group members to check in.

As the talk moves around the table, members share information on drug treatments, describe their medical condition, offer advice, complain about a benefits nurse "who went to Auschwitz U," dish up tales of life in the gay bars, commiserate with those who tell how exhausted the preceding Sunday's group-sponsored picnic left them. There is an edgy humor, gallows humor, in the talk. One man, off to visit his parents in Ohio, imagines the local headlines if he were to die—Gay Comes Home to Die—and his mother's reaction: "How can you do this to us—again?" The employees also talk about the strength they draw from the group, about how it helps to have a place to discuss questions that arise on the job, conflicts with colleagues, and guilt about not being able to work as hard as they once could.

A few years earlier, no one at Pacific would have imagined such a group on company premises and on company time. "When I first proposed it in 1985, there were no takers," says Dragotta. Employees with AIDS were afraid to come forward. "At the time I started doing AIDS education," counselor Jean Taylor recalls, "an embarrassed official buttonholed me and said, 'Do anything you want, Jean, just don't talk about condoms.'" Now everything related to AIDS is open to discussion. Union steward Tim O'Hara, relying on a poll detailing workers' interests, promoted the idea of a corporate-produced video on the correct use of condoms. The concern that some employees might be offended by frank talk about sex is receding.

In organizing discussions of safe sexual practices or running AIDS support groups, Pacific, like any company, has to walk a fine line. AIDS is still encased in moral debate, but discussions of private morality have no place in the business setting. What is relevant are sound business practices and sensible personal precautions. The AIDS support group is both a humane gesture and an appropriate business move. Taylor says, "We started seeing people with the AIDS virus, and those who were well but worried, going out on disability. These groups are a way to help people stay productive, a way for people to begin processing their own grief."

Evidence of Pacific's support for AIDS education is clear not only in these groups but also throughout the organization. At the second annual AIDS Walk, a city-wide fund-raising event in July 1988, more than 400 Pacific employees sporting company T-shirts walked together under the company's banner. Elsewhere in the company, AIDS-related causes have become almost as familiar and noncontroversial as the United Way. At Pacific Telesis Foundation, the staff has made AIDS causes a top priority for charitable giving.

Still, there remain important and unresolved AIDS issues on Pacific's agenda. AIDS education is not a part of an overall corporatewide strategy. Whether employees ever see the AIDS video or get to talk through their concerns about AIDS depends entirely on whether a supervisor volunteers to organize such a session. This bottom-up approach means that, where such education is least needed—in San Francisco and Los Angeles, two cities where public knowledge about the disease is high—it is most likely to be provided. But elsewhere in California, in the fortress at San Ramon and the outposts beyond, where a majority of phone company workers are employed, many managers still treat AIDS as someone else's problem.

Those supervisors who phoned their colleague Chuck Woodman, asking how to handle an AIDS case on their work force, may still regard it as just a once-in-a-career concern; and their workers are still unwilling to talk openly about AIDS. "Whenever I get an AIDS call from Fresno," says counselor Jean Taylor at San Francisco headquarters, "it's always like Deep Throat, and it's always, 'Someone I know was wondering. . . .' "

For Pacific, an AIDS education effort pitched to the varying concerns of its employees is not only enlightened practice. It is sound business. Pacific may be among the companies with the most AIDS cases in the country. As those numbers continue to mount—and they will—the work force problem will become more critical. In 1988, Chuck Woodman had some twenty-five workers with AIDS, requiring regular shuffling of his 750-person roster. According to company sources, a 1987 estimate prepared by medical director Ralph Alexander—but never made public—indicated that as many as 2,000 employees might be infected with the AIDS virus.

There is little that the company can do for these employees with AIDS that it isn't already doing—treating them just as it would treat anyone with a life-threatening illness—but it can do more to slow the spread of the disease. If Pacific can strengthen and expand the scope of its in-house AIDS education, intelligently implementing a program that will reach a quarter of a million lives, then this unlikely corporate pioneer will continue to enlighten others coming to terms with AIDS.

Across the country, the corporate time clock of AIDS policy has run quickly if unevenly, with wide variations in responses reported. According to the 1987

American Society for Personnel Administration survey, some companies persist in punishing workers with AIDS, firing them or limiting their health benefits. A majority of companies offer no AIDS education and have no contingency plans for handling employees refusing to work with an AIDS victim. Barely one business in ten has a written AIDS policy. As discouraging as these data are, they probably exaggerate the degree of corporate responsiveness, since companies that deny the corporate reality of AIDS are unlikely to answer such a survey.

On the other side of the ledger, since the landmark 1986 Bay Area "AIDS in the Workplace" conference, there have been dozens of similar conferences across the country. In February 1988, thirty prominent corporations—among them IBM, Warner-Lambert, Time Inc., Chemical Bank, and Johnson & Johnson—endorsed an AIDS "bill of rights," ensuring that employees with AIDS would receive evenhanded treatment.

For the CEOs in Knoxville or Kansas City still wondering whether their companies should deal with AIDS, the answer should be plain: there is little choice. Nor can handling AIDS be just the province of corporate doctors or human resources specialists. Everyone has a stake in this boundary-crossing issue—that's one of the things that makes AIDS both so hard to manage and so important.

There is considerable help available to businesses. The groundbreaking experience at Pacific is instructive, AIDS educational materials are now widely marketed, and groups like the Red Cross and local AIDS organizations can assist. But to confront AIDS intelligently means having a new look at a wide range of business practices. It means rethinking a company's approach to medical benefits. Those issues Pacific found readily manageable several years ago have become tougher now because recent scientific advances have reshaped the equation. New medication like the antiviral "cocktail" is now prolonging the productive lives of workers, but at a cost—one insurance company estimates that AIDS-related illnesses constitute between 2 and 5 percent of all group health claims in the 1990s.

Devising an AIDS policy also means reexamining the company's approach to wellness education, its concern for prevention, and its willingness to talk about once-forbidden subjects like sex. It means rethinking relations between employer and employee, rethinking relations among units within the company, rethinking the boundaries between the company and the public domain.

The outcome of that reanalysis will likely reach far beyond AIDS education to produce a telling portrait of the corporation as a community. For American business, as for Americans generally, AIDS is something like a mirror that, unwillingly and unexpectedly, we have come upon. The meaning of Chuck Woodman's and Pacific's, odyssey is this: in our reactions to AIDS, something of significance about ourselves and about the character of our enterprises is revealed.

The Politics of
Needle Exchange:
Why What's Banned in Boston
Is "Best Practice" in Seattle

THROUGHOUT much of Western Europe and in Australia, users of heroin and other injection drugs have had ready legal access to clean needles since the mid-1980s. Pharmacies sell needles over the counter, much like aspirin, and some cities run needle exchanges where addicts can swap used needles for new, sterile ones. Most public health experts in these countries believe that providing clean needles is an effective strategy for reducing the risk of transmitting the human immunodeficiency virus (HIV) among drug addicts and those with whom they have intimate contact. So widespread is this belief and so consistently supportive is the research that needle exchange increasingly is regarded as a routine standard of care, akin to providing insulin to people with diabetes. Indeed, the failure

This chapter was coauthored with Ronald Bayer. Much of the material in this chapter is based on the authors' site visits and personal discussions with key figures in the shaping of needle exchange policy at the state and local level.

to ease access to clean needles, whether through market availability or subsidized exchange, is increasingly regarded as medical malpractice.

Some of the strongest support for this policy comes from American research, which indicates that widespread adoption of needle exchange in the United States could save tens of thousands of lives. Increasingly, AIDS in America is a needle-borne epidemic centered in predominantly African-American and Latino ghettos that affects intravenous drug users, their sexual partners, and their children. Injection drug users account for about one-third of the 250,000 cases of acquired immune deficiency syndrome (AIDS), and they constitute the fastest-growing risk group. Sharing needles is the main reason. Before the advent of AIDS, researchers typically described this practice as a ritual of solidarity for a widely despised segment of the population that has few other ways to show solidarity. Sometimes it amounts to a tacit suicide pact among those who will give up anything for the formidable, if fleeting, pleasure of a fix. But as users have become knowledgeable about how AIDS is transmitted, needle sharing is mainly an act of desperation by those without ready access to clean needles.

Nonetheless, mainstream American politicians still mostly dismiss the idea of making clean syringes available to drug users as misguided and dangerous—as sending the wrong message" in the midst of the official war on drugs. American law reflects this hostility. A doctor's prescription is necessary to buy needles in many states, including those where drug injection is most common. And in almost every state, needle possession for the purpose of illegal drug use is outlawed by drug paraphernalia statutes. The United States unintentionally has become the control group in an international investigation of the effectiveness of needle exchange.

With the notable and short-lived exception of New York City, few of the needle exchanges in the United States are situated at epicenters of the twin scourges of AIDS and intravenous drug use. Though the estimated number of exchanged needles has substantially grown in recent years, more needles—700,000 for an estimated 3,000 injection drug users—are exchanged in Amsterdam (population 750,000) than in any American city.

1

It is easy enough to understand why needle exchange in this country is so generally unacceptable. It has been opposed on deep-rooted ideological grounds by the unusual and powerful coalition of "just say no" conservatives, law enforcement agencies, and establishment figures in the black community.

President Reagan and Bush rejected needle exchange, even when effective AIDS prevention appeared to hang in the balance, because they saw it as undercutting the national message of "zero tolerance" for drug use. The Clinton administration almost endorsed needle exchange, then backed off in the face of certain congressional defeat. Former Los Angeles police chief Daryl Gates bluntly encapsulated the antagonism to needle exchange: "We should take users and shoot them." Although Gates's statement is hyperbolic, it does reflect widespread police hostility toward heroin addicts. Urban police departments could have discouraged needle sharing by aggressively shutting down the shooting galleries where much of the sharing has occurred, but his has not happened—a course of inaction that UCLA drug policy expert Mark Kleiman believes to be deliberate. Shooting galleries, Kleiman contends, have not been closed precisely because they are such effective vectors of AIDS transmission.

The public debate about needle exchange has been mostly a whites-only affair. But many black politicians and ministers, whose constituents have been decimated by the twin plagues of drugs and AIDS, have been vocal opponents. Legislation that prevents cities from spending federal dollars on needle exchange or even the distribution of bleach was promoted in Congress by a political odd couple: conservative Republican Sen. Jesse Helms of North Carolina and Rep. Charles Rangel, a progressive African-American Democrat whose New York City district has one of the nation's highest rates of HIV infection.

Blacks' deep distrust of social experimentation, which looks like experimentation on *them*, is a major explanation for this hostility. Benjamin Ward, a former New York City police commissioner, told the *New York Times* that "as a black person, I have a particular sensitivity to doctors conducting experiments, and they too frequently seem to be conducted against blacks." According to surveys conducted by Stephen Thomas, director of the Minority Health Research Laboratory at the University of Maryland in College Park, only one black person in five—compared with two-thirds of all

Maryland households—trusts federal reports on AIDS. Two of every three blacks think there might be some truth to reports that AIDS was developed in a germ-warfare laboratory. While 85 percent of Maryland households generally dismiss the idea that AIDS is a form of genocide against blacks, some two-thirds of black church members entertain that possibility. So do some black leaders. Needle exchange is "genocide," said Harlem City Councilman Hilton Clark, who, damning the New York City experiment, added that its promoters "should be arrested for murder and drug distribution." Similar sentiments have been expressed by black leaders in such typically liberal locales as San Francisco and Boston.

To be sure, the black community is divided on the wisdom of needle exchange. Those African Americans, mostly young and mainly gay, who identify more with the style of AIDS activism favored by the AIDS Coalition to Unleash Power (ACT UP) than with black churches, regard opposition to needle exchange by establishment black leaders as an instance of literally deadly denial; they too have sometimes turned to the language of genocide. That charge is usually a conversation-stopper—and a policy-stopper too.

To say that all needle exchange supporters could be crammed into a phone booth is an exaggeration—but not much of an exaggeration. Needle exchange is promoted by AIDS activists; by some public health officials, AIDS researchers, and political liberals; and by some members of the largely disenfranchised community of intravenous drug users. These groups do not make for a politically powerful coalition. Therefore, the infrequently asked question about the politics of needle exchange is: Why has the program been implemented at all, given such formidable obstacles? In its contentiousness, needle exchange does not stand alone among public health issues; others include the distribution of condoms in schools and, historically, fluoridation of the water supply. The effort to explain why needle exchange has been successful in some locales but not others increases our understanding of the trajectory of this policy—and also of the possibilities and limits of radical public health reform generally.

2

Nearly everywhere that a needle exchange is operating, a single activist or a handful of individuals has served as the catalyst. In this initial phase, charisma matters. The names of these contemporary Johnny Appleseeds are well known in the needle exchange world: Dave Purchase in Tacoma, Jon Parker in New Haven and Boston, Robert Elovich and Yolanda Serrano in New York City, George Clark in San Francisco, and Aaron Peak of Honolulu, who left Hawaii to run an exchange in Nepal. Usually, an act of civil disobedience—the willingness to court arrest for distributing clean needles illegally—has been necessary to attract the attention of public health officials, the press, and particularly politicians and police, all of whom must eventually acquiesce if needle exchange is to be sustained.

These individuals have used different strategies—or, more precisely, differences in personality have led to

different strategies. Sometimes, as with Elovich and
Parker, a cadre such as an ACT UP chapter or the
AIDS Brigade has formed around them. In other instances, as with Purchase and Peak, the individual *is*
the program, at least at the outset. Because these typically are activists who have come to needle exchange
with a history of organizing, their initial inclination is
to be confrontational. Some have opted to remain outsiders, seeing themselves as organizers in the Saul
Alinsky mold rather than as members of the community. Parker, for example, prefers an us-versus-them
approach, and he wears his dozens of arrests in eight
states as a badge of courage. Others—including Kathleen Oliver in Portland; Purchase in Tacoma; and Pat-
rick Haggerty in Seattle—more closely fit the Jane Ad-
dams tradition of social work activism. They have
relied on their long-standing membership in a community to counter the charge that they are carpetbaggers;
to shame the opposition (Oliver once declared, "What
you're really saying is that these people are expend-
able, that you'd rather have them die of AIDS than
give them needles"); and, vitally, to win support for
their initiative by drawing on connections they have
developed over the years.

Outsiders gain real power from their remarkable
willingness to take personal risks. In Portland, Bill
Reese, Ph.D., known as "Dr. Bill," who legally sold
needles to local drug users, saw his store firebombed
by antagonists. Despite complaints from store owners
in Tacoma, authorities were unwilling to jail veteran
drug counselor Purchase when he set up his one-man

operation, a card table on a downtown sidewalk, and that gave him influence over public decision making. Public health officials in Hawaii sought to avoid the embarrassment that would follow if Park distributed needles on the streets, as he threatened to do, and were arrested; they enlisted his participation in a coalition that supported state legalization of needle exchange. In New York City, Elovich and other activists were arrested and tried under the state's drug paraphernalia law. A jury acquitted them on grounds of public health "necessity," which gave them a moral authority they could rely on for broader political purposes.

But charisma is an inherently unstable base for a continuous social enterprise. Needle exchange requires an organization to arrange regular staffing of sites, to obtain clean needles, and to dispose of used needles. While volunteers often operate the exchanges, needles cost money, and there isn't a reliable private source of support. The generally held view is that clients cannot subsidize the service, that their participation and the personal responsibility it evinces are a sufficient contribution.

In some cities, notably San Francisco, contributions from private donors have kept needle exchanges operating. The American Foundation for AIDS Research (AmFAR) has delivered the support essential to run needle exchanges in several cities, including Portland and Boulder, and to vastly expand New York City's program. In this sense, AmFAR has been an agent of change, much as the Ford Foundation nurtured community action through its "gray areas" program in the late 1950s, developing a model that the federal government could draw on in the War on Poverty.

But these efforts cannot survive for very long on grants alone. Private money is scarce for something as controversial as needle exchange. In San Francisco, for instance, corporate donors such as Levi Strauss have not been eager to publicize their involvement. And though foundations such as AmFAR are enthusiastic about launching new ventures and are even willing to fund needle exchange where it is illegal, they have neither the resources nor the interest to deliver aid in perpetuity. The Portland program, the first one launched in this country, still depends on private largesse; it has been in constant danger of closing because of a lack of funds.

In the not-so-long term, then, public endorsement is essential to maintain needle exchange. It ensures, at the least, an end to police harassment of those handing out needles; it may also bring money, legitimacy, and the institutionalization of these programs under the umbrella of public health services. But securing public funds is another matter. Indeed, the limited prospect of finding such support has prompted many needle exchange proponents to advocate changes in the nation's drug paraphernalia laws so drug injectors can easily purchase needles in pharmacies. Yet advocates of needle exchange often stress that changing the behavior of drug users by linking them to treatment requires the personal contact and the development of trusting relationships that only programs can provide—"open arms more than open doors [to pharmacies]," as one program director phrased it.

3

Since the early days of the AIDS epidemic, many leading public health officials in America have supported the concept of needle exchange. More than fifteen years ago, David Sencer, then New York City's health commissioner, publicly warned that failure to distribute clean needles meant "condemning large numbers of addicts to death from AIDS." His successor, Steven Joseph, who pushed for a needle exchange clinical trial, told the *New York Times* in 1988 that "we don't have that much time." These officials perceived the issue not as a moral or law-enforcement concern but as a straightforward, if politically volatile, public health concern. They did not believe, as many politicians did, that providing needles would invite a new contagion of drug use. "I never heard of anybody starting drugs because needles were available or stopping because they couldn't find a clean one," declared Mervyn Silverman, president of AmFAR and former health director in San Francisco. Many public health officials visited Amsterdam, and even more attended the annual international AIDS conferences, so they learned of needle exchange successes in Western Europe and Australia. Although these experts never saw needle exchange as a panacea, intuitively it has seemed to be a promising strategy for harm reduction—an approach that could accomplish in the realm of drug use what condom campaigns were meant to achieve in the domain of sex.

The endorsement of public health officials is essential to bring needle exchange into being. Although private ventures can survive where, as in Portland, the public health department has largely distanced itself from the enterprise, no community has embraced needle exchange as public policy without more explicit official backing. However, for health officials endorsement can be personally costly. It means testing the credibility and clout of public health authorities in confronting such powerful antagonists as law-enforcement officials, politicians at all levels of government who see the issue from a law-enforcement or moral perspective, well-organized members of the "moral majority", and some leaders of the very communities—African American and Latino—whose members apparently stand to gain most from needle exchange. Endorsement also means developing ties with activists who may be difficult allies because they instinctively distrust "the system" and who lack experience operating within it. Interestingly, such support has come from across the ideological spectrum, including health officials identified with a more traditional public health approach to the AIDS epidemic, such as public health directors Stephen Joseph in New York City, Christine Gebbie in Oregon and then Washington, and Molly Coye, first in New Jersey and then in California.

On occasion, endorsement of needle exchange has come directly from the top of the public health hierarchy. In New York City, health commissioners Sencer and Joseph spoke out early, despite opposition from the state health director, David Axelrod. In Philadelphia, the public health director, with the mayor's support, expressed his willingness to distribute needles—

and risk arrest if necessary—to defy the governor. Elsewhere, as in Seattle, Tacoma, and Hawaii, the needle exchange idea filtered up the organizational ladder—from the street-level bureaucrats who have daily contact with drug users to those who manage the drug-treatment or AIDS program, and eventually to department heads, who took up the matter with their counterparts in law enforcement and with politicians. Public health officials don't always win these contests. Coye, California's health director, could not convince Gov. Pete Wilson to sign legislation legalizing needle exchange, just as she had failed several years earlier in New Jersey when Gov. Thomas Kean rejected her efforts to organize a needle exchange clinical trial. Regardless of whether they succeed, such efforts demand leadership and risk-taking not ordinarily associated with bureaucrats.

This crazy-quilt pattern of adoption and rejection of needle exchange in the United States reflects a diffusion—and confusion—of authority in a federal system. Sometimes reformers have taken advantage of this division of responsibility, despite what has been Washington's adamant opposition to needle exchange. Similarly, local autonomy has enabled county or municipal health officials to undertake needle exchange where state health departments have been cautious, reluctant, or unsympathetic.

But divisions of authority also can hinder innovation. In New York, for example, state health officials were unwilling to endorse needle exchange because David Dinkins, then New York City's mayor, was ambivalent. More often, states have blocked local initiatives. Conservative Democratic governors in Pennsylvania and Maryland have opposed initiatives from Philadelphia and Baltimore. On several occasions, the socially conservative legislature in Massachusetts rebuffed efforts by former Boston mayor Raymond Flynn to legalize needle exchange. Baltimore's police chief threatened to arrest anyone who distributes needles, which drove that city's effort underground. Washington, D.C., launched a ninety-day needle exchange clinical trial, rather than a full-scale program, only because the brief experiment did not require the approval of the capitol's congressional oversight committee; for District of Columbia officials, this episode offered another argument for statehood.

4

Efficacy research has been a source of support in the effort to launch needle swapping. Studies, particularly those in New Haven and Tacoma, have helped overcome policy makers' doubts, and in some places needle exchange has been promoted as an experiment to be scientifically evaluated, not as a policy to be implemented generally. Not surprisingly, though, the strong ideological dimension of the issue means that political considerations often trump the data. As science historian Warwick Anderson notes, the issue has become "so enmeshed in politics that no one can now say who was talking as a scientist and who as a politician: There was no room left for relatively autonomous science."

New York City's experience, about which Anderson writes, is instructive. In 1988, when health commissioner Joseph received the go-ahead to start a needle exchange experiment, opposition from the city's black and Latino leadership was vitriolic. The fact that this was just a study, not an entire program, mattered not at all. The black and Latino caucus on the city council denounced the scheme as "beyond all human reason." In a letter published in the *Amsterdam News*, the city's leading black newspaper, and signed by a number of luminaries, the idea was assailed as "a very serious mistake" that would lead to the legalization of drugs.

A little more than a year later, David Dinkins, who had became the city's first black mayor, fulfilled a campaign promise to black constituents and abruptly ended the experiment. Newly appointed health commissioner Woodrow Myers, an African American, announced that he was "ideologically opposed" to needle exchange and could "not imagine any data" that would change his mind. Myers took his ideologically based antagonism even further when he sought to cancel a city contract to educate addicts on how to sterilize their works with bleach. The city's Black Leadership Coalition on AIDS, a politically powerful group, backed Myers, labeling bleach-and-teach a "Trojan horse for the African American community."

Within two years, however, Mayor Dinkins had changed his mind. The illegal but widely publicized needle exchange efforts of New York City's AIDS activists had put the item back on the public agenda. Another relevant factor was the Yale University–sponsored study, released in mid-1991, suggesting that a needle exchange clinical trial had slowed the spread of HIV but did not increase drug use, as had been feared. Those preliminary findings received a great deal of press attention, partly because they carried Yale's imprimatur. The fact that New Haven's black major, John Daniels, an opponent of needle exchange when he was a state legislator, had supported the trial and boldly announced its success put great pressure on Dinkins. Myers, the New York City health commissioner, had resigned and been replaced by Margaret Hamburg, a public health pragmatist; this made the mayor's shift easier to stage-manage. Hamburg cited the New Haven findings in an analysis recommending a shift in policy. Moreover, James Dumpson, a senior black figure in the city's social welfare circles who was the chairman of the Black Leadership Coalition on AIDS and a member of Hamburg's working group, announced that he favored distributing sterile injection equipment to addicts. Although many leading black politicians remained unconvinced, they recognized that Dinkins was politically vulnerable, and so agreed to let the mayor reverse himself without sparking a political explosion. When Dinkins announced in 1992 that he would permit state- and privately supported needle exchange in New York City, it was vital for him literally to surround himself with a broad spectrum of black leaders.

Elsewhere, though, the efficacy studies have had less impact on policy. Advocates often have referred loosely to findings from Amsterdam, New Haven, and Tacoma, but this has been more rhetorical flourish amid political argument than a re-examination. The fact that Tacoma had a needle-swapping program was more pertinent to officials in nearby Seattle than the New Haven study was. A key legislator in Hawaii rejected all European research as irrelevant to the American experience.

The research project in Tacoma has regularly been redesigned in response to complaints from critics, while the New Haven study has been criticized for depending in part on mathematical projections rather than concrete data. That's to be expected, even though the empirical evidence supporting needle exchange is quite as strong as, say, the evidence supporting Head Start. But this has not kept opponents from dismissing the findings as unconvincing. The researchers, many of whom have become vocal enthusiasts of the programs they are investigating, claim that they have been unfairly held to a higher standard of proof than the standard for other programs. That proposition, though true, is politically irrelevant. It is difficult to imagine *any* findings that would satisfy political opponents, because their skepticism rests on ideological concerns; for them, data are essentially beside the point. On the other hand, those who are more sympathetic to needle exchange often acknowledge privately that conclusive proof of the effectiveness of exchange would be difficult to establish. In the face of this uncertainty, they nonetheless consider the risks worthwhile—certainly less than the risk of inaction. Doug Sutherland, who as the mayor of Tacoma made an about-face on the issue and became a supporter of needle exchange, noted: "We cannot tell [how effective needle exchange is], and we will never be able to tell. We are trying to prevent something from happening. How can you know you've been successful?"

5

As New York City's experience indicates, race has been a vital and volatile factor in the politics of needle exchange, at least in cities most devastated by the needle-borne AIDS epidemic. Concern about racial conflict may be one reason why the idea has not been taken seriously—indeed, has barely been mentioned—in such major centers as Newark, Detroit, Cleveland, and Miami.

Yet there are signs that blacks' objections to needle exchange have lessened, and this creates new political opportunities for proponents. The policy-stopping talk of genocide is no longer so widely heard. The endorsement of needle exchange in the past few years by black mayors in New Haven, Philadelphia, Washington, D.C., and New York City has made it more difficult for minority community leaders to sound the charge of racism. Tacit acquiescence by the black establishment is increasingly replacing resistance as the norm. In Baltimore, for instance, needle exchange was rejected when Mayor Kurt Schmoke proposed it, dismissed in the outcry over Schmoke's call for an open discussion of drug legalization. The idea quietly resurfaced when Schmoke backed away from legalization; a key state legislator, who is black and represents Baltimore, endorsed needle exchange; the state attorney general was supportive; and no vocal opposition came from the city's powerful black clergy.

Minority unhappiness with needle exchange has been much less evident in the western states, where many programs operate. There, with the instructive exception of Los Angeles, African-American communities generally are smaller, and drug addiction is not viewed as a predominantly minority problem. Not that race has been irrelevant. Black leaders in Tacoma opposed situating a needle exchange in their neighborhood, and their wishes were honored. Seattle, which has had a program since 1990, waited three years and sought support from local African-American leaders before it proposed expanding the effort into a predominantly black area.

Race has also shaped the discussion of needle exchange in a very different way—as a buttress for conservative and white opposition. Strong resistance from law-enforcement officials and politicians is likely in a state such as New Jersey, where race, drugs, and crime are perceived as closely linked phenomena and are particularly salient concerns. In contrast, in places such as Seattle, Portland, Boulder, and Hawaii, the belief that drug addiction has fueled a crime wave among nonwhites is less widely held. There is less fear of drug-related crime generally and less concern that needle exchange will boost the number of addicts. All of this translates into less opposition to needle swapping. Police in Tacoma saw the issue as a health concern, not a law-enforcement matter. Honolulu police initially were disinclined to testify against a needle exchange bill, and did so only when the state prosecutor pushed them to say something; in their testimony, the police expressed opposition to the legislation in pro forma terms that really bespoke their indifference. Hawaii's legislators were unimpressed when the U.S. attorney appointed by President Bush provocatively warned them that they

243

risked creating a "needle park" in Honolulu. The opposition in Seattle and Portland has been so miniscule that now, several years after needle exchange programs were adopted, local elected officials express some surprise that the issue still is controversial in other cities.

6

When John Daniels was a member of the Connecticut legislature, he was outspoken in his opposition to needle exchange. What changed his mind, he says, was a visit to the neonatal intensive care unit at New Haven's city hospital. The legislator-turned-mayor left the hospital sick at heart about the AIDS-blighted lives there, convinced that if needle exchange could save a single child from such a fate, it was worth implementing.

Daniels's conversion story is not unusual. The primary selling point of needle exchange is not that it will slow the spread of HIV among drug users but rather the impact that needle-borne HIV transmission has had on the "innocents": women and especially children. In Hawaii, for instance, a septuagenarian pediatrician was a major force behind passage of state legislation.

Concerning the effect of needle exchange on addicts, the most politically persuasive contention is that the exchanges are a bridge to treatment, not merely dispensaries for reducing the number of infected needles circulating among drug users. The addict, it is said, comes to recognize that someone cares about his fate: from the contact, treatment for addiction, job training,

housing support, and welfare—in short, full membership in the commonweal—can follow. This argument
seeks to neutralize the charge that needle exchange
represents a capitulation to addictive behavior. The argument is used even though advocates acknowledge
that it is crucial to reach out even to people who are
not interested in treatment.

The needle user who persists in maintaining his habit
is socially problematic—an enemy deviant, as sociologists might say—while the addict who seizes on the
needle exchange as a way to end her addiction is more
acceptable because she is repentant. This explains the
emphasis on treatment in rhetoric favoring needle exchange, even though everywhere there are waiting lists
for methadone treatment programs and no funds to expand those programs. Moreover, because of the perception that exchanges do only what their name implies
(exchange needles), they have been regarded not as
permanent arrangements but rather as public health
"experiments" that must be carefully monitored. The
European concept of providing clean needles as a routine standard of care has not caught on in this country.
Only in Seattle is the expansion of needle exchange being promoted with the public health argument that the
targeted area "deserves" this state-of-the-art program.

7

Choosing these arguments for needle exchange—em-
phasizing the benefits for women and children, the
bridge to treatment, and the experimental nature of exchange—while de-emphasizing the problems of addic-

tion may be necessary to secure adoption. These arguments intentionally neutralize the perceived social threat and make needle exchange (unlikely, say, condom distribution in high schools) seem like a goodwill gesture from "us" to "them." Yet at the same time such arguments camouflage the reality that at the card table in Seattle's skid row and inside New Haven's mobile van, the government is using taxpayers' dollars to supply "works" to drug users. Although there are sound public health reasons for these ventures, politicians do not willingly discuss those reasons. Former New Haven mayor Daniels perceives needle exchanges as a political millstone. "Don't ask for a signing ceremony," the governor of Hawaii told advocates when the bill authorizing a needle exchange reached his desk, expressing his wish to avoid calling attention to what had been done.

Although the Clinton administration has been far less hostile to needle exchange, at the local level, where needle exchanges operate, programs live a fragile life after their inception. The political coalitions that brought many exchanges into existence were short-lived, their members having moved on to other issues. When the charismatic figure who launches a venture leaves, the program may suffer because it is not fully integrated into the public health bureaucracy. In Hawaii, needle exchange founder Peak departed for Nepal shortly after that state passed needle exchange legislation in 1990, worn out by politicking; that law is simply a symbolic accomplishment. Even if they stay on, those who advocate radical policy change are not necessarily capable of making the transition to program managers. There is little in the way of a national network to provide information or assistance to beleaguered programs, although efforts to create a network are afoot. Furthermore, while the media have been mostly supportive, the possibility of a mediagenic scandal is always present; possibilities include the child who pricks himself with a used needle bearing the code of a needle exchange, the fifteen-year-old who overdoses with drugs using a needle supplied by an exchange, or the dealer who swaps hundreds of needles at the exchange and then resells them on the street.

One way that skeptical politicians have been persuaded to vote for needle exchange is by stressing how cheap it is, but this too is a problematic strategy. Politicians have typically been reluctant to provide more than token funding because invariably they perceive priorities that are more pressing or more politically attractive. In Portland, for example, where budgetary retrenchment has had a profound impact on the needle exchange program, exchange activist Kathleen Oliver points out the difficulty of asking for funds to buy sterile needles when libraries are being closed.

Meanwhile, those politicians who are searching for a reason not to increase support for methadone treatment and drug education will seize on needle exchange as a convenient rationale. "See, we're doing something," will be the claim. This argument confuses the part for the whole. More important, it invites a new epidemic of denial concerning the scope of the drug issue. To deal with these second-generation challenges to the implementation of needle exchange—which should be seen not as an end in itself but rather as part of a far broader drug education, treatment, and control policy—will require a type of politics quite different from what has thus far emerged.

Look Back in Anger:
Hemophilia Activism and
the Politics of
Medical Disaster

O<small>N A WARM</small> afternoon in the autumn of 1996, a limousine pulled up at the gates of the Bayer AG plant in Berkeley, California, and a handful of young men piled out of the car, megaphones at the ready. "We are here to take your name away!" they shouted. "I.G. Farben, I.G. Farben, Zyklon B, Zyklon B"—an unsubtle reference to the lethal gas manufactured by the German pharmaceutical house and used to chilling effect in the Holocaust—"four thousand dead, four thousand dead, four thousand dead." A cameraman recorded the scene, preparing "great source tape" for television stations to air.

During the late 1980s and early 1990s, similar "zaps" were regularly launched by AIDS activists against drug companies. Then, the demonstrators were mainly young gay men, members of ACT UP, protesting the pricing practices of pharmaceutical houses that made AZT and other drugs unaffordable to many people with AIDS. Though the focus of the 1996 protest remained AIDS, the protesters were hemophiliacs, not homosexuals. A few years earlier, they would have praised the drug company for manufacturing Factor VIII, the blood-clotting concentrate that enabled them to lead normal lives, but this lifeline had proved to be the source of HIV contamination. Consequently, more than half of those with severe or moderate hemophilia were infected with the deadly virus; and, since many nations relied on U.S. suppliers for blood-clotting products, similar calamities were reported not just in the United States but across the globe.

A tragic accident, the pharmaceutical houses called it, but to many hemophilia activists these casualties were the inevitable result of decisions driven by corporate greed.

Out of the nightmare of AIDS a new social movement has emerged. Not only in the United States but in scores of other nations, people with hemophilia, historically quiescent, became a vocal group with an identity, an animus, and a strategy. Their anger has been directed at firms like Bayer, which manufactured Factor VIII, as well as at governments, for their supposed failure to warn of the danger; at their doctors, who, they asserted, misled them; and even at their own organizations, which allegedly minimized the risk of exposure to HIV. This newly energized movement has demanded compensation from drug companies and governments, as well as apologies for wrongdoing and justice in the criminal courts.

In the midst of the AIDS devastation, people with hemophilia have claimed a degree of control over their own lives and, in so doing, they have obliged govern-

249

ments and transnational corporations to take them very seriously. Although this is good news, there is also another, less noticed and less happy, tale to be told—about the fissioning of the AIDS-infected universe along the fault line of the deserving and the undeserving, the innocent and the guilty.

HISTORICALLY, people with hemophilia were united only in stigma and suffering. The first scientific advance came in 1941, with the separation of plasma from whole blood, which meant that people with hemophilia could be treated without the many complications of ordinary blood transfusions; until then, there had been no way to replenish Factor VIII, the protein in blood plasma, absent in people with hemophilia, that helps blood to clot. This was only modest progress, however, because the plasma treatment was painful and protracted, keeping many hemophiliacs from holding steady jobs and obliging them to depend on welfare. A generation later, when the first blood-clotting product, cryoprecipitate, became available, things changed dramatically. One dose of cryoprecipitate contains Factor VIII drawn from five to fifteen donors, not just one, and the treatment is faster, infinitely less painful, and far more effective than the administration of whole plasma. This was a major advance—still, many hemophilia sufferers hoped for more than an approximation of normality. Hemophilia is an inherited disease that strikes only males, and young men in particular had a hard time coming to terms with their genetic inheritance. They wanted to be entirely normal—to be able, as the director of the French Hemophilia Association said, to climb Mont Blanc.

Factor VIII concentrate, which first came on the market in 1970, held out the hope of total liberation. Unlike cryoprecipitate, this blood product could be kept at home without refrigeration, and could be used prophylactically. It revolutionized the lives of hemophilia sufferers, as school and work became taken-for-granted activities. But the very reason the concentrate is so effective, the fact that a single dose is drawn from thousands of donors, is also why it posed potentially grave risks—why the gift of life could also be a poisoned gift. The possible dangers became evident soon after the concentrate went on the market, when substantial quantities were found to be contaminated with hepatitis B.

Then, a decade later, came the advent of AIDS. Although this mysterious new disease, identified in 1981, was originally believed to affect only gay men (the U.S. Centers for Disease Control initially referred to this condition as GRID, a gay-related immune deficiency), within a year the first cases of blood-borne transmission were being reported. Yet instead of switching back to cryoprecipitate, with its far lower risk of contamination, most people with hemophilia continued, faithfully as it turned out, to rely on the concentrate until the middle of the 1980s. The professionally run organizations that spoke on behalf of people with hemophilia were chiefly concerned about maintaining the widespread availability of Factor VIII concentrate, and so were inclined to minimize the AIDS risk. There was only the remotest possibility that tainted blood was used, these spokes-persons averred, and that threat was outweighed by the risks of diminished mobility for people with hemophilia denied access to Factor VIII concentrate. In arguing that hemophilia sufferers preferred the risk, presumably minute, of being exposed to contaminated blood to the loss of access to Factor VIII concentrate, the specialists made risk calculations on behalf of their clients—calcu-lations that turned out to be terribly wrong.

1

By the mid-1980s, as the death toll mounted among people with hemophilia exposed to the virus through blood transfusions and Factor VIII concentrate, the vic-tims' anger crescendoed. In modern societies, which purport to be able to manage risk, such calamities are not regarded fatalistically, but instead invite a search for causes and culprits.

Hemophilia groups had long been dominated by the medical and pharmaceutical establishments, and con-sequently reacted cautiously to the news of tainted Factor VIII. Commenting in 1983 on one drug com-pany's decision to withdraw a batch of Factor VIII, the U.S. National Hemophilia Foundation declared: "It is not the role of the NHF to judge the appropriate-ness of corporate decisions made by individual phar-maceutical companies. . . . [Such corporate decisions] *should not* cause anxiety or changes in treatment pro-grams" (emphasis added). At the international level, so substantial was the dependency of the medical specialists on their pharmaceutical patrons that until its 1994 conference, the World Federation of Hemophilia forbade any public criticism of the drug companies.

In country after country, newly energized people with hemophilia shattered these cozy arrangements, seizing control from the supposed experts. At the outset of the epidemic, the French Hemophilia Association had adopted a policy of quiet diplomacy and backdoor overtures to government, in order "not to have hemophiliacs talked about" and not "to accuse either doctors or the State"; an activist splinter group, the French Hemophilia Association of Poly-Transfused Persons, brought charges against the blood banks and the French Hemophilia Association as well. In the United States, the insurgent Committee of 10,000 issued a scathing report, "The Trail of AIDS in the Hemophilia Community," drawn from documents discovered in legal proceedings, which summarized "evidence that demands a verdict" against, among others, the established hemophilia organization.

These newly energized groups turned to tactics that, although the staples of other social movements, were anathema to traditionalists. In Holland, usually known for its consensual manner of decision making, a debate over the purity of the blood supply became known as "Bloody Sunday" for its acrimony. Doctors and people with hemophilia in Denmark split over the propriety of a confrontationist strategy, and the fact that the chairman of the Danish association's medical committee was also a blood products manufacturer became a point of controversy. The Canadian Hemophilia Society, in the words of its president, started "crying scandal" on behalf of self-styled "victims," as people with hemophilia publicized their own plight and demanded a state investigation. In Italy and Denmark, insurgent hemophilia rights groups abandoned the practice of insisting on the privacy of people with hemophilia; television stations were invited to record the plight of hemophilia sufferers as a strategy for boosting public support.

DURING this initial spate of activism, the principal demand in most of the thirty-three member nations of the World Federation of Hemophilia was that hemophiliacs with AIDS and their families receive financial compensation from the government and/or drug companies. Most people with AIDS, of course, did not contract the disease from factor concentrate, but rather through sex or dirty needles shared by drug users. In distinguishing hemophilia sufferers from other people with AIDS, and claiming they were uniquely entitled to compensation, the activists were doing more than practicing interest group politics; they were also making a judgment about who was and wasn't deserving. The international federation nurtured these efforts, even as it tiptoed through the social minefield of guilt and innocence. In a memo to member national organizations, it observed that "the public has to be convinced that haemophiliacs are *particularly eligible* for compensation, especially with respect to psychic and social aspects" (emphasis added). A few months later, it urged that governments recognize "the *uniquely tragic position* of people with haemophilia who have become HIV-seropositive through the use of medically indicated blood products" (emphasis added).

As new information has continued to surface about what was known about AIDS and blood, when it was known, and by whom, the sense of outrage has heightened among activists. Pharmaceutical houses were accused of putting hemophilia sufferers' lives at risk by knowingly distributing tainted batches of Factor VIII. Over a period of months, sometimes years, those companies failed to test the blood they used to manufacture concentrate in order to determine whether it was infected with HIV, and failed to switch to heat-treated Factor VIII, a process that destroys HIV, until their stocks of the non-heat-treated product had been used up. For their part, public health officials were charged with criminal indifference to the plight of people with hemophilia.

Nowhere was the drumbeat of betrayal and evildoing heard more loudly than in the United States. A "genocide" was occurring, the newly formed U.S. Hemophilia/HIV Peer Association declared in 1991, because of the "commercially driven practices of certain large pharmaceutical corporations." Those firms had failed to counter the earlier threat of hepatitis B. Had they done so, "they would have prevented the transmission of HIV." Moreover, "with the exception of persons who were transfused with contaminated blood, only our community has been brought down by AIDS precisely because we followed the advice of our doctors." These activists condemned the National Hemophilia Foundation in equally strong language. "It is difficult to comprehend how the NHF could have failed to sound an alarm" about hepatitis B. Once AIDS appeared, the bill of particulars noted, "the NHF . . . advised hemophiliacs not to be alarmed and not to change their treatment methods. . . . That remained the advice we were given . . . into 1985. . . . In effect we were told by NHF to use [Factor VIII] just as though there were no danger of AIDS." Under those circumstances, the foundation's reassurances were acts of betrayal, the manifesto continued. "We—the alienated—do not identify with the hemophilia institutions. After all the debacle of the 80s, we do not need an organization that cozies up to the corporate decision makers."

At the 1992 NHF convention, protesters wearing death masks confronted "the corporate mass murderers." The NHF had refused to seek financial compensation, believing that such a move would be dangerous because socially divisive, "an ideological throwback to Elizabethan Poor Laws, with notions of 'deserved' and undeserved populations." The new generation of activists demanded compensation—which by this time had been provided by every other postindustrial democracy—not only as financial relief but also as "a partial payment for wrongs that had been done." They insisted, as well, on an apology for the infliction of needless suffering and death. "Today we demand justice," exclaimed a mother of two hemophiliac sons, both dead from AIDS, "and shout to the world and to this committee, 'How did you let this happen to us?'"

Across the globe, hemophilia rights movements were similarly strident. In France, which has a centuries-long tradition of venerating its blood donors, the revelation that, for financial reasons, batches of Factor VIII (and whole blood) had been used despite knowledge of their likely impurity, led to an alliance of rebellious hemophiliacs, journalists, and lawyers. So enraged were these activists that at the criminal trial of a senior health official, police feared that infected syringes would be thrown at the accused. In Japan, lawsuits and street theater were the twin prongs of the hemophilia rights campaign. One attorney explained the dual strategy: "We have learned on other occasions that rights will not be bestowed from above if we are silent." On World AIDS Day 1995, 1,400 students gathered at Waseda University; two weeks later, rallies were held in eight Japanese cities, as two thousand demonstrators massed at Tokyo's Ministry of Health and Welfare. This public campaign forced the heads of pharmaceutical houses and health officials in Japan to rethink their attitude of cavalier dismissal. In 1995, Green Cross, the country's primary supplier of blood products, had patronizingly said that "[w]e feel pity for the patients rather than being sorry for them." Less than a year later, though, amid a widening blood scandal, the Green Cross president reversed his position. At a meeting with spokesmen for the hemophilia rights group, he bowed deeply in apology, his forehead touching the floor, and this display of physical and psychological vulnerability became the defining moment of the conflict. Subsequently, a high-ranking Japanese government official has been sentenced to prison for his role in the blood products scandal, and officials at companies that manufacture blood products stand accused of falsifying data.

In Canada, more than a hundred policymakers were the focus of a multiyear investigation, conducted by an official commission of inquiry at a cost of more than $14 million (Canadian), and the commission's report was sharply critical of their actions. Variations on these themes have been played out in half a dozen other countries, including Ireland, Germany, and the Netherlands. Even Switzerland, home of the International Red Cross, widely believed to have set the gold standard of purity of the blood supply, has had its own blood scandal.

2

Across the globe, the story of AIDS and people with hemophilia is told the same way: a tiny and vulnerable group, born with a medical condition that it has struggled to overcome with the help of modern science, guilty of nothing except faith in its doctors, is decimated by the very forces that it regarded as its saviors. It's an irresistible narrative, and politicians of varying stripes have been drawn to the cause like moths to flame. In Japan, a health minister seized upon hemophiliacs' grievance to clean house in his bureaucracy, so boosting his own political career. Hemophiliacs formed an alliance with the ultra-right National Front, which stood to gain politically from the hemophilia sufferers' plight. Jean-Marie Le Pen's party nominated a hemophiliac candidate for Parliament. Across France, posters featured a torch with a flame of letters that spelled out the party's favorite scapegoats—*"Socialisme, Immigra-*

tion, Délinquance, Affairisme"—equating them with SIDA, the French acronym for AIDS.

Even where innocence and its shadow weren't so sharply contrasted, gays and hemophilia sufferers often found themselves at odds. The fact that hemophilia was often confounded in the popular imagination with homosexuality exacerbated the divide. Hemophilia activists in France relied on homophobic fears as a reason for maintaining the separation between groups led by gays and those led by people with hemophilia. Because hemophilia sufferers are men, these spokesmen contended, their joining forces with gay groups could be read as confirming the belief that people with hemophilia were homosexual. ("Hemo-homo," a common schoolyard taunt in many nations, graphically expresses this popularly conceived connection.) For its part, the Italian Hemophilia Association demanded hospitalization for people with hemophilia apart from other terminally ill AIDS patients, who were mainly gay and intravenous drug users.

These quarrels reflected more profound differences in how the gay and hemophilia movements responded to the AIDS epidemic. Gay-led AIDS organizations neither sought special compensation nor placed much stress on identifying and punishing the culpable parties, as did people with hemophilia. At the outset of the epidemic, it was rumored that AIDS was a CIA plot to kill off homosexuals, but that claim was quickly dismissed as paranoid. For gays, there was little support for conspiracy theories; AIDS wasn't a metaphor, just a virus. The gay AIDS message has emphasized empowerment rather than victimhood (tellingly, "people with AIDS," or "people living with AIDS," not "AIDS victims," is the preferred expression), as well as the need for the AIDS-infected to become involved in influencing policy that directly affects their lives. Such participation has been conceived as altering the curve of the future: promoting effective treatment, a vaccine, and eventually a cure for the disease. For that reason, gay activists have pressed for greater public support for AIDS research, and some have schooled themselves in the language of science in order to participate in forums usually dominated by scientists.

Hemophilia groups, by contrast, have mainly presented themselves as victims entitled to compensation. Perhaps because, unlike gays, they already expected to receive care, they concentrated their energies on the misdeeds of the blood products industry rather than on AIDS treatments of vaccines. Their demands have been expressed in terms of tangible entitlements—financial settlements—as well as symbolic acts of contrition. To a remarkable extent, the movement has achieved its goals. In that success are to be found the seeds of its possible demise.

3

The future of the hemophilia rights movement is uncertain. Having achieved much of what it set out to do, the movement has only the power of solidarity, or the possibility of a new threat to the purity of the blood concentrate supply, upon which to pitch its appeal. The movement has spoken about the price of death but not the need for treatment. It conceives of justice as being therapeutic, but justice is a discipline, not a cure. Despite all the criticisms hemophiliacs have leveled against their doctors, they remain dependent on those physicians, and this reality also limits the potential for mobilization. If solidarity and fearfulness prove to be insufficient glue, this new social movement will have exhausted itself in the battle over AIDS-tainted blood.

Not just hemophilia rights organizations but social movements generally stress the grievances of a narrowly defined constituency because that is the easiest way to provide coherence, to gain members, to construct a shared narrative. This isn't necessarily a measure of social justice, however. In a polis where such groups hold sway, the public interest gets defined as the aggregation of these groups' grievances. Meanwhile, equally valid claims are ignored because there's no group prepared to press them. In France, the budget for indemnifying people with hemophilia is more than twice the annual outlay for AIDS prevention (and many times the budget for AIDS research). In the United States, individuals exposed to HIV through blood transfusions will not benefit from pending federal legislation, which provides compensation only for people with hemophilia. Nor were these transfusees invited to appear before the national commission that reviewed the operation of the U.S. blood supply system, since that commission's mandate was expressly limited to hemophilia sufferers.

Identity politics of this kind is inherently divisive, for it thrives when a particular worldview, a tale of blame, gains popular support, even when this means rejecting rival claims for justice. When hemophilia groups described themselves as "innocent victims," they invited hostility toward other people with AIDS, especially homosexuals and intravenous drug users, who could not so readily occupy the moral high ground. Their argument from innocence made it easier for public officials to focus on these favored groups, especially people with hemophilia and children with AIDS (who have also received disproportionate government aid), while paying less attention to the vast majority of AIDS cases, which are not blood-linked.

The narrative of fault and blame, as well as the focus on the plight of appealing individuals—Kimberly Bergalis in Florida, the sweet-faced teenager allegedly infected with HIV by an irresponsible gay dentist; in Japan, a charismatic adolescent who has been the symbol of the hemophilia movement—represent the successful adoption of familiar tactics of identity politics. But if emotion-laden appeals assume pride of place in democratized policy conversations, rational public officials will become more risk-averse, unwilling to invite the political fallout that comes from taking on those who can take to the television studios. In the aftermath of the hemophilia rights movement, who will risk being known as "Blood Britta," the Danish health minister who, AIDS activists claimed, "wants dead bodies on her table"? Who will weather the insult hurled at an American doctor whose professional life had been devoted to the care of people with hemophilia, and suffer being called "the Mengele of the Hemophilia AIDS Holocaust"?

The successes of the hemophilia rights movement have meant help for a handful of people who needed it. Yet in another kind of society—one less committed to the justice of Elizabethan Poor Laws, more inclined to shared responsibility—the fact that a person is seriously ill would be reason enough to deliver such help. Moral tests would not be imposed before assistance was forthcoming. The prevailing calculus of support, which invites distinctions between the deserving and the undeserving in the delivery of assistance, signals prudent public health officials how to respond to the next health crisis, and the one after that. One current public health debate concerns whether all blood should be screened, at enormous expense, for the rare and nonfatal virus hepatitis C; another has to do with whether blood found to be contaminated with Creutzfeldt-Jakob (mad cow) disease should be recalled, and recipients of such blood informed—even though there is no evidence that this disease can be transmitted by blood—because there is no way to prove the absence of risk.

In such instances, the politically safe decision is to insist on zero risk—even if this means expenditures that would not withstand cost/benefit scrutiny, and even as far larger risks that won't be captured in vivid policy dramas are ignored.

Lives

||||||||||||||||||||||||||||||

A Boy's Life:
Deadly Sexual Secrets
in a Southern
Town

Fʀᴏᴍ ᴛʜᴇ moment he arrived in the slow-motion southern town of Fletchers Crossing in March 1985, fifteen-year-old Marcus Robinson was a curiosity and a threat. If you had asked him back then whether he was gay, Marcus would have said no. But his gaudy appearance gave him away, the manicured fingernails gleaming red, the dangling earring, the fluttery walk, a dance on spiders' legs performed by this very black and painfully thin adolescent.

Marcus Robinson was soon to become something else: a troubled, runaway child made a ward of the state. And then, a ward of the state who, it would be learned, carried the virus that causes AIDS. Public officials would find themselves facing a truly novel problem, for this is the first time any community in the country is known to have taken responsibility for a teenager exposed to AIDS through gay sex. School, family, and sex—above all, Marcus's sex life—would become the government's business.

1

There is no town on the map named Fletchers Crossing, although the place is very real. And "Marcus Robinson," like all the other characters who inhabit this story, actually goes by another name. That camouflaging is necessary because vital details are drawn from the usually sealed records of the juvenile court, which insisted on the pseudonyms; and even now this teenager's life would be wrecked if his identity became public. (Any similarity of the names to real persons or places is purely coincidental.)

Among teenagers AIDS is an epidemic. By some knowledgeable estimates, on the streets of New York City 10 to 30 percent of adolescent runaways may be HIV-positive. And while the number of AIDS cases among youngsters thirteen to nineteen remains relatively low—350 as of February 1989—that number significantly understates the magnitude of the problem. The long incubation period of the virus, estimated at up to ten years, means that most of the twenty- to twenty-nine-year-olds with AIDS—21 percent of all AIDS cases—actually contracted the disease during adolescence.

To the newly re-puritanized United States, adolescence spells the unchecked id; and black adolescence translates into threat as well. Gay teenagers look especially menacing, immoralists with sex and not social responsibility uppermost in their minds. A boy like Marcus Robinson, black and gay, a teenager with a history of anonymous and unsafe sex with older men, becomes the magnet for all these emotions.

MARCUS Robinson is one smart boy; his 117 IQ only confirms what everyone agrees on. As long as anyone can remember, he had also been different from the other kids on the block, a boy raised by a woman who really wanted a daughter, and who taught him knitting, crocheting, and cooking. When he was growing up in Philadelphia, most of his friends were girls. But when he hit puberty, Marcus discovered boys.

"I got beatings for staying out," says Marcus, yet that didn't keep him home, for "mom had no control over me." As an impressionable ten-year-old, he discovered that the woman he called "mom" wasn't his mother—his real mother had actually died from a drug overdose and "mom" was in fact his aunt. "You ain't my mother," he announced. "You can't tell me what to do."

The first time he had sex with another boy, Marcus was twelve years old. "I was shocked then. I went on like nothing had ever happened. . . . My mom had told me that homosexuals are bad people, and so I thought this means I'm bad." But soon enough there was lots of sex, usually with older men he would pick up at the neighborhood park. "I'd stay out all night, start walking around, get into something with someone, come home. I never thought much about it."

When Marcus was thirteen, his aunt petitioned the court to have him declared an uncontrollable child. "We sat together in court, my mom and I, the judge reading the case. My mom started crying; I did too. I was hurting. 'We're going to have to take him away from you,' the judge told mom. After the hearing was over I was in a room alone, waiting for them to take

269

me, when I saw the open door and ran home." Two years and much heartache later, there was no reprieve. Marcus was on his way south, sent to live with his elderly aunt and uncle. Perhaps spending some time with Aunt Bess, known in the family as the praying aunt, would straighten him out.

In Philadelphia, Marcus Robinson was used to the freedom of the streets. What he found in Fletchers Crossing was a tradition-minded, God-fearing family. "We disagreed about everything," says Marcus. He was desperate to return home, and when his aunt in Philadelphia wouldn't give him bus fare, he took off. In June 1985, Marcus appeared in Fletchers Crossing juvenile court as a runaway.

The judge tried to send him north, only to be informed that the woman who had raised him wasn't even his legal guardian. When Marcus learned he wasn't returning to Philadelphia, he tried to kill himself with an overdose of sleeping pills. Three months later he was back in court, again as a runaway. This time he was locked up for three days in the holding tank for juveniles.

From that moment until he was finally sprung from Fletchers Crossing a year and a half later, Marcus was ringed by grown-ups who pried into his life and made conflicting plans for his future. He took to petty crime during the succeeding months and landed in a halfway house for juveniles, where he wrote a suicide note specifying to the minute—8:39 P.M.—the time of his intended death.

Marcus's screams for attention kept escalating. What

he got, by order of an anxious juvenile-court judge, was a month in a nearby private psychiatric hospital. Inside the institution, Marcus quickly worked his way out of the locked facility, earning the privileges—the chance to smoke, to take meals in the cafeteria and not in the ward—that come with following the rules. Still, he refused to open up. Even though Marcus continued to deny ever having had any sexual relations, homosexual or heterosexual, the hospital psychiatrist decided to "check him for AIDS just in case there has been some homosexual experience." The test results showed that he carried the HIV antibody. Instantly he became a pariah.

On March 27, 1986, with no other placement available in the entire county, Marcus Robinson was dumped into a boardinghouse filled with derelict adults, which agreed to take him only because another resident had AIDS. The man who ran the place "kept hitting on me," Marcus remembers. Three months later, clinically depressed, he was sent to the county hospital psychiatric ward.

While there, Marcus repeated professions of chastity to his social worker, an ex-marine and tough-love advocate named Jim Parsons, a man fascinated by black history and made visibly uneasy by homosexuality. Yet to his psychiatrist Marcus admitted that he had continued to have sex for several months after his diagnosis, including one-nighters with two local teenagers.

After being released from the county hospital in July, Marcus was placed in the home of Grace Lamont—his last, best hope in Fletchers Crossing, for no one else in town would have him. For more than three decades, Lamont—a brassy and durable black woman, uneducated and God-fearing, called "mama" by the dozens of children who have lived with her—has taken in the hardest cases: a six-year-old who is blind, retarded, and wheelchair-bound; an eighteen-year-old who is just a judge's whim away from prison. She has made their reclamation her project.

"You better behave or you're out on the streets," Lamont constantly told Marcus, and that summer and fall she tried to "straighten him out."

"That boy can type anything," says Grace Lamont. "He's good at making up poems, stories. He can crochet and knit too. He has the smarts." Eventually, though, Lamont was scandalized by Marcus's effeminate ways. "I cut his hair when it started getting girlish. He began hanging around the kitchen, but I told him, 'There ain't no way two women are going to do the cooking in this house.'"

One day in October, rifling through Marcus's desk, Grace Lamont came upon the scribbled draft of a love letter addressed to another boy in Fletchers Crossing. It is as sweetly evocative and, in the context, as suggestive of impending tragedy as anything a modern Romeo would write. *"So I saw you down on Main Street. I called a friend and told him how you looked—how cute you are to me, wearing white pants with a gray two-tone shirt. . . . My heart almost stopped when you waved and said hi. I want you and I love you."* That note was never sent, but an outraged Grace Lamont delivered it to

Parsons, who began to have nightmares about Marcus spreading AIDS among the teenagers of his town.

There was full-scale panic that same month when Marcus came home one afternoon with his undershorts all bloody. He had had surgery for rectal abscesses a few weeks earlier, and bleeding is common after that operation. But neither that fact, nor the unbearable pain that would accompany sex so soon after surgery, allayed Grace Lamont's suspicions. She told Jim Parsons that she wanted the boy out.

In fact, during the months he spent with Lamont, Marcus began to grow up emotionally. His psychiatrist was persuaded that he had finally stopped denying both his homosexuality and the implications of AIDS for his life. But social worker Parsons was unconvinced.

"THIS boy has to be locked up someplace," Parsons told Judge Robert Smithers in November 1986. The county's mental health director said the same thing: "Marcus Robinson currently demonstrates a lack of appropriate social judgment and irresponsible sexual behavior. His presence in the community represents an immediate danger to other juveniles."

Judge Smithers wasn't about to be stampeded. He was the judge who had sent Marcus to his first psychiatric evaluation. While new options were being floated now—training school, the "structured therapeutic environment" of a state mental hospital, jail—none of them seemed right. In the middle of the interminable court proceedings, Jim Parsons popped up with a solution Swiftian in its simplicity: "Why don't we put him on a bus and ship him where he came from?" To that proposal, Joan Browning, the longtime head of the state's Family Services Unit, delivered a blunt answer: "We do not put children on buses."

"I am not subject to pressures to do anything that I don't think ought to be done," says Browning. "That's my job." It was Joan Browning's insistence on searching out a place that could plausibly be called home (contacting nearly two hundred different organizations in her search), and Judge Smithers's commitment to the best interests of his young charge, that ultimately made a far happier second act possible for Marcus Robinson.

2

The lives of bureaucrats are filled with missions unaccomplished, thwarted hopes. Occasionally, though, they accomplish wonders—or at least set wonders in motion. That is what happened in the case of Marcus Robinson. The cumbersome social services machinery, prodded by the juvenile court, launched a new life.

But by February 1987, four months after the latest round of court hearings had begun, those wonders weren't visible to Marcus. His hopes had been raised, then carelessly smashed, and he had just about given up.

A month earlier had come the good part. Marcus had spent a wondrous weekend in Lorraine, a city several hundred miles from Fletchers Crossing. He stayed in the cheerful, family-photo-filled home of Carole Walker, a preschool teacher in her late forties who was his prospective foster mother, and her grown daughter. He met Walker's son and daughter-in-law. He was introduced to neighbors, went shopping at the flea market, and even willingly attended church.

From the start, Marcus and Carole Walker hit it off. She had endless questions to ask, not to judge but to understand. She wasn't nervous about taking in a boy with AIDS, Walker told Terri Breen, the social worker at Caring for Kids, the university-affiliated organization that was going to manage the case; she had already read up on how the disease was—and was not—transmitted. Marcus's past behavior was another matter: "If he's going to stay with me he will have to be part of the family and follow the rules."

"I wanted the challenge," Carole Walker says. "I knew I could win." After the weekend, Walker told her family what she was going to do. " 'He has *what?*' my son said, more amazed than asking a question. Then he walked around and walked around some more. Finally he shook his head and said, 'Mom, you must know what you're doing.' "

The minute he got back to Fletchers Crossing, Marcus wrote the Walkers a letter: "*I can't wait to come back.*" But then, for many weeks, nothing happened. The Caring for Kids board of directors balked at first: some of the board members feared bad publicity and lawsuits, others quoted scripture to express their antipathy to Marcus's gayness. One of the members quit when his colleagues made their decision: accepting the hardest cases was the organization's real mission. Then Lorraine's high school officials waffled on accepting Marcus, and that stalled Judge Smithers's decision.

On February 26, 1987, with temperatures dipping into the twenties, Marcus got dressed in short-shorts, a tank top, and plastic flip-flops, and went parading in the neighborhood. An hour later, he came back to Grace Lamont's and collapsed. That night, he was admitted to the county hospital, diagnosed as having what was then called AIDS Related Complex (ARC).

Marcus Robinson's desperation walk changed the equation. With his pediatrician unwilling to release the boy from the hospital until a better home could be found for him than the Lamonts', Judge Smithers approved the move to Lorraine, even without a firm commitment from the school administrators there. Jim Parsons, wondering aloud how to get reimbursed for the gas, drove Marcus to his new home.

"THE first time I met Marcus," says Terri Breen, the social worker at Caring for Kids, "he reminded me of a pup that had been beaten too much. He was superthin. He spoke in a whisper—you had to put your ear right alongside his mouth to hear him. He answered questions in mm-hmms and un-unhs. As I watched him with Carole, he started opening up, getting back his confidence. Now you can't stop him from talking. The more Marcus told her, the more Carole said 'I still like you, that's okay,' the more the real Marcus came out, teasing and cracking jokes, sitting up straight and stating his opinions."

"That first Saturday morning," Marcus told me when I talked with him for the first time, in the fall of 1987, "I began laughing: 'You're all so crazy, so silly.'" During that summer, the Walkers took a trip to Florida. "We saw everything, Saint Augustine and Disney World and

Jacksonville. The only time I got bored is when I had to go to bed. And the one time I got upset is when I lost my best shoes at Jacksonville Beach." The family went fishing, too. "Marcus didn't know how to bait a hook," Carole Walker says, "but he caught a fish." Back home, every night the two of them would walk three miles around the track at the nearby high school.

Carole Walker urged Marcus to tone down his act so that he could fit in better, and he acquiesced; the nail polish and the earring became history. The two would talk for hours on end, thoroughly sifting events and feelings, pleasures relived and pains explored. When Walker cut herself with a kitchen knife, she reminded Marcus that "an open wound is the one thing we have to be careful with." "I know," he replied. "I'll be real careful. I wouldn't want what I have to happen to anyone, especially to you."

Even sex, the most delicate issue for Marcus to manage in his day-to-day life, was on the table. He hasn't had sex since the summer of 1986, Marcus says, and it's all but impossible that he is lying. Even if he wanted to, he couldn't conceal the briefest encounter from Walker, so intense was their relationship. "It's not so hard anymore, not to have sex," Marcus says, "but I still think a lot about it. I told [Carole] about this boy, what he looks like. I could talk to him, but he's going to want to do more than talk and then I have to make up lies."

"We talked about safe sex," says Walker, "about condoms, but he said there's no way. Kids here didn't think AIDS had anything to do with them."

In Lorraine, the Marcus Robinson who emerged was someone who wanted to give—give back he says— something of value. When a man named Frank, who had befriended him in the AIDS support group he went to, was hospitalized with pneumocystis pneumonia, Marcus visited him every day. "Other people may be scared of AIDS, but I'm not. I've got the disease. I can bring something to people who are all alone and dying, even if it's just reading a book out loud." Safe in this place, safe too from the pull of his past, Marcus Robinson was, in a sense, reborn.

IT WAS early in July 1987—his third day on the job, Lorraine school superintendent Sam Hannon recalls—when his deputy brought the news that a student with ARC was planning to enroll at Lorraine High. Hannon had been through some tough encounters during his career, but AIDS was in another league entirely. So far as Hannon knew, no child with AIDS had enrolled in any public school in the state.

The deputy superintendent argued for keeping Marcus Robinson out. He recalled the fights over integration a few years earlier, when white parents had pulled their youngsters out of Lorraine High—for a while the school was dubbed Congo High—and he feared a repetition. "This will cause all our children to withdraw," he said.

The possibility of panicky parents didn't entirely sway Hannon. A professional who prides himself on being guided by his head, he was reassured when local medical experts confirmed his understanding that AIDS was not easily spread. Moreover, he knew that Marcus was legally entitled to be in school. Yet what the superintendent had learned about the would-be student's personal history was deeply worrying. Judging from the record, Marcus Robinson was a sexually active gay teenager entirely capable of spreading a deadly disease to unknowing classmates.

"As long as the boy behaves responsibly and wants a new lease on life, I'm not going to stand in his way," Hannon informed social worker Terri Breen. "But with the first evidence that he isn't acting up to standards, out he goes."

The Lorraine High principal spelled out to Marcus exactly what these expectations were. Not only was unsafe sex forbidden, anything that might look like sex, safe or unsafe—anything that might even lead to sex—was unacceptable. There was to be no flirting with boys, no dating. Indeed, it would be best not to hang around with the gay crowd. The principal was sure he could keep tabs on Marcus's not-so-private life outside as well as inside the school. The dean of boys at Lorraine High, the disciplinarian whose door carries a sign reading THE OFFICE OF THE AFFAIRS OF MALE STUDENTS, also organized the town's rec program, and that gave him instant access to the adolescent grapevine.

"You've got to be superhuman," Carole Walker told Marcus when she heard how he was expected to comport himself.

As THE school year began, things seemed to be going according to Hannon's best-case scenario. In closed session, the superintendent had quickly gotten the school board to endorse his decision, and he had launched a series of talks on AIDS for students, teachers, and parents. Hannon was sitting in his office at the end of the second day of classes, his feet propped up on the desk, feeling tolerably pleased.

Then, with one phone call, all the orderly arrangements collapsed. "We have an unsigned letter that a student with AIDS is in your school," said the editor of the *Lorraine Gazette;* apparently one of Marcus's teachers, though pledged to secrecy, had gone to the press. "Do you care to comment?"

"I'll give your reporter all the facts," the superintendent promised, even as he feared what might come. Just one week earlier in Arcadia, Florida, the enrollment of three young brothers, hemophiliacs with the AIDS virus, led to a massive student boycott and, ultimately, to the torching of the family's home. That act drove them away, even as it made Arcadia the national symbol of know-nothingism. Would Lorraine be another Arcadia?

What actually transpired in Lorraine, though, was better than anyone could have dared hope for. The *Gazette's* page-one story about an unnamed high school student with ARC did not try to track down the student. Instead, it stressed the scientific evidence that the virus could not be casually spread. Moreover, a panel of experts, the *Gazette* pointed out, had found no reason to bar the teenager.

That evening, Superintendent Hannon went on TV to deliver a message of reassurance. He was joined by the county's health department director and its AIDS specialist, whose own children attended Lorraine High. The story topped the news and ignited no protest. School attendance figures remained normal.

"No one seems bothered," one sophomore told a TV reporter. "I don't feel like I'm in danger. I'm just not going to get around people's blood." By week's end, the *Gazette* could publish an editorial patting everyone in Lorraine on the back: school officials for their "sensible approach," parents for not "overreacting," and the community for its "compassion."

THE morning after the *Gazette*'s story ran, Marcus Robinson was in school—scared, he says, that "hundreds of parents might find out who I was and come after me." He was walking down a corridor, at that moment the only student in the hall, when a bevy of reporters appeared. Quickly, he slipped behind a door.

Other students would point at him during those first days and whisper. "I'll bet that's the one. He'll be dead soon." And some students warned the county health worker who had delivered the AIDS lectures that "if anyone finds out who the person is, they'll kill him."

Yet the whispering soon died down. "People usually like me," says Marcus. From his first semester at Lorraine High, Marcus Robinson was an honors student. One teacher who had once dismissed him as a "sissy little kid" changed her mind. "The day of that news story, with the TV all around, it must have taken a mountain of courage to walk through those doors and act normal. He's the bravest person I know."

There was a sadness beneath the surface, Marcus's teachers recall. Being normal became his constant preoccupation, and this meant "passing": not as white, but as healthy and heterosexual. The smallest incidents—not drinking from the water fountain, turning down a bite of a classmate's candy bar (or not being able to offer a bite of his candy bar)—came laden with significance. Though Marcus knew AIDS wasn't transmitted this way, he shied from even the remotest possibility of danger. Besides, people's understanding, though broadened, was still not broad enough, and Marcus feared a backlash if classmates learned that he had the virus. "I'm glad people don't know. This way, they treat you as a normal person."

In Lorraine, for the very first time, Marcus Robinson allowed himself to have ambitions. "I want to be in the yearbook ten times," he said in the flush of his success. "I want to make an impression on the world before I die."

3

Marcus Robinson turned eighteen on March 4, 1988. Now he was legally an adult, eligible for disability benefits because of his health. No longer would he be under the custody of the social services officials, no longer would he be "placed" in a successions of homes. Now his whole life was filled with choices.

Only in geometry or fiction do lines run straight. The paths of real lives are constantly turning back on themselves, coming upon emotional daylight and then slipping away again. In June, at the very end of his junior year, Marcus was halfway through his final exam in English when, without a word of explanation, he bolted from the classroom. Teachers and friends telephoned to find out what was wrong. Why would a gifted student do such a crazy thing?

Marcus felt he'd let people down at school, he'd let

everyone in Lorraine down. "I broke my leg," he told them, just for something to say.

Marcus Robinson never returned to Lorraine High. In a matter of days he had left town. He was headed not for his first home, Philadelphia, for there, he thought, everyone would tell him how thin he'd gotten, everyone would guess he had AIDS. Instead he went back to Fletchers Crossing. Although just fifteen months earlier Marcus couldn't bear the place, he had convinced himself that "life could be better there than it used to be. At least I have friends there."

"I felt like I needed more freedom," said Marcus when I talked to him again in March 1989, "needed to be part of the gay life, to make up my own rules." His teachers at school were watching him too closely, he felt, and Carole Walker was holding the reins too tight. Though people in Lorraine offered him love, it was love that came with a high price tag. He was expected to be celibate, and even more, to deny his own sexuality. He was supposed to act middle-class, white, straight, southern, "normal."

"I can't be the person you'd like me to be," Marcus told Walker. "I can no longer live under your roof, because I don't have my freedom."

"If you leave," she answered, "that's it. You can't turn around and come back." By then, however, Marcus felt he'd pushed things too far. He needed to find out who he really was, and with some urgency, because he was already exhibiting AIDS-related symptoms.

On his last day in Lorraine, social worker Terri Breen came to see him. "What'll you do in Fletchers Crossing?" she asked him. "Maybe I'll just lay down and die," he replied, shoving the hard words in her face, and Breen drove off, angry. Half an hour later, she came back and handed Marcus a single rose.

Breen is sad about what happened. She also sees the events through the distancing lens of a social worker. "When an adolescent's self-image is damaged enough, he feels he doesn't deserve success. As soon as things start going well, he'll sabotage his life." At those moments, there isn't much that even the ablest child-minder can do.

WHAT Marcus recalls about his leavetaking is that he wept on the bus all the way from Lorraine to Fletchers Crossing. Once there, life didn't match his fantasies, and two weeks later, he phoned Terri Breen, asking whether he could return to Carole Walker's home. "Carole was away that weekend," Marcus remembers, "so I wouldn't hear officially 'til Monday, but I kept dancing and saying. 'I'm going home!'" Walker, however, was true to her conviction that actions have consequences— even for adolescents. "I still love you," she said, "and I care for you, but you can't come back."

"I hung up the phone," says Marcus, "and I ran out and I was crying, crying; I never thought she would say no."

Marcus and Walker talk on the telephone every week, reminding one another that the good feelings are still there; that conversation is the emotional centerpiece of Marcus's week. The rest of the time, he mostly hangs around his apartment, watches TV, and talks to his girlfriends. The telephone, with two extensions, call-forwarding, and call-waiting, is his lifeline.

No longer does Marcus talk about wanting to make an impression on the world. "Now it's a matter of day-to-day. Maybe this story will make me famous," he says, forgetting that no one will know that the story is about him. Sex is still only a memory and a dream. "There's no way in the world I would mess up anybody's life," he tells Walker. "When I even think about sex, the first thing that comes into my head is what *you'd* think."

On Halloween, Marcus went to a party in drag, wearing three-inch heels, a sequined blouse, and a size-four black leather miniskirt. It was his first time, and he was a smash. Now, perfectly made up and able to pass for a girl, Marcus sometimes goes to a straight bar with one of his girlfriends.

The paraphernalia of drag offers Marcus a new mask and a new way to acknowledge that he is, in fact, a sexual being. But drag, like AIDS, also creates a link between sex and the possibility of death. "It's fine in the bar," Marcus says, "'til some guy starts talking to me and I open my mouth. Once this dude came after me, calling me 'faggot,' and I had to run for my life."

MARCUS Robinson returned to Fletchers Crossing High on the first day of school in September 1988. But in the halls, he thought students were pointing at him, whispering that he had AIDS. Not wanting word to spread, he quit for good. Now he talks about going for his high school equivalency degree, about enrolling in community college. So far, though, it's only talk—like the promises to get back on AZT, which he stopped taking when he left Lorraine.

Among Marcus's peers, only his girlfriends know he is HIV-infected. It pains him that he can't even talk honestly with a buddy who recently came down with AIDS, can't help someone come to terms with an illness he knows so well, but that would mean letting his secret loose in the world. "He gets drunk a lot and he'd start blabbing," Marcus says of his friend, "and pretty soon everyone would know."

Not a day goes by that he doesn't think about Lorraine. "I was watching *The Jeffersons* on TV and Mr. Jefferson had this magic clock. He could rewind time, start it over. If I could do that, I'd be back in Lorraine right now. I should have been born there, it seems so right—more right for me than my real family."

In all the phone conversations with Carole Walker, though, Marcus has never confessed the depth of his true feelings. "'Cause I can't," he declares. "When you break up with someone you love, it's hard to go back."

Events, not a sense of purpose, run his life today. There's no one looking out for him in the unbenign universe of Fletchers Crossing, so he hides out in his room, physically removed from the world for days on end. It is AIDS—the secret more than the disease itself—that is really in control.

Marcus can imagine one more bend in the road. "Maybe I'll just get myself on that bus and go surprise Carole. Now wouldn't that be something!"

tent of Our Character, attracted considerable press attention and made him famous and financially secure—"mammon serving God, as it were," says Bill Thomas, his editor at St. Martin's Press.

For at least a generation, the discourse on race has had all the formal predictability of a duel, with conservatives, mostly white, railing against racial quotas and forced integration, and liberals, mostly black, decrying the persistence and awful power of white racism. By now, the arguments having been made and made again, what matters to the partisans is grabbing those TV sight bites, boosting spirits, and keeping the faith—not winning hearts and minds. Smack into the middle of this increasingly tiresome duel steps Steele—a very different kind of voice, at once more bookish and more personal, reframing both the questions and the answers.

The reaction to Steele has largely traced familiar ideological divisions. Conservatives have embraced him, often treating him as a black apologist for do-nothing-ism, an exhibit in the litany of "we told you so's." He has also been heralded by some liberals, white and black, as a teller of painful truths. But many black politicians and civil rights activists dismiss him as a sell-out, delivering to white America just the message it wants to hear. Civil rights leader and former Georgia state senator Julian Bond attacked one of Steele's essays in *Harper's* by claiming that Bull Connor or George Wallace could have said the same things thirty years earlier.

On a National Public Radio show, Steele debated Eleanor Holmes Norton, a Georgetown University law

No Angels, No Demons:
Shelby Steele
Refuses to See Things in
Black and White

ON A TYPICAL California autumn morning in 1975, a twenty-nine-year-old black man named Shelby Steele, then in his second year as an assistant professor of English at San Jose State University, sprinted to catch his bus. He was often late like this—his hair was still wet from the shower, his coffee sat untouched on the kitchen table—aand under his arm he clutched the five student papers he planned to read during the twenty-minute ride to campus.

Everthing in his life was regimented, every minute accounted for. There was time measured out for his wife and two very young children, time to prepare and teach his four courses, time to labor over essays about black literature that he hoped would earn him tenure.

"At the next bus stop," says Steele, the moment coming alive again as we talk, "a black guy my age gets on. He has a radio. He sees me reading the students' papers. 'Are you a teacher?' he asks. Then he tells me he's on unemployment, he's going to see a girl-friend. He's happy about everything, no strain, and it's brother this, brother that, black power this, black power that.

"That guy opened a crack in my mind. He was free as a breeze, while I wouldn't quit working till midnight, then I'd be woken up an hour later by my baby's cries. Something was wrong."

A different soul inhabiting Shelby Steele's body might have decided it was the grinding routine that was wrong, the ceaseless seriousness of his own life, but to Steele the parts that did not fit all belonged to the man who shared his seat on the bus. "The black rhetoric of power, his drifting through the day unconcerned, seeing it as putting one over on the system, on the man. An adult male, thirty years old, not working—it made no sense.

"Those attitudes and ideas about how the world worked were keeping him back. They had nothing to do with race."

Although the days of commuting on the bus are long gone, that day's revelation became Shelby Steele's obsession. In essays that began appearing a few years ago in major national publications, including *Harper's*, *Commentary*, the *Washington Post*, and the *New York Times*, Steele has "followed the road from the private self to the public reality," as he says, to describe with elegance and complexity how the fact of race sometimes explains—and in his view often distorts—relations between blacks and whites.

Whites and blacks both see the world in terms of their own "innocence, the essence of racism—using others as

a means to our own goodness and superiority," Steele argues. Whites' fixation on their racial innocence makes them feel entitled to power; Ronald Reagan, for example, insisted that he was no racist—which allowed him to rest easy while resisting policies aimed at bettering the lives of black people. Meanwhile, blacks' fixation on their own victimization "leaves us with an identity that is at war with our best interests, that magnifies our oppression and diminishes our sense of possibility," according to Steele.

It's time, says Steele, for blacks to drop the crutch of victimization and make it on their own. He criticizes affirmative action programs for inviting racial tensions and also for fostering a sense of inferiority among blacks. Those blacks who wind up in integrated settings because of racial preferences, he writes, are prone to "integration shock"—beset by doubts about their own capabilities. This abiding sense of uncertainty encourages blacks to pull back for fear they will fail in the competition for academic and professional prizes, and to "recompose" the situation, blaming whites for their failures. The key to black progress, he states, is for blacks to master, and not be mastered by, their own fate. "We need (non-racial) social policies that attack poverty rather than *black* poverty and that instill those values that make for self-reliance."

These essays brought Steele a certain controversial celebrity. He won fans and enemies with his PBS-TV *Frontline* show on the killing of Yusuf K. Hawkins, the sixteen-year-old shot to death in the Bensonhurst neighborhood of Brooklyn, merely for being a black teenager in a white no-go zone. Steele's book, *The Con-*

professor and former director of the U.S. Equal Employment Opportunity Commission. "A quota is designed around color or sex, it is not designed around competence," said Steele, and Norton slammed the censor's stamp on his words: "I'm not sure that that message is the message we ought to be putting out over the air." That's precisely the kind of lockstep thinking Shelby Steele is challenging.

1

In the opening scene of the *Frontline* show on Bensonhurst, a camera pans the tidy and ornamented middle-class Italian neighborhood that, in the aftermath of Yusuf Hawkins's killing, had become a racial *danse macabre*. When tensions ran highest, blacks led by Reverend Al Sharpton, a master of *Eyewitness News* incitements, marched tauntingly through these streets while the white residents grossly pantomimed eating watermelons and shouted obscenities at the marchers.

Then Shelby Steele appears on camera, a passenger on the subway to Bensonhurst. The viewer doesn't know the problems he has had getting on the air, doesn't know that Steele was almost shut out of the PBS documentary because of pressure from civil rights activists who wanted a more politically correct voice to be heard. With his horn-rimmed glasses and button-down shirt, Steele looks as innocuous as a bookkeeper, and his voice is as smooth as syrup. In his hands the Bensonhurst story becomes the vehicle for displaying his way of understanding race.

"Race," he says, shifting from the immediate events to the universal, using a language at once psychological and moral, "is a mask through which other human needs manifest themselves. For many new immigrants, racism was a means to power. Blacks too could derive power from Hawkins's death, a power that comes from being victimized by whites."

The killing angers Steele and grieves him. It brings to mind his feeling as a nine-year-old in 1955 when Emmett Till, a black boy about his own age, was slain by two white men in Mississippi for whistling at a white woman. Yet now, Steele announces, we need to get beyond the flashbacks of race. "I feel an overwhelming sense of racial fatigue."

The escalation of hostilities in Bensonhurst, the charges and indignant denials of racism, let the local politicians preen but otherwise accomplished nothing, he says. And much of the show meticulously documents the equal opportunity posturing, the black ministers on the make and that carnival barker of the airwaves, Morton Downey Jr., mugging for the bigots. To Steele, Bensonhurst represents, tragically, an opportunity missed. Attention could have been paid to the barrier that keep the poor—black and white alike—in their place, but instead there was only politicking.

This racial posturing, says Steele, is a "luxurious indulgence" for a place like East New York, the burnt-out hulk of a neighborhood where Yusuf Hawkins came from. The camera surveys the wrecked buildings and carcasses of abandoned cars, as Steele himself drives through this sad terrain. He is the visitor in the beige, raglan-sleeved raincoat, pointing out the sights to the passenger-viewer but never getting out of the car. East New York seems a no-go zone for Steele, and in phrases that could have come from those *Harper's* essays, he talks calmly about the "impulse to move away" and "a certain guilt" stirred up by his visit.

Racism endures—racism remains intolerable—says Steele, a point that his critics refuse to acknowledge is part of his message, but discrimination counts for so much less now than in the past. The civil rights movement has lost power "because its target was no longer clear." What's needed to rescue the people living in East New York—in *all* the East New Yorks—is economic development, helping people "who may be victimized but who refuse to think of themselves as victims."

The message echoes lines from a chapter in *The Content of Our Character* on the perils of black unity, in which Steele calls on black leaders to "tell us of the freedom and opportunity they have discovered . . . tell us what they tell their own children . . . to study hard, to pursue their dreams with discipline and effort, to be responsible for themselves, to have concern for others, to cherish their race." This sounds too easy and rhetorical, more like the dream life retailed on *The Cosby Show* or the pieties of Ronald Reagan than the hardscrabble reality of wrecked lives in the ghetto. But on PBS, Steele insists that to focus on racism just "drains off energy. The memory of injustice can become its own form of oppression."

2

"I don't aspire to have my life be like *The Cosby Show*," Steele tells me. "What's crucial are the underlying values—self-discipline, responsibility, and so on." We are sitting in Steele's cubicle of an office in a suburban Los Gatos shopping center. He was on leave from San Jose State; soon thereafter, he would be named a fellow at Stanford's famously conservative Hoover Institute. This ascetic's space, which Steele rents for $85 a month, was once a doctor's examining room, and some of the lab equipment, as well as the "Payment Due at the Time Services Rendered" sign, remain. Down the hall is a business called Odysseus Exploration and Research, Inc., a New Age enterprise that offers, among other enticements, workshops that explain to women what men really want.

As we talk, ashes from a succession of True menthol 100s scatter on Steele's pink and black pin-striped button-down shirt; he has recently taken up smoking again after having quit for twelve years. The room is packed with milk crates full of papers. The bookshelves overflow with the collected essays of Ralph Waldo Emerson, the nineteenth-century American who, famously, extolled self-reliance, and Christopher Lasch, who inveighed against the culture of narcissism. There's Erik Erikson's psychoanalytic portrait, *Gandhi's Truth*, and Camus's *The Rebel*, and James Baldwin's essays, *The Price of the Ticket*. A poster showing Robert Mapplethorpe's famous photo of a black man's profile overlapping a white man's profile, a gift from Steele's fifteen-year-old daughter, is the only decoration on walls plastered with Post-it reminders.

In all his writing and TV appearances, Steele is delivering not only social commentary but also his own life story, for in his case autobiography is destiny. The town he grew up in during the 1950s—Phoenix, Illinois, on the edge of Chicago's notorious South Side ghetto—has the look and feel of Yusuf Hawkins's East New York.

The Steeles weren't the typical inner city family, though. His father, Shelby Sr., was a truck driver with only a third-grade education, but his mother, Ruth, had her masters in social work from the University of Chicago, and she is white. Although Steele is at pains to minimize the significance of that fact ("I knew I was black. I lived in a segregated neighborhood, my friends were black"), his capacity to see from both sides of the racial divide is literally in his blood.

"It was a deeply American family, with all the familiar stresses of American life, living together, having children, getting involved in the community. The special blessing was that, one day, I could be in Kentucky with my black relatives, the next day I'd be talking to my white building-contractor grandfather. I could see these supposedly virulent strains getting along, and that harmony informs my vision."

This elementary school that Steele attended was staffed by white teachers, rejects from the neighboring, mostly white school, who knew how to make the lives of children miserable. His first-grade teacher used to demand that parents buy new boxes of crayons, then she'd confiscate them, Steele tells me, and there were days when she made the class draw stick figures for hour after hour. This third-grade teacher forced the students to sit on the cold, bare concrete floor for the entire day as punishment.

Steele's sixth-grade teacher, an ex-Marine, determined from a single missed question that he was dumb, then constantly punished him for his classroom mistakes. One day, the boy was ordered to pick up with his bare hands all the shards of broken glass that littered the concrete playground. When he sat down after a half-hour of this, angry and bleeding and exhausted, the teacher seized a bicycle, gave it, together with a baseball bat, to an eighth grader, and ordered him to chase Shelby around the schoolyard "until he passes out." Steele ran two laps and then pretended to faint. When the eighth grader rode off, Shelby ran away into the cornfields and never went back.

Blacks who have lived through traumas similar to Steele's humiliation in the schoolyard are sometimes led to question the possibility of achieving anything more than an uneasy coexistence between the races, a relationship built not out of trust but from the raw power of black solidarity. But Steele, looking back at the moment in an essay titled "Being Black and Feeling Blue," extracts a different lesson—about how, out of this event, a black child can build an anti-self "that believes our wounds are justified by our own unworthiness, and that entrenches itself as a lifelong voice of doubt."

What may have preserved Steele's sense of himself is the fact that his parents didn't blame the victim. On the contrary: When Shelby's brother told them what had happened, they met with other parents in the neighborhood, organizing a boycott that got the ex-Marine fired and eventually closed the school.

It's not that the Steeles didn't regularly know the sting of racism—you couldn't live in Chicago, America's most segregated city, during the 1950s and 1960s, and not know racism—but they kept finding ways within the system to win back their dignity. When the family was kicked out of a whites-only church, they founded their own church, the first integrated church in the area, taking half the congregation with them. Years later, Shelby's parents tried to purchase a house in Park Forest, then a brand-new suburb, and when they were turned down because of race they went to court and won. In the early 1970s, as a graduate student at the University of Utah, Steele was denied a rental apartment in Salt Lake City when the landlord, who hadn't met him before OK'ing the lease, learned he was black. He sued, and the judge leveled the heaviest possible penalty against the landlord.

"My parents were strong people," says Steele, "with a very certain sense of what was fair. They told us, 'You are a citizen, you have rights, stand up and make the system respond to your needs.' They were civilized and genteel people, but they had no fear, took no guff from anybody. They showed us, a thousand times." The four Steele children have all made the system work for them. Shelby's twin brother, Claude, is a social psychology professor at Stanford University; one sister, Marilyn, is a psychologist in Los Angeles; and the other, Karen, is an executive with McDonald's in Seattle.

"Nothing angered my parents more than people who didn't fight back—that's how they believed change occurred," Steele continues. "In my house, Martin Luther King Jr. was a Johnny-come-lately—Gandhi had been their hero. I went through the world with that attitude. In high school, if I wanted to take a girl to a downtown hotel that was supposed to be for whites, I went anyway. We blacks—all of us—have to do that. *That* is the real black power."

At Coe College, an almost all-white school in Cedar Rapids, Iowa, Steele organized the first campus civil rights group, which he headed until his junior year. By then, though, traditional civil rights seemed too tame. "I had grown up in the movement, been indoctrinated with King's adaptation of Gandhi's way; it was a central part of my family's philosophy. The idea was to hammer away slowly until change came. But at the time I was angry and outraged. If you were black and of my generation, you had to feel outraged at the discrimination. Even today, if somebody is going to block my life path because of my race, I'm absolutely militant. I'm Malcolm X. By any means necessary."

As a senior, the radicalized Steele led a band of black students into the college president's office, shouting out demands for black teachers and a blackened curriculum. "I was yelling at the man, who previously had been kind to me, letting the ashes from my cigarette drop all over the carpet—for someone raised to be respectful, that was something!"

After Steele graduated in 1968 with his B.A. in sociology, he went to teach American history, Afro-American literature, and African literature at a high school in East St. Louis, among the most decimated towns in America. Almost all the teachers and students in the Southern Illinois University–run high school were black. "It was a 'black black' kind of program, a nation-building program, and I wanted to be part of that."

Three years later, Steele left to pursue an old dream, a doctorate in English. Although he remained a fellow traveler in the black power movement, he determined that the time had come to get on with his own life. "It came as something of a disappointment to me," he recalls, "to realize that being black in no way spared me the necessity of being myself." Steele had always been a voracious reader, always had a novel under his nose, always suspected he might want to write. He enrolled at an unlikely place, the University of Utah, mostly because an old friend said good things about it, and the department "turned out to be perfect, a liberal island in a Mormon world." He got his degree in 1974, then packed his bags for San Jose and the beginnings of a new career.

His wife, Rita, who is white, lived through it all with him, the black power days and the ghetto days in East St. Louis and the battle with the Salt Lake City landlord and the killing schedule in San Jose. While he was getting his Ph.D. in English, she was getting her degree in psychology, and she now has a practice in San Jose.

The fascination that surrounded what was once called miscegenation now attaches to interracial marriages. The topic is a staple of the TV talks shows and gossipy dinner parties. It is routinely mentioned in profiles of Shelby Steele. "My wife loathes that reference to herself as a white woman," he says. (Rita Steele keeps her distance from the press, determined to maintain her privacy.) "'She is white, she is Jewish'—that plays into those stupid stereotypes." For Steele, too, the subject is loaded, since some of his most vociferous critics insist that his interracial marriage distorts his entire way of seeing.

"The subject puts me in a double bind," Steele tells me. "If I say I'm writing to validate that relationship,

CHAPTER 12

I'm guilty. If I say I'm not, I'm held in suspicion. People of both races have a quick capacity to get past race, to see each other as human beings. Marriage has redundantly, boringly impressed that on me."

Steele also gets mad at critics who point to his suburban tract home in a white middle-class neighborhood as proof that he is, as the new jibe goes, an "incog-negro." "We are punishing blacks for success, rewarding them for failure," he says, and the memory returns of that thirty-year-old black man riding the bus on his way to see his girlfriend, without a job and free as a breeze.

"I tried that way of life myself in the '60s," says Steele, circling back to the story, "and it didn't work for me. Maybe there's an element of envy, maybe it pricked me enough to build an elaborate defense of the life I've been living.

"It took me twenty-nine years to get to that moment on the bus, to connect with the reality. It's not just my story, though," he adds. "The stereotype of the lazy black SOB is common, and the fear is profound that I'll be judged by that stereotype. They will judge our race by him—and they'll overlook me, quietly sitting on that bus grading those papers."

3

Staffers from the White House have been vainly trying to reach him, Steele tells me, apologizing for cutting short one of our meetings. They've been faxing him materials on the civil rights bill that President Bush is threatening to veto because of its affirmative action provisions, and are hoping for a reaction from Steele. He's unsure what he'll say, whether he'll say anything. While we are talking the phone rings; it's a reporter from *Time* magazine calling to make an appointment. The phone rings again a few minutes later and an editor is asking whether he would write a magazine article on how it feels to become—suddenly—famous. Politely he declines the invitation.

"I just don't have enough time these days," he says. "I guess *that's* how it feels to be suddenly famous."

This rise to attention—a profile in the *New York Times*, appearances on *Nightline* as the black professor-in-residence, and all the rest—has given Steele's critics more ammunition. If jealousy is at work here, there's also righteous indignation that this buffed and polished and allegedly inauthentic voice is getting such prominent play.

"It is very rare for blacks to move from obscurity to prominence in four years," observes Roger Wilkins, lawyer and journalist and, these days, history professor at George Mason University. "White people don't make a practice of giving black people meteoric success—not unless they find them comforting."

"Having Steele do the Bensonhurst show is like asking a Protestant to interview Irish Catholics in Ulster," thunders novelist Ishmael Reed. "Here's a man who has fair skin, who can avoid all the problems that people with darker skin face, who doesn't understand the miseries of the ghetto communities in the East. Why him?"

Quickly, Reed answers his own question. "The 'black pathology' industry is booming. In the new colonialism, whites tell Third World people who their spokesmen are. Steele's just another mouth for hire, pushing the self-development line: 'If you're good, they'll let you drink out of the mainstream.' He's taken the easiest way to assimilation—jumping on blacks."

Steele answers the personal attacks in kind. He dismisses Reed's swipe as "romantic bullshit," then says: "Roger Wilkins just loves the agony and angst of the black experience; it confirms a victim-focused identity. He would cherish being cursed out in the street, for the power he can find in that.

"I get in trouble with those blacks who are vested—invested—with civil rights victimology. Their careers depend on it, they're in Fat City. When I talk about how (black) college administrators undermine the confidence of black students, encouraging them to dis-identify with the ethos of the university, I'm taking bread off their table."

A prime example of civil rights victimology at work, says Steele, came during the drug trial of Washington, D.C., mayor Marion Barry, "when black leaders like Benjamin Hooks of the NAACP claimed that Barry was being persecuted by white society." By waving the bloody flag of racial discrimination, "someone who's been caught with what amounts to a smoking gun is made innocent."

To be a public figure on racial issues these days invites being used. The national media has a way of boiling a person down to two or three sentences, then asking him to repeat those sentences over and over again, but Steele is not a reductive thinker. Public life vexes Steele and his friends worry that it will consume him. "He has the temper of a literary critic, not a politician," says Gerald Mazorati, his onetime editor at *Harper*'s. John Bunzel, the former president of San Jose State University, now at Stanford's Hoover Institute, describes Steele as "interested in learning with a capital L."

The part of Shelby Steele that's a writer, the "intensely private person," is wary of what's happening to him. He refuses to discuss his icy relationship with his brother, Stanford psychologist Claude Steele, who has a very different take on the relevance of race in America. He has seen his family life changing, with TV cameras in the living room and reporters calling at all hours. "Neighbors who once said 'Shelby, when are you are going to help me put up that fence?' now come up to me in a different way. 'Mr. Steele, I saw you on TV.'" Steele turned down an invitation to join a gathering of black leaders with President Bush at the White House, fearing that the occasion would be just a photo opportunity for the old civil rights crowd. He wrote a piece for the liberal magazine *Dissent*, a tacit rebuke to those who think they can pigeonhole him by pointing out that he has published in the stridently conservative magazine *Commentary*.

"I am somebody else every morning," says Steele the existentialist, quoting novelist James Dickey, and that attitude encourages a certain fatalism about the shape his life is taking. But Steele the entrepreneur appreciates that marketing himself is a "part of the business, paying your dues." And he knows himself well enough to realize that fame can be an intoxicant. "There's a part of me that enjoys it. I loathe posturing," he tells me, "though I see it as part of my personality. In my work I try to operate beneath that."

This is midlife for Shelby Steele, a time of intense personal reckoning. "There's a painful parting, a tremendous sense of loss of illusion about my power to write, to teach, to be a good husband and father. I'm not as good as I thought I was. I've had to accept what really is there"—in himself and the world he inhabits. What he wants, he says wistfully, sounding a bit like that man boarding the bus on his way to the university, is more time—time to carefully polish his essays on the aesthetic of Spike Lee ("confused," he calls it) and the strains of multicultural America, to recount more of his life stories, maybe to write a novel.

Meanwhile, Shelby Steele's voice is growing more influential, and other black intellectuals are advancing similar themes. "Highly educated black readers do not enjoy reading [what Steele says] but many need to," observes Howard University education professor Kenneth Tollett. Writing in the inaugural issue of the influential liberal quarterly *This American Prospect*, William Julius Wilson, one of the nation's most distinguished sociologists, urged an emphasis on "race-neutral" programs such as full employment strategies, comprehensive health care, and public school reform instead of affirmative action efforts that are "perceived to benefit only racial minorities." Poverty, says Wilson, now counts for much more than race.

Even Benjamin Hooks, a leading practitioner of what Steele calls "the politics of division," delivered a Steele-like message at an NAACP convention. "I'm calling for a moratorium on excuses. I challenge black America—all of us—to set aside our alibis. We must take responsibility for our own lives, for our own destiny. We must not wallow in self-pity and blame someone else."

Yet Steele's own contribution to this very different way of seeing the world, his efforts to move beyond "victimology" to a realization of individualism, may go unappreciated for reasons that have less to do with substance than psychodrama. His way of truth-telling is not impersonal, like much social science, but instead the vividly personal dissection of how blacks use race "to shield us from what we do not want to see in ourselves"—namely, "the internal antagonist that believes our wounds are justified by our own unworthiness."

That is a statement as stunning in its directness as a body blow. But the punch may be too powerful to be endured: As Kenneth Tollett says, relating a friend's observation, "finding out he wanted to sleep with his mother during his childhood was neither liberating nor therapeutic."

"I want to get closer to the heart of things," says Steele. "A writer has to put some blood on the table, give his all. When people reduce my passionate commitment to craft to racial politics or opportunism, then my buttons are pushed."

Steele confesses a certain nostalgia for what he remembers as "the integrity and genuineness" of the early civil rights years, when blacks and whites could truly talk to one another. Steele says that he hopes against the odds that his words can "help heal the racial wounds"—can encourage the duelists, black and white, to give up their racial agendas and the power those agendas bring.

Yet as Steele himself has written, in words that could be his epitaph: "The most dangerous threat to the black identity is not the racism of white society (this actually confirms the black identity), but the black who insists on his or her own individuality."

The Many Masks of
Richard Rodriguez

In his well-thumbed copy of George Steiner's *Language and Silence*, an autobiography he much admires, Richard Rodriguez, perhaps the best-known Latino writer and PBS personality in America, has marked a passage he might as well have written about himself. "I am often out of touch with my own generation. . . . That which haunts me and controls my habits of feeling strikes many of those I should be intimate with in my personal world as remotely sinister and artificial. . . . Men are accomplices to that which leaves them indifferent."

These days, when the focus is on race, ethnicity, gender, sexual preference—the critical fault lines of our society—the give-and-take of genuine conversation ceases. Intellectual battle lines are clearly drawn: Political correctness, a term originally coined as an admonition against taking one's own politics too seriously, now is deployed as an ideological weapon. *Speak the truth*, goes the command, and that means, tell the story that we—the community of the elect, those who script the party line, the one true church—have decided is the truth for today. In this all-too-familiar environment, subtlety of expression becomes moral backsliding.

Richard Rodriguez, who traffics in complexity and nuance, who resists being shoehorned into categories or conscripted into causes, finds himself caught in the crossfire. His first book, *Hunger of Memory*, an account of his coming of age, brought him instant renown, and much controversy, when it was published a decade ago. What attracted the most attention was Rodriguez's opposition to bilingual education and affirmative action, the two brightest stars in the firmament of ethnic PC. Bilingual education is wrong, Rodriguez argued, because it imports into American classrooms the private and intimate language of the home, the language of *mamacita*, when immigrant children really need to master English, the public language. Affirmative action also is misguided, he contended, since it doesn't help the poor and dispossessed who really need help but only those who, like himself, have already made it.

Such views made Rodriguez a *pocho*, a traitor, to the ethnic left. Yet even when he wrote about these polarizing public matters, his angle of vision was less polemical than personal. *Hunger of Memory* is not really a political tract but rather the autobiographical account of how a single self gets formed. It is not the story of a Chicano, a term he despises because of its very un-Mexican slanginess. Instead, it tells the tale of an ambitious boy whose desire to become part of the American establishment draws him away from the family he loves, who returns home in the end, only to realize that this home can no longer be his. When he abandons Spanish, the language of his parents, for the English that the nuns teach, hiding in shame when his father mangles English in public, he is re-enacting D. H. Lawrence's refusal to speak his father's Derbyshire dialect. Rodriguez's own unwillingness to be labeled an ethnic, which led him to turn down a teaching job in Yale's English Department to pursue a writer's lonelier, riskier life, is not so much a political rejection of the policy of affirmative action as a more deeply felt act, one that confirms his truest sense of himself.

On both sides of the ideological divide, though, those subtleties have mostly been ignored. "I am convenient," Rodriguez says, "to people with an agenda." *Hunger of Memory* has drawn raves from conservatives, who read it as confirming their belief that Americanization is an unambiguous blessing, that "native languages" should have no official place in English-only America. Linda Chavez, a more straightforward proponent of the virtues of assimilation who herself has been treated as a Hispanic traitor ever since she headed the U.S. Civil Rights Commission during the Reagan presidency, thinks these conservative attempts to claim Rodriguez as one of their own are "unfair. Richard has always been an intellectual who writes in a very personal way," she says, "and he seems uncomfortable as a spokesman for policy positions."

Yet intellectuals do get used, and not entirely unwillingly, either. When the National Endowment for the Humanities recently honored three writers, they selected the late Allan Bloom, who in *The Closing of the American Mind* recounted America's cultural collapse at the hands of the mongrel young; Shelby Steele, who argues in *The Content of Our Character* against affirmative action and takes an eloquently revisionist view of race relations; and Richard Rodriguez—a selection so politically loaded that the prize might as well have been called the "Anti-PC Award." "They asked me if I would accept the award and I said, 'Of course, I'd be honored,'" Rodriguez says, not mentioning the political implications of his civil response.

Meanwhile, many Latinos and leftists angrily denounced *Hunger of Memory* as a neurotic's tale and a sellout's story. To the generation of militant Latinos who have come after him, whose voices now deliver lectures in Chicano studies classes and from political podiums, Richard Rodriguez stands accused as *Tío Tom*—a traitor to his people, his family and himself. "I cannot imagine anyone being more thoroughly colonized," says Tomás Almaguér, sociology professor at UC Santa Cruz. "He was seduced early by the English language, by middle-class culture. He lusts after the whole package, he wants to be the son of the master."

Rodriguez's presence can still inspire rage. After he spoke at Harvard, a Latino in the audience stood up to address the crowd. "I want all you Anglos to hear this," he said, wagging an accusing finger at Rodriguez. "That man does not represent the Chicano experience! He is no role model! He is screwed up!"

Rodriguez loves to recycle this story, so that he can have the last word. "Of *course* I am not a role model!" he says to me. "Of *course* I am screwed up! Why else do you think I am a writer?"

In *Hunger of Memory*, Rodriguez imagined the world

as a stage on which he got to be the playwright and play all the parts. And he still believes he can assume any role. "I think of myself as Irish," he tells me, beginning a characteristic riff by fondly recalling his boyhood among the Irish nuns in Sacramento. "And most of the people who have been closest to me in my life have been Irish. When I read William Saroyan I discovered I was Armenian. When I read Philip Roth I discovered I was Jewish, too. Passing that white church on Fremont Street in Sacramento, hearing those hymns sung with so much optimism, I saw myself as a Protestant—as someone, who had moved from the Catholic 'we' to 'I,' who believes in jogging and working on machines that improve my body. I became an American when I learned the impatience at having to wait 30 seconds for a burger at McDonald's, when at age 12 I had a newspaper route that made me independent of my father. Increasingly I see myself as Indian, though I never thought I'd say that. I live in a gay, Chinese city, from which I take my identity. When Bill Moyers asked me on TV whether I was Hispanic or American, I told him I was Chinese.

"And you"—he is looking squarely at the face of a gay man wearing round tortoise-shell glasses and a black T-shirt from The Gap, who traces his family back to Manhattan and Germany and Russia—"you are Kit Carson to me."

Richard Rodriguez as Chinese, myself as Kit Carson: This belief in an individual's almost-infinite capacity to become someone else enrages his Chicano critics. That's too bad, he says: "Never is the Chicano being more American than when he insists on rejecting his culture, which is really surfboards and James Dean and pizza, *Ozzie and Harriet* and Elvis, to invent another culture out of the past that his parents left behind in Mexico."

Although this argument is clever, it is also too facile. No matter how hard he imagines himself into the role, Richard Rodriguez can never really become Chinese. Nor, and more to the biographical point, can he pass as the blond Californian of his childhood dreams or as a John Cheever, that artful WASP-y concealer. His own past *does* matter. He is deeply Mexican and middle-class and Catholic, and his ability to draw on that shaping history accounts for much of his popular appeal. When Richard Rodriguez does his star turns— delivers his "essays" for *The NewsHour with Jim Lehrer* analyzing the meaning of Columbus's voyage to the New World or appraising Los Angeles after the riots, submits to a Bill Moyers interview that in its solemnity stands as a caricature of such events—he is not really the playwright but a Mexican-American player on an American stage.

Rodriguez knows all this. In *Days of Obligation: An Argument with My Mexican Father*, he takes seriously the charge of ethnic amnesia. As he pulls apart his cultural identity, piece by piece, he examines his Mexican and Indian identities in ways that keepers of the flame will often find unflattering, sometimes offensive. Even the word "Indian," Columbus's mis-description, is used with his trademark indifference to conventional sensibilities. Literally as well as figuratively, he refuses to drink the Mexican water. There is more tinder for provocation when he reflects on the sorrows and consolations of his Catholic faith and discreetly plumbs the meanings of his own homosexuality.

Yet Rodriguez's real interest is not in being a provocateur. He aspires to construct an account of the Californian and Mexican landscapes that shows, through stories, how the great contending forces of optimism-comedy and fatalism-tragedy have been played out across national and cultural borders. Meanwhile, he is constructing a parallel account of the forces at play across the topography of his soul.

These travels take him beyond the safe harbors of the conventional, past the comforting stories most of us repeat to cheer ourselves, out into lonelier seas. In the ten loosely joined chapters, many reprinted from *Harper's* and other magazines, that comprise *Days of Obligation*, Richard Rodriguez does not sort out everything that he has witnessed, all the bits and pieces of himself he has stared at so hard. Indeed, he seems to have barely survived his encounter with the barrenness he finds at his core.

In a nuanced *LA Weekly* essay-review of *Days of Obligation*, "My Argument with Richard Rodriguez—Or, A Defense of the Mexican-American Chicanos Love to Hate," Ruben Martinez writes an open letter to "Richard, father." "If Richard Rodriguez remains an 'assimilated man,' then the terms of assimilation—American 'culture' itself—have changed. . . . He has peeled off a layer of the self-loathing . . . but his journeys have only compounded his own contradictions." For Martinez, who was a harsh critic of *Hunger of Memory*, the fact that this gay, Catholic, Indian writer can choose to be "American" without renouncing any of those as-

313

pects of his identity is cause for reflection, not condemnation: "Whose future do we live now?"

"I am making a career out of studying the million different shades of gray," Martinez continues, but Rodriguez's ethnic critics may insist upon a palette of black and white. The *SF Weekly*'s Marcelo Rodriguez, for example, uses *Days of Obligation* as a vehicle for co-opting his namesake, the Chicano who went astray, and welcoming him back into the PC fold. In a piece called "The Re-Education of Richard Rodriguez" (the title unwittingly suggesting leftist brainwashing), he describes him as a man who finally has found his "Mexican side," who has all but disowned his earlier heresies on bilingualism and affirmative action. In fact, neither implicitly nor explicitly has Richard Rodriguez repudiated *Hunger of Memory*, as he hastens to point out. But in the *SF Weekly* piece, the possibility that *Days of Obligation* changes—broadens—the subject doesn't arise.

Rodriguez is resigned to such simplifications. "I cannot teach people to read for the pleasure of listening to another life."

Days of Obligation deepens and fragments the search for identity that began in *Hunger of Memory*. The dust jacket copy contends that Rodriguez deserves to be ranked with the greatest essayists, with Swift, Carlyle, and Montaigne—all dead for centuries, all certifiably part of the literary canon, none Hispanic. "Imagine Jonathan Swift sitting in a nightclub in Mexico City," intones the blurb's blitzed-out prose, but this is carrying a good joke too far. Swift wielded his prose with malevolent precision; Rodriguez at times seems to lose himself in fractured images. Where the language of

Hunger of Memory bit cleanly and sharply, *Days of Obligation* is lyrical, convoluted. Sometimes the style is overly filigreed, as if all that matters is the slipstream of words, not what they mean. Complexities sit disconnectedly alongside one other. Shards of thought, contradictory in their implications, are set out like fragments of a crystal vase that cannot be pieced together. How do Richard the Indian and Richard the Dandy and Richard the Failed Saint coexist? What keeps Richard the Catholic Traditionalist a faithful communicant in a church that officially regards him, a gay man, as an unrepentant sinner?

Yet just as this isn't an account of ethnic acceptance or ethnic rejection, neither is it meant to be read for the strength of its linear argument. *Days of Obligation* balances pessimism and the defeat of too-easy expectations against the discovery of the unanticipated. The shimmer of those fragments, the brilliance of the epiphanies, can be extraordinary. So too, in a very different way, is the life.

1

It is nearly the end of a week-long stay in Tijuana when one of those epiphanies arrives, unbidden. Richard Rodriguez has spent his days in Tijuana the way people paid to write about such places usually do—being driven by taxi down "El Main Street," pondering the culture of *mañana*, being chatted up by a guide from the tourist office, forever fretting about whether it's safe to drink the funny-colored drinks he is offered. He appreciates Tijuana because the city, like the writer himself, has multiple identities: Americans think of Tijuana as part of Mexico, but Mexicans dismiss Tijuana as the southernmost outpost of the United States. Yet every night he crosses the border to sequester himself in the air-conditioned comfort of the San Diego Inter-Continental.

On Holy Thursday, at the invitation of a Jesuit priest from Berkeley named Tom Lucas, he takes a taxi to La Casa de Los Pobres, a Tijuana mission that serves the poor. He has been in worse neighborhoods, he writes, but "because Mexico is brown and I am brown, I fear being lost in Mexico." That theme—the nightmare of being left behind, alone and unable to return home, pinned down by endless brown hands—haunts his nights, twists his sheets.

As he distributes sacks of groceries to a line of patiently waiting women, he describes himself as a kind of priest. "What a relief it is, after days of dream-walking, invisible, through an inedible city, to feel myself actually doing something, picking up something to hand to someone. Thus Mexico's poor pass through my hands." Later, acting the role of a latter-day Marie Antoinette, he tosses stale cakes to overeager young *pobres* who crowd around. As night comes, he leaves in the supposedly safe company of Tom the Jesuit.

But instead of finding safety, Tom and Richard become terrifyingly lost. "There are few streetlights, no street names. After several dead ends, we are lost. Down one road we come upon a pack of snarling dogs. Backing up, we come near to backing off a cliff. Once more we drive up a hill. Then Tom recognizes a house. A right turn, a left," and they have found themselves once again. "At the base of the canyon we see the highway leading to Ensenada. In the distance, I can see the lights of downtown Tijuana, and beyond, the glamorous lights that cradle San Diego Bay. It is a sight I never expected to see with Mexican eyes."

"With Mexican eyes": While San Diego, seen through his American eyes, may be lifeless and emptied of people, it represents the promised land to the thousands who try slipping across this border every night. Back in the 1970s, when Richard Rodriguez was modeling in liquor ads for Latin American magazines, his face was at once familiar and glamorous to those who dreamed of crossing the border. *I am here and I am like you*, the advertisements implied. *You can make it too, you can make it big, in the land of opportunity.* Looking north from the base of the canyon toward San Diego, it is as if he sees the reflection of his own celebrity.

This sense of his Mexican-ness slips away, though, and on Easter Sunday he passes up the celebration at Casa de los Pobres for an elegant brunch in La Jolla, across the border. "What is Tijuana like?" he is asked, but he does not reply. Instead he goes walking on the beach. He is swept up by the sight of the Salk Institute, the vision of California's brave future that this futuristic building of the 1950s represented, a future that he perceives as overtaken by tragedy.

Yet in La Jolla and in Mexico City—where he begins his story kneeling on a bathroom floor, vomiting up bits of Mexico—indeed, in almost every location he describes, Richard Rodriguez feels alone, out of place. It is as if he is always wishing he could be anywhere but here, as if there might be life someplace else, rather than the hollowness he keeps sensing.

THE first time I came to the crossing at San Diego," Richard Rodriguez tells me, "I went up to the border patrol and asked what to do. I didn't believe I could go in and come out. I was the ultimate ridiculous gringo."

We are sitting across from one another in his Victorian apartment on a warm September day, separated by a wide curly-legged wooden writing table, in the room where he entertains callers. In person, he looks very different from the riveting image that stares out at readers from the cover of *Hunger of Memory*—a striking-looking, confident man-boy who in the late 1970s earned decent money as a model in L.A., a sexy exotic among all the Tab Hunters. Now he wears the pouchier, more deeply etched face of middle age. A small nineteenth-century California landscape and a print of Antwerp are the only objects, besides the books, on the wall behind him. Although I have known him for some time, he has remained a very private man; not by happenstance have we always met in public places, in bookstores and cafes. In the bedroom, a blank-eyed bust of Virginia Woolf stares at the bed, over which hangs a print depicting the bullet-riddled shirt of Maximilian. The print graphically recalls the bloody fate of the last European who dared to try ruling over Mexico.

This is the apartment of a solitary man who has lived alone during all of his adult life, out of a fear that what he describes as the small intimacies, "false teeth in a bathroom glass, questions about whether there is cream for the coffee," would keep him from his calling

duced to the beauty of darkness. Sensuality fills the room. There are subtle gestures, plays of the hands, talk of seduction. What matters here, says Huerta, is the body language and the talk; for one Latino to call another *mijo*, my son, is to speak the word that will melt the most macho of hearts.

That ambitious child of California, Richard Rodriguez, whose dreams were all of families rich enough to own second homes in Laguna Beach, has learned that he too can be *mijo*. "Where, then, is the famous conquistador?" he writes in *Days of Obligation*. "*We have eaten him*, the crowd tells me, *we have eaten him with our eyes*. I run to the mirror to see if this is true. It is true."

Neither the quest for an outlaw's head nor the restored missions nor even the prayers spoken by penitents kneeling on cool stone floors, but rather this world of *mamacita* who pours the drinks and *mijo*: this is the great gift, a world of meanings more sensual than intellectual, that Father Huerta, Virgil to Richard Rodriguez's Dante, has given him. The boy who wanted to be one of the golden children of the West—who once tried to scrape away his own darkness with a razor—has begun to acknowledge that Indian-ness as his own.

But the knowledge, as always, brings only a transient consolation. There are things that not even *mijo* can redeem; there is a darkness that not even the embrace of one's own color can escape. The California that Richard Rodriguez quested after in *Hunger of Memory* was a cheerful place, but in the years since both it and he have grown older. Tragedy and a sense

as a writer. It is the apartment of a monk with a pronounced aesthetic streak—a monk who glories in the small effect, who even as we are talking is mulling over whether to buy a chinoiserie lamp that a decorator has located for him.

"It was not until 1983, after *Hunger of Memory* was published," he says, "when I got a letter from Al Huerta inviting me on the quest for the head of Joaquin Murieta, that I began to discover the Mexican part of California and of myself." Alberto Huerta, S.J., University of San Francisco professor and liberationist theologian, had written an article describing Rodriguez as a "sad case," a man fleeing his ethnic shadow. Some time later, the Jesuit went on his crusade, sending hundreds of letters to everyone from Joan Didion to George Deukmejian. Those letters recounted the story of Joaquin Murieta, the much-feared and loved, largely mythical bandit-hero of nineteenth-century California, hunted down and beheaded by the government of the new state—a man variously remembered as blond and raven-haired, a "perfectly bilingual" man who "straddles two worlds."

Murieta's head had long been missing. Locating and burying it seemed to Huerta an act of piety as well as a gesture of reconciliation between cultures. The priest can be a persistent and persuasive man; and Rodriguez, "called to a kind of Hispanic confrontation," goes along for the ride. During the journey, recounted in *Days of Obligation*, the head becomes a kind of joke, the trip itself is full of fear and loathing among the saints and sinners, and Huerta himself comes across as a curiosity piece. But Rodriguez makes a point of thanking Huerta in print for his "intellectual companionship," and during our meetings his name keeps coming up. When Huerta invites me on a San Francisco version of the journey into Hispanic-ness, in order to introduce me to what he has shown Rodriguez, I gladly accept.

Our tour has its magical mystery moments. "I will always find a parking place," Huerta tells me, his borrowed, battered tan Toyota bucking and swaying as he gestures, "because I believe in angels." Even as I wonder what to make of this—"Doesn't God have bigger things to worry about?" I ask; "God has time for so many things," he replies in apparent seriousness—I observe that a parking space appears at each stop, exactly where it is needed.

"Mexico was here, suffering and strong": Mission Dolores is our first stop. The idea is to feel a sense of the displaced Mexican soul that Huerta has imparted to Rodriguez—rescuing him, as Huerta tells me, from "the fog of London." A chapter in *Days of Obligation* recounts his travels through all the California missions, a trip that began here. The tourists "come for the history," the mission priests tell Rodriguez, but he actually hears a tourist mom inform her child that a baptismal font is "where the Indians cooked their food." Meanwhile, as Huerta and I walk through the rose-strewn Mission Dolores graveyard, the names I read on the tombstones are all Irish, not Hispanic.

There is another, more austere side of Mexican Catholicism in San Francisco, says my priest-guide as we drive up to a Carmelite monastery adjacent to USF, a home for cloistered nuns who fled Mexico in the early

years of the century, when priests and nuns were being hanged from trees. Richard Rodriguez's father saw such sights as a child; that is why the father is so unsentimental toward Mexico. "This is the church where Richard has prayers said," Huerta informs me. "Can you see the simplicity of the place, a place to surrender yourself to fate? . . . Richard fears for the death of the church, but Hispanics cannot stay away from Catholicism. The rituals will bring them back. Those wild Latino stallions on the street, when they get sick they want a priest." In this cloistered atmosphere, I detect an aspect of Richard Rodriguez. But what I mostly see is the gleaming gold cross that stares down at the worshippers—that cross, and a wooden crucifix from which a bloodied Jesus hangs, in front of which the faithful are praying.

Our tour ends at a cantina in the Mission District. A dozen people are gathered in this cool, dark place. Two or three are playing pool, egging on one another—*pollo*, the others derisively call a man who hesitates to take a risky shot. I ask for a Corona. Huerta has a brandy. A woman is pouring the drinks, and although she is the only woman in the place, she is as safe as if she were in church, says Huerta, because she is the *mamacita* of the cantina. The faces in the bar convey the same mixture of Indian and Spaniard that Richard Rodriguez sees when he looks in his mirror.

In *Hunger of Memory*, Rodriguez lacerated himself with the "shame and sexual inferiority" he felt because of his dark complexion. "I was to grow up an ugly child. Or one who thought himself ugly." But since then, in places like this cantina, he has been intro-

of fatalism have invaded the land of the skateboarders and the modernist Salk Institute, the place of limitless futures.

"The wonder of California," he says in his sunny apartment, "was that you could make yourself over, become someone new, dye your hair blond, never again see your grandmother in Kansas." But now the sunlight in Los Angeles feels older and more Mexican somehow, the city bathed in tragedy. "L.A. is not the carefree blond city anymore." He too is less able, and maybe less anxious, to remake himself. "'As you see me now you will see yourself,'" my father said to me, reciting the old Mexican proverb. "'It all goes in a circle.'" No matter how much jogging I did, how often I went to the weightlifting salon, I was going to become that little old man—and more to the point, I was going to die."

"I have come at last to Mexico, the country of my parents' birth," he writes in the first pages of *Days of Obligation*. "I do not expect to find anything that pertains to me." He *does* find something. But Mexico, ironically, refuses to conform to its sentimental role as the land of loss, fatalism, noble suffering. "What I feared most about Mexico," he tells me, "was not the brownness but the pessimism, the sense communicated all my life through my father that life was hard, that it would catch you in the end." Yet the Mexico he discovers in bustling, industrializing Tijuana is getting younger by the day, fast losing memory—losing tragedy, becoming a land of comedy where everyone is fifteen years old and wears a T-shirt. In his search for some enduring thing to cling to—culture, ethnicity, even one's own history, refracted in a thousand moments—Richard Rodriguez finds himself, once again, asking questions for which there are no answers.

None of this fits the conventional categories of ethnic pride or ethnic denial. A talent coordinator for the mistress of convention, Oprah Winfrey, recently telephoned, inviting Rodriguez to appear on a TV discussion with other "self-hating ethnics. You know, Norwegians who hate Norway, French people who can't stand French food." He demurred. "My relationship with my Mexican self is complicated but I feel a real love for Mexico." That was not what the talent coordinator wanted to hear and so she hurriedly hung up.

2

At the end of the chapter on the California missions in *Days of Obligation*, Richard Rodriguez is touring Mission San Jose, the last stop on his tour of the California missions. It is the most recently restored, "rebuilt from the ground up—a complete fake," he writes, but his attention is really focused on something more riveting and real: the appearance of a young man. "A boy wanders down the center aisle, naked to his waist, his thongs slap, slap, slapping upon the tiles of the mission floor. He pushes his sunglasses up to rest on the crown of his head. He pauses with savage innocence and a certain grace."

In Richard Rodriguez's prose, bare-chested boys whom he endows with savage innocence intrude even in the church. The youthful Rodriguez in *Hunger of*

Memory longs for the "shirtless construction workers," the sweaty braceros with their muscled arms. "I was unwilling to admit the attraction of their lives. I tried to deny it by looking away. But what was denied became strongly desired."

As an adolescent growing up in the '50s, in a middle-class Sacramento home, Rodriguez spent a single summer working in the fields. But his ambitions always pointed him far away, toward the most prestigious fortresses of academe. In the early 1960s he went to Stanford, where he earned a bachelor's degree, then to Union Theological Seminary, where he spent two years studying with leading Protestant and Jewish theologians. There was more study, interspersed with a stint as one of the beautiful people of L.A., two years at London's Warburg Institute and Oxford. Finally came Berkeley, and a Ph.D. in Renaissance literature.

The real attraction of those shirtless men he describes is not their poetic lives but their muscled bodies. But this he cannot—at least he will not—say. Fittingly, the final chapter of *Hunger of Memory* is called "Mr. Secrets." The well-crafted mask, the intellectual's Mardi Gras costume, kept this part of Richard Rodriguez's identity hidden from his straight audience. But gay readers knew how to read between the lines in order to find the beads of identity being dropped. "I was sure he was gay when I read *Hunger of Memory*," says Eric Rofes, director of the Shanti Project in San Francisco. "That was a part of his life I identified with, the perpetual outsider. He was really writing about how being culturally marginal changes a person."

In "Late Victorians," the second chapter of *Days of*

Obligation, homosexuals occupy center stage, yet still there is no declaration of his own homosexuality. Rodriguez writes of San Francisco's elaborately redone Victorians as "dollhouses for libertines" and of their occupants as "barren as Shakers and interestingly, as concerned with the small effect," who "have made a covenant against nature. Homosexual survival lay in artifice, in plumage, in lampshapes . . . lacquer, irony. . . . *We'll put a little skirt here. . . . We'll bring out the highlights there."*

Such prose infuriated GLAAD, the Gay and Lesbian Alliance Against Defamation, for many of the same reasons that *Hunger of Memory* angered so many Mexican Americans. In letters to *Harper's*, where the essay was first published nationally, GLAAD complained that "Late Victorians" recycles all the homophobic chestnuts about gays as pitiful, peripheral, unnatural people whose fate is to become tired old queens—and embraces the new homophobia that condemns gays as morally irresponsible children whose insistence on endless play brought AIDS upon themselves. This is dangerous stuff, one *Harper's* letter-writer insisted, which would scare back into the closet any adolescent coming to terms with a gay or lesbian identity.

These angry critics believe Richard Rodriguez is Pat Robertson in drag—that, as one correspondent contended, Rodriguez would destroy all homosexuals if he had the power. Gay Chicano intellectuals like Tomás Almaguér hold different suspicions. "We've walked the same streets, but he carries so much personal baggage! He probably entered the gay world through back streets, furtive encounters." For Rodriguez, this reticence and evasiveness define his well-defended life. "There is nothing that I have to say . . . nothing, that is, that I would like to say," a man who may, or may not, be Rodriguez's lover sweetly tells me. Wearing masks is also a literary strategy. "I don't want to sound like Randy Shilts," Rodriguez tells me. "Who is Randy Shilts? A journalist who writes about bathhouses. I don't want to sound like Armistead Maupin. I am after a different kind of prose."

In "Late Victorians," Rodriguez describes the Castro in the 1970s, where for the first time in history homosexuality defines a community, as "the revolutionary place . . . utopia," the last, best embodiment of the California dream. He tells of César, a man who possessed a great mind, talent, and style, and who introduced him to the beauties of gayness beyond the dream of eternal youth, to the Latin style, something subtler, more evocative—for this, too, has been part of Richard Rodriguez's education, part of his turn to Mexico, toward the uncertainties of history and culture. César, who is dying of AIDS, accuses him of being "too circumspect" to risk death—too timid to live life—and he turns the accusation on himself. "So was I going to live to see that the garden of earthly delights was, after all, only wallpaper—was that it, César? Hadn't I always said so? It was then I saw that the greater sin against heaven was my unwillingness to embrace life."

To Paul Monette, author of *Borrowed Time: An AIDS Memoir*, a writer who found his true voice in his hand-to-hand combat with the plague, "Rodriguez blunts the power of his writing by not acknowledging his gayness—and he is wrong to separate himself from the community in the midst of AIDS." But not every writer has to be a polemicist; and not every gay San Francisco needs to demonstrate his authenticity by living in César's Castro. Richard Rodriguez is confronting something more painful, the void in his own soul.

At the end of the piece there appears the old queen who drew the GLAAD critics' ire. He is a congregant at Holy Redeemer Church in the Castro, a man with "something of the old dear about him, wizened butterfly, powdered old pouf . . . what I fear becoming," who in the eighth decade of his life has dedicated himself to those with AIDS. As the old man joins the other AIDS volunteers in front of the congregation—"takes his place in the company of the Blessed"—Richard Rodriguez stands aside in humility. "These learned to love what is corruptible"—that is, to love another human being—"while I, barren skeptic, reader of St. Augustine, curator of the earthly paradise, inheritor of the empty mirror, I shift my tailbone upon the cold, hard pew."

3

It is the beginning of October 1992, and Richard Rodriguez has just returned from a quick trip to the East Coast. He has received a less than warm reception at Vermont's Middlebury College, facing more shouted accusations that he is "Tío Tom." As a teenager he dreamed of being able to stay at the Plaza Hotel in New York City. Now he has spent a day in New York City modeling for *Vogue*—"a middle-aged man in a magazine for the young," he describes the scene. I imagine him being costumed by the *Vogue* photographer in a serape by Giorgio Armani or else in the hooded cloak of a monk.

The man of many masks has shed another mask. In a *Los Angeles Times Magazine* essay, Rodriguez writes of sitting in his car outside his parents' home in the fog of San Francisco's Sunset District, waiting for the right moment to go inside. Mr. Secrets is deploying this secret, the story of his closeted existence, very directly and for a very public purpose: to lambaste the Republicans for their diatribes about family values. The pointedness of the prose excites him: "I never thought I would use that voice. I want to say that Quayle and Robertson and the rest of that crowd despise what America really stands for. I want to say that the transsexual in the Tenderloin, dying of AIDS, has seen and known so much more about life than the people who shout about family values. I want to say that we"—we gay men and lesbians, we queers living in the age of AIDS—"are the holiest people of our times."

That rare moment of political clarity passes. Today, as on most days, Richard Rodriguez remains alone. On this Indian summer day, as on most days, he will run for miles through the city, alone and bare-chested. Then he will pump up his biceps at the Pacific Heights Health Club. On Sunday, dressed in white shirt and dark pants, he will walk to a Catholic church, passing the joggers and the pretty people in the cafes. He won't attend mass at Holy Redeemer, a place that seems to him "too good," too vibrant a community, but instead will go to a church where he feels the solitude of his own and others' lives.

There is an unfinished assignment, to interview

Georgio Armani and write about why Milan has been such an important capital of *haute couture*, yet the man who once called himself a dandy is not anxious to make the trip. Instead, he will keep writing about AIDS, "the downer that one wants to read about," and he will also spend some time in Hong Kong and mainland China "to find the Asian within the Indian."

What he wants to do most of all is to learn how ordinary Americans live their lives, to become the modern-day counterpart of the king who disguised himself to pass unnoticed among his people. "I want to know whether people in Walnut Creek, in the Mission, in Hillsborough, know what love is, whether they experience God, whether they are afraid of death. I want to know what it feels like to be lying in a hospital bed when someone keeps poking at your veins." Richard Rodriguez is really wondering whether there actually is anything out there—anything other than tragedy, hollowness, barrenness—waiting to be known. For now, he says, he is so very tried of examining his own soul.

Fault Lines

WE LIVE IN a time of peace and prosperity without precedent. By rights we should be rejoicing, but from every corner the wails of Cassandras drown out the Whitmanesque song-singers. Why, if we are so rich, do we feel so poor?

Laments about the present condition are eloquent— Arthur Schlesinger's *Disuniting of America,* Todd Gitlin's *Twilight of the Common Dream*—but the path that leads out of this cul-de-sac is not well sign-posted. And in the wrong hands, lamentation can dissolve into nostalgia or coercion. The Disney Company can turn the New Urbanism vision of neighborhood life, intended to revive the public square, into a company-run town called Celebration. In practice, character education can become groupthink or else an everything-goes relativism. Scolds like William Bennett reduce the idea of civic virtue to moralistic preaching.

Small wonder, then, that those who proffer a different vision of the commonweal—the promoters of civil society or a communitarian ethos—frequently find themselves warding off antagonists of all political shades. Partisans on the Right dismiss civil society and communitarian thinking as conservatism gone soft. Libertarian conservatives, Don Eberly observes in *America's Promise,* complain that the communitarian movement diverts attention from the project of dismantling the welfare state. Traditional conservatives attack the movement for failing to "discourage—that is, to stigmatize—immoral behavior" by restoring public shaming. Those on the Left, Amatai Etzioni notes in *The Spirit of Community,* "dub the fledgling movement 'neopuritanism,'" and complain that the emphasis on character and community splits the nation into a good "us" and a despicable "them."

Even *Time* magazine joined the chorus of "antis," with a cover story assailing those who embrace communitarianism and the civil society as busybodies "humorlessly imposing on others arbitrary (meaning their own) standards of behavior, health and thought." *Nineteen eighty-four,* here we come.

THESE stories offer a reminder that, whether the idea of community provokes praise or condemnation, it is a reality in our day-to-day lives. Despite the dominance of individualism in thought and deed, no one can float freely through society. No one is unencumbered by ties and obligations, whether to family, workplace, neighborhood, affinity group, or church. For good or bad—as these histories show, for good *and* bad—we live in a thick network of associations, a world where character counts.

"The republican tradition," Michael Sandel writes in *Democracy's Discontent,* "reminds us that to every virtue there corresponds a characteristic form of corruption and decay." One form this corruption takes "is the tendency to fundamentalism, the response of those who cannot abide the ambiguity associated with divided sovereignty and multiply-encumbered selves . . . who would banish ambiguity, shore up borders, harden the distinction between insiders and outsiders." This is the corrupted behavior of the caseworker who washes his hands of Marcus Robinson, the people on Brussels Street who believe that a gay man somehow invited his own murder at the hands of a teenage neighbor, the residents of Mount Laurel who hope to banish the poorest members of their community.

"The second corruption to which multiply-encumbered citizens are prone is the drift to formless, protean, storyless selves, unable to weave the various strands of their identity into a coherent whole." Recall the denizens of the Berkeley hills whose aspirations to create a new Eden are subverted by unsociability driven by narrow self-interest—modern-day Mrs. Jellybys who, like Dickens's famous character, shed copious tears over the plight of poor people in the Third World but simply cannot imagine allowing Berkeley's poor to live in their midst.

This loss of a story line, a social narrative, is a tragedy of the commons, for "without narrative there is no continuity between the present and the past, and therefore no responsibility, and therefore no possibility of acting together to govern ourselves." Still, we hunger for stories—not homilies or tales from civics class, but truer-to-life tales, stories to live by. Sometimes that hunger is sated by sensation, soap operas that no one would dream of scripting, such as the long-running tale of the presidential DNA. But we are also drawn to stories laden with moral meaning, such as the brutal murder of a gay college student named Matthew Shepard in Laramie, Wyoming, an event that evoked a spontaneous outpouring of grief across the nation.

What happened in the town of Laramie after that murder is also worth recalling. "We are not a community that tolerates such violence," the citizens insisted, telling themselves and anyone else who would listen a tale about who they were. "We are good people and this is a good place." The killers had no place in that narrative. They were depicted as loners who lived outside the pale.

Sometimes, as in Ronald Reagan's invocation of "morning in America," our common stories are the merest sentiment, the wish (or ad) as father to the thought. But a great deal of value can be extracted from the histories of ordinary people—individuals who under extraordinary circumstances discovered their better selves, and in the process helped to repair civic life.

What better ordinary heroes for these times than Ethel Lawrence in Mount Laurel and Deborah Meier in East Harlem, the AIDS activists within the corporate culture of Pacific Bell, the crusaders for needle exchange in Tacoma, the volunteers at San Francisco Community Boards, and the hemophilia activists who forced an indifferent government to pay attention? None of these individuals has any pretensions to sainthood. On the contrary: "They" are really "us," their faces the very same faces we confront in the mirror—if that is the part of ourselves we decide to become.

334

IIIIIIIIIIIIIIIIIII ACKNOWLEDGMENTS IIIIIIIIIIIIIIIIIIIII

A DECADE or so ago, having just returned to UC-Berkeley after a stint as an editorial writer with the *Sacramento Bee*, I decided to try my hand at writing magazine pieces. My intention was to tell stories that signified beyond their particulars, but as I quickly learned, writing newspaper editorials or columns, let alone writing books for academic audiences, has little in common with reporting and writing for magazines. Without the mentoring of smart and patient editors and publishers, among them Dave Beers, Rhea Wilson, David Talbot, Jeffrey Kittay, Douglas Foster, Cullen Murphy, Allan Webber, Elsa Dixler, Alice Chasan, Lewis Lapham, Peter Schrag, and Frank McCulloch, none of this prose would have seen the light of day.

Friends and colleagues read and reread many of these pieces in earlier versions, saving me from endless embarrassments. To try naming them all is to risk the sin of omission; you know who you are. I have, as well, learned much from my coauthors: John Dwyer and Larry Rosenthal, with whom I wrote *Our Town*, from which the essay on Mount Laurel is adapted; Ronald Bayer, with whom I wrote the piece on the politics of needle exchange; and Elliot Marseille, with whom I have worked on several articles about Community Boards in San Francisco, one of which is included in this collection.

Each of these projects has involved a considerable

335

amount of time on the road. It is the part of the work I like best, because it gives me a license to be curious about the way the world works. Not long ago, a school superintendent asked me why I was spending so much time in his out-of-the-way town. "Because I really enjoy learning about new places," I said. "Well," he replied, a puzzled look on his face, "I really like fishing."

In cities and towns from Florida to California, public officials and ordinary citizens patiently answered my questions, introduced me to people to whom I otherwise would not have had access, and foraged through their files to dig out unpublished papers, faded-ink letters, and mimeographed reports. Perhaps our conversations provided them with their own Andy Warhol "fifteen minutes of fame" moment or perhaps they just appreciated having someone take an interest in their lives. Whatever the reason, I can count on the fingers of one hand the number of people who, over the years, have refused to talk to me. I have always depended, as the Tennessee Williams line goes, on the kindness of strangers. Though not all of them agree with what I have written, I have done my best not to betray their kindness.

The research for several of these pieces was supported by various foundations. At a critical moment in the project, the Gerbode Foundation came through with a grant that helped defray the travel expenses for the Mount Laurel book. The Kaiser Family Foundation provided a travel grant for the article on needle exchange. The Spencer Foundation underwrote *Learning by Heart: AIDS and Schoolchildren in America's Communities;* "A Boy's Life" is adapted from that book. The

Toyota Foundation and the Japan Foundation's Center for Global Partnership subsidized the research on hemophilia activism as part of a book-length study, *Blood Feuds: AIDS, Blood, and the Politics of Medical Disaster.*

I thought I was past being surprised, at least in my professional life, but when Peter Dougherty, my editor at the Press, asked whether I would be interested in turning my magazine articles into a book I was, for once in my life, left momentarily mute. I had bought into the journalists' adage that articles, once published, found their true home as canary cage liners, but Peter saw it differently. He has been instrumental in shaping this material into a book: helping to pick and choose which pieces to include, coming up with a title after scores of near-misses, and helping to produce a jacket design that is meant to convey "community" in a non-nostalgic way. Every author should be so lucky. Copy editor Madeleine Adams gently buffed the prose and located errors of fact that the editors of the articles had missed.